ax Facts 6

Y0-AAA-989

Tax Facts 6

The Canadian Consumer Tax Index and You

Sally Pipes and
Michael Walker
with
Isabella Horry

Canadian Cataloguing in Publication Data

Pipes, Sally, date.

  Tax facts 6

  First ed. published 1976 under title:
How much tax do you really pay?
  Bibliography: p.
  ISBN 0-88975-120-X
  1. Taxation - Canada. 2. Tax incidence -
Canada. I. Walker, Michael, 1945-
II. Fraser Institute (Vancouver, B.C.).
III. Title.   LL328
HJ2451.H69 1988   336.2'00971   C88-091332-0

SIXTH EDITION

Printed in Canada.

Contents

Preface / xi
About the Authors / xiii

Chapter 1
The Canadian Tax System / 1
The Many Faces of the Tax Collector / 1
Income taxes predominate / 1
Dividing the Spoils / 6
The Fifth Column / 9
Hidden taxation / 9
Indirect taxes / 9
The hot potatoes—passing tax forward / 13
Who pays the indirect taxes? / 14
Other Taxes by Other Names / 17
Clothing and textile taxes / 17
Marketing board taxes / 18
Regulatory taxation / 18
Deferred taxation / 18

Chapter 2
Personal Income Taxation in Canada / 21
The Current Income Tax Structure / 21
The Proposed Income Tax System / 24
Who Pays the Income Tax Bill? / 25
Get It from the Rich / 27
How rich is rich? / 27
Counting the rich / 28
Taxing the "rich" not the source of wealth / 28

Chapter 3
How Much Tax Do You Really Pay? / 29
  How Much Income Do You Really Earn? / 29
    Cash income / 29
    Full cash income and underreporting / 30
    Total income / 30
    Total income before tax / 32
  Calculating the Total Tax Bill / 33

Chapter 4
The Canadian Consumer Tax Index / 41
  Introduction / 41
    Why construct a Consumer Tax Index? / 41
    What is the Canadian Consumer Tax Index? / 42
    What the Consumer Tax Index shows / 46
  Taxes Versus the Necessities of Life / 46
    The average burden of tax versus the average
    family's tax burden / 53

Chapter 5
The Relative Burden of Tax / 57
  The Distribution of Income / 57
  Tax Distribution and Tax Rates / 60
  Who Pays the Tax Bill? / 67
  The Rags-to Riches Tax Burden / 67

Chapter 6
Taxes Across Canada / 71
  Accounting for the Future Tax Burden / 79
Appendix / 83
Notes / 175
Glossary / 177
Bibliography / 181

Tables and Figures

Tables

1. The Different Taxes Paid by Canadians and the Proportion that they Represent of the Total / 2

2. Total Taxes as a Percentage of Total Canadian Income / 5

3. Taxes Collected by Federal, Provincial, and Municipal Governments / 7

4. 1986 and 1987 Combined Federal and Provincial Personal Income Tax - Marginal Rates / 22

5. Personal Income Tax Paid (Single Taxpayer—No Dependents) at Selected levels of Income 1986 / 23

6. Personal Income Tax Paid (Married Taxpayer—Two Dependent Children under Sixteen Years of Age) at Selected Levels of Income 1986 / 23

7. Tax Rates and Numbers of Earners, 1986 / 24

8. An Analysis of Income, Taxes, and Tax Returns by Income Class, 1985 / 26

9. Full Cash Income, 1987 / 31

10. Total Income, 1987 / 32

11. Total Income Before Tax, 1987 / 34

12. Tax Bill of the Average Canadian Family / 35

13. 1987 Income Table for Canada / 36

14. 1987 Tax Table for Canada / 38

15. Taxes Paid by the Average Canadian Family, 1961-1987 / 43

16. The Canadian Consumer Tax Index / 44

17. The Consumer Tax Index Based on 1971 Dollars of Purchasing Power / 44

18. The Consumer Tax Index Versus the Balanced Budget Tax Index / 47

19. Income, Taxes, and Selected Expenditures of the Average Canadian Family / 49

20. Indices of Income, Taxes, and Selected Expenditures of the Average Canadian Family / 51

21. Taxes and Selected Expenditures of the Average Canadian Family Expressed as a Percentage of Total Income Before Tax / 53

22. Average Tax Rates for All Canadian Families Versus Tax Rates of the Average Canadian Family / 55

23. Decile Distribution of Income / 58

24. Income in Age Groups as a Percentage of Average for All Groups, Male Canadian, 1985 / 59

25. Decile Distribution of Taxes / 61

26. Decile Distribution of the Personal Income Tax / 61

27. Decile Distribution of Profit Taxes and Property Taxes / 63

28. Decile Distribution of Capital Income / 63

29. Decile Distribution of Tax Rates / 66

30. Increase in Tax Rates by Decile Since 1961 / 66

31. The Rages-To-Riches Tax Burden / 68

32. Taxes of the Average Family by province, 1987 / 72

33. Provincial Tax Rates* as a Percentage of Cash Income, Full Income, and Total Income Before Tax, 1987 / 74

34. Decile Distribution of Taxes by Provinces, 1987 / 76

35. Tax Rates by Decile by Province, 1987 / 78

36. Taxes of the Average Family Including Deficits by province, 1987 / 80

37. Total Spending and Spending per Capita by Province, 1987 / 81

Figures

1. Where Governments Obtained Their Revenue in 1961 and 1986 / 3

2. Government Take from a Litre of Gasoline / 10

3. Government Take from a Bottle of Liquor / 12

4. Take Home Pay Versus Gross Pay / 14

5. The Canadian Consumer Tax Index 1961-1987 / 45

6. The Canadian Consumer Tax Index Versus the Balanced Budget Tax Index 1961-1987 / 48

7. Taxes and Selected Expenditures of the Average Canadian Family, 1961-1986 / 50

8. How the Canadian Consumer Tax Index (CTI) Has Increased, Relative to Other Selected Indices, 1961-1986 / 52

9. Taxes and Selected Expenditures*of the Average Canadian Family Expressed as a Percentage of Total Income Before Tax / 54

Preface

This book is a summary of the latest results of a Fraser Institute project that began in July, 1975. The objective of the project was to find out how much tax, in all forms, Canadians pay to federal, provincial and municipal governments and how the size of this tax bill has changed from 1961 to the present. The study analyzes Canada's tax system in each of nine years, 1961, 1969, 1972, 1974, 1976, 1978, 1981, 1984 and 1987. The years 1961 and 1969 were chosen because they have been the focus of major studies in the past. Neither of these major studies attempted to link their findings together over several years. The Fraser Institute studies integrate and link the various past studies.

The book has been written with two distinct purposes in mind: first, to provide a non-technical do-it-yourself manual so that the average Canadian family can calculate how much tax they pay; second, to update a statistic, first published in 1976, that we call the Canadian Consumer Tax Index. This index measures how much the tax bill of an average Canadian family has increased since 1961 and by how much it is changing currently. In other words, it measures changes in the price that Canadians pay for government.

This book does not attempt to look at the benefits that Canadians receive from government in return for their taxes. Rather, it looks at the price that is paid for a product—government. It has nothing to say about the quality of the product, how much of it each of us receives, or whether we get our money's worth. These questions, essential though they are, must be considered in another study. Evidently, the Institute reflected a general curiosity—perhaps anxiety —about the price we pay for government when it first published its work on taxation in 1976. *How Much Tax Do You Really Pay?* was judged to be a bestseller in Canada.

A defect of the first two studies was the fact that they did not contain province-by-province data on the burden of taxation. Some readers indicated that they wanted to know their tax burden in the province of residence. Commencing with Tax Facts 3 they were able to compare their own tax burden with the burden which exists in other provinces.

A criticism levied at our previous study, *How Much Tax Do You Really Pay?* was that it ignored the extent to which governments finance their expenditures by issuing debt. As one observer remarked, "Governments can only finance their expenditures by taxing or printing money. When they issue bonds they are only deferring the process of taxation or delaying the printing of money. There is a limit on the extent they can do this and we should therefore peer through the veil of debt to the ultimate tax and money printing implications of government finance." Accordingly, since the fifth edition, published in 1986, we have made explicit calculations of the tax burden including and excluding the current deficit position of governments at all levels.

The Fraser Institute calculations of tax burden are part of an ongoing program of research. In making these results available to the public we seek both to inform and to be informed. Readers who disagree with our methods or conclusions are invited to write to the Institute to convey the nature of their reservations. In this way, our methods and our estimates can be refined and hopefully perfected.

We are pleased to acknowledge the assistance of Statistics Canada, which provided certain unpublished background data which were essential to the study. The Canadian Tax Simulator computer programs were written originally by David Gill whose unsparing efforts we are pleased to acknowledge. The sixth edition has been computed on a set of programs modified to run on a micro-computer system. These modifications were completed by Douglas T. Wills who has gone on to climb other mountains.

Sally C. Pipes
Michael A. Walker

About the Authors

SALLY C. PIPES

Sally C. Pipes is Assistant Director of the Vancouver-based Fraser Institute. Born in Vancouver, Canada, she graduated with a Bachelor of Arts in Economics (Honours) from the University of British Columbia in 1967. Prior to joining the Fraser Institute in 1974 as Research Economist, Ms. Pipes held a variety of research positions in both the private and public sectors, including the Policy and Planning Branch, Federal Department of Energy, Mines and Resources, and the Bureau of Economics and Statistics of the B.C. Ministry of Economic and Small Business Development. In 1969, she joined the Employers' Council of British Columbia as a Research Economist and in 1973 became a member of the Economics and Statistics Department of the Council of Forest Industries of British Columbia. In that position she was responsible for preparing the B.C. forest industry's brief for the Geneva Round of the GATT negotiations.

A Past President of the Association of Professional Economists of British Columbia, she is a Past President of the Canadian Association for Business Economics, a position she held for two terms. In 1982, the B.C. Ministry of Finance and Corporate Relations appointed her a Director of the Credit Union Deposit Insurance Corporation of British Columbia. She is currently serving her first term as a Board Member of the Vancouver City Planning Commission.

She co-authored with Spencer Star, *Income and Taxation in Canada, 1961-1975* and co-authored with Michael Walker *How Much Tax Do You Really Pay?* (1976), *Tax Facts* (1979), *Tax Facts 3* (1982) *Tax Facts 4* (1984), and *Tax Facts 5* (1986). Ms. Pipes is a member of the Mont Pèlerin Society, the Canadian Association for Business Economics and the Association of Professional Economists of B.C.

MICHAEL A. WALKER

Michael Walker is Director of the Fraser Institute. Born in Newfoundland in 1945, he received his B.A. (summa) at St. Francis Xavier University in 1966 and his Ph.D. in Economics at the University of Western Ontario in 1969. From 1969 to 1973, he worked in various research capacities at the Bank of Canada, Ottawa, and when he left in 1973 was Research Officer in charge of the Special Studies and Monetary Policy Group in the Department of Banking. Immediately prior to joining the Fraser Institute, Dr. Walker was Econometric Model Consultant to the Federal Department of Finance, Ottawa. Dr. Walker has also taught Monetary Economics and Statistics at the University of Western Ontario and Carleton University.

Dr. Walker writes regularly for daily newspapers and financial periodicals. His articles have also appeared in technical journals, including the *Canadian Journal of Economics, Canadian Public Policy, Canadian Taxation* and the *Canadian Tax Journal.* He has been a columnist in *The Province,* the *Toronto Sun, The Ottawa Citizen, The Financial Post,* the Sterling newspaper chain, and community newspapers across Canada, as well as a regular contributor to CBC's "As It Happens." He prepares a daily, syndicated radio program and speaks on a regular basis to a wide variety of groups, conferences, and associations throughout Canada and the U.S.

He is an author, editor, and contributor to more than twenty books on economic matters, some of which include *Balancing the Budget; Flat-Rate Tax Proposals; Reaction: The National Energy Program; Rent Control: A Popular Paradox; Unions and the Public Interest; Discrimination, Affirmative Action and Equal Opportunity; Privatization: Theory and Practice; Trade Unions and Society, Privatization: Tactics and Techniques;* and *Freedom, Democracy and Economic Welfare.*

Dr. Walker is a member of the Mont Pèlerin Society, the Canadian and American Economic Associations, and the International Association of Energy Economists.

ISABELLA D. HORRY

Isabella D. Horry was born in 1963 in Vancouver, Canada. She attended the University of British Columbia, and graduated in 1985 with a B.A. (economics), and then in 1987 with an M.A. (economics). Since February 1988, she has been employed by The Fraser Institute as a Research Economist.

Chapter 1

The Canadian Tax System

THE MANY FACES OF THE TAX COLLECTOR

Under the Canadian constitution, the federal government and the provincial governments are essentially given unlimited powers of taxation. In the British North America Act, the immediate predecessor of the Canadian constitution, the provinces are limited to the collection of taxes which are paid directly by the person being taxed—so-called direct taxes. But because of the broad judicial interpretation given to the meaning of "direct," the provinces have been able to levy all sorts of taxes except import duties and taxes on sales which cross provincial borders. Given this unlimited scope for taxation and the 100 years of ingenuity that have elapsed, it is not surprising that Canada now has a very complicated tax system.[1]

Some understanding of this complexity can be obtained simply by noting the twenty-two categories of tax set out in Table 1. This number has grown over the past few years as new taxes, like those on energy and the airport tax have been implemented. In the not too distant future another major tax in the form of an extension of the federal sales tax will be visited on Canadians. The exact form of this tax has not been decided.

Income taxes predominate

It is evident from Table 1 and Figure 1 that personal income taxes are the largest single source of government revenue. During 1986 some 56.9 billion dollars were extracted by federal and provincial income tax—a sum which represented 35.3 percent of the total taxes that Canadians pay. Second in line as a source of federal and provincial revenues was the sales tax—representing 13.1 percent of tax revenue and 21.1 billion tax dollars. Corporate profits taxes, at 8.3

TABLE 1

The Different Taxes Paid by Canadians and the Proportion that they Represent of the Total

Category of Tax	$ millions 1986	% of total taxes	$ millions 1961	% of total taxes
Personal income tax	56,863	35.3	2,099	22.7
Sales tax	21,136	13.1	1,351	14.6
Profits tax	13,363	8.3	1,199	13.0
Property tax	15,923	9.9	1,285	13.9
Resources tax	10,953	6.8	266	2.9
Federal social security tax	8,783	5.5	388	4.2
Canada Pension Plan(inc. QPP)	5,754	3.6	0	0.0
Import duties	3,975	2.5	438	4.7
Auto, fuel, and gas tax	4,348	2.7	525	5.7
Provincial social security tax	3,099	1.9	155	1.7
Liquor tax	886	0.6	450	4.9
Hospital and medical premiums	3,678	2.3	120	1.3
Tobacco tax	3,601	2.2	387	4.2
Motor vehicle registrations	1,594	1.0	179	1.9
Other provincial fees, licences fees	2,972	1.8	11	0.1
Other municipal business taxes	252	0.2	46	0.5
Other municipal taxes and levies	114	0.1	104	1.1
Provincial insurance premiums	491	0.3	31	0.3
Amusement and admission tax	192	0.1	24	0.3
Other federal excise taxes	1,443	0.8	28	0.4
Federal excise; other	1,582	1.0	0	0.0
Succession and estate duties	0	0.0	145	1.6
Total	161,002	100.0	9,231	100.0

Source: Statistics Canada, *Federal Government Finance, Provincial Government Finance, Local Government Finance,* Catalogue Nos. 68-211, 68-207, 68-203, 1961 and 1988.
Revenue Canada, Statistical Services Division.

Figure 1—Where Governments Obtained Their Revenue in 1961 and 1986

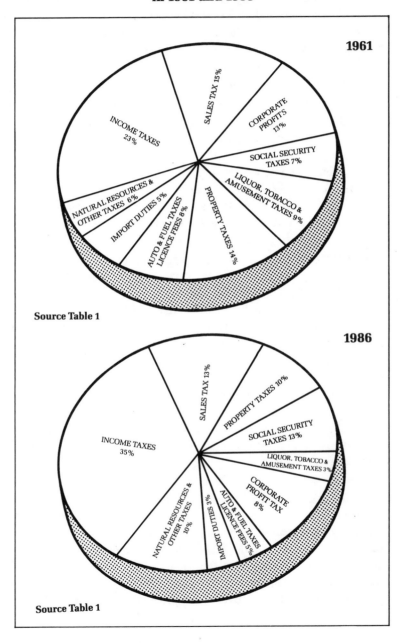

1961

SALES TAX 15%

CORPORATE PROFITS 13%

INCOME TAXES 23%

SOCIAL SECURITY TAXES 7%

LIQUOR, TOBACCO & AMUSEMENT TAXES 9%

NATURAL RESOURCES & OTHER TAXES 6%

IMPORT DUTIES 5%

AUTO & FUEL TAXES LICENCE FEES 8%

PROPERTY TAXES 14%

Source Table 1

1986

SALES TAX 13%

PROPERTY TAXES 10%

INCOME TAXES 35%

SOCIAL SECURITY TAXES 13%

LIQUOR, TOBACCO & AMUSEMENT TAXES 3%

CORPORATE PROFIT TAX 8%

NATURAL RESOURCES & OTHER TAXES 10%

IMPORT DUTIES 3%

AUTO & FUEL TAXES LICENCE FEES 5%

Source Table 1

percent of total taxes, accounted for a further 13.4 billion dollars, while the total of property and natural resource taxes accounted for 26.9 billion dollars and 16.7 percent collectively. Together these five kinds of tax accounted for nearly 73 percent of total government revenue during 1986. (It is interesting to note that both the corporate profits tax and the income tax were implemented in 1916 and 1917 as "temporary" measures to finance World War I.)

Table 1 also illustrates how the Canadian tax structure has evolved over the twenty-five years since 1961. The most obvious change has been the evolution of the personal income tax. While always a prominent feature of the tax system, the income tax has, in recent years, become increasingly important. In 1961 income taxes represented only 22.7 cents out of every tax dollar Canadians paid, but by 1986 income taxes accounted for 35.3 cents—more than two and a half times the revenue generated by the second-running sales tax.

This increase came about largely through passive interaction between the progressive income tax system and money incomes swollen by inflation.[2] Until the income tax was indexed to the inflation rate in 1974, all income increases were taxed at progressively higher rates in spite of the fact that much of the increased income represented illusory inflation-based gains.

As a consequence of this revenue growth, government was able to rely less on other forms of taxation and to allow the burden of some of these taxes to fall. However, in some important cases—notably sales tax and resource taxes—the rate of tax was increased despite rapidly growing revenues from personal income tax. (Table 2 presents the burden of the top eleven taxes contributing to government revenue in 1986. The figures in the table are the effective rates of taxation relative to total Canadian income.)

Unlike income taxes, sales taxes are levied principally by the provincial governments—though the federal government has gradually increased its participation in this revenue source through such taxes as the federal manufacturers' sales tax. As a consequence, while revenue from the income tax explosion poured into the federal government's coffers, the provinces were led by their perceived need for tax revenue to gradually boost their sales tax

TABLE 2

Total Taxes as a Percentage of Total Canadian Income

Category of tax	1986 %	1961 %
Personal income tax	11.9	6.4
Sales tax	4.4	4.1
Profits tax	2.8	3.7
Property tax	3.3	3.9
Resources tax	2.3	1.0
Federal Social Security tax	1.8	1.2
Canada Pension Plan (incl. QPP)	1.2	0.0
Import duties	.8	1.6
Auto, fuel and gas tax	.9	1.4
Liquor tax	.2	1.3
Other taxes	4.0	3.7
TOTAL	33.6	28.3

Source: See Table 1 and Statistics Canada, *System of National Income and Expenditure Accounts*, Catalogue No.13-001, 1961 and 1986.

rates (except for the Province of Alberta which has no sales tax and in British Columbia where the sales tax has been adjusted up and down. It was reduced from 7 percent to 5 percent on April 11, 1978, on April 1, 1979 a further reduction to 4 percent was made. However, on March 10, 1981 it was increased to 6 percent and in July, 1983 to 7 percent. In the 1987 budget, the tax was once again dropped to 6 percent).

The rise in resource taxation in the 1970s and 1980s resulted primarily from rises in the price of oil and gas, triggered by the oil embargo and subsequent cartelization of oil pricing by the OPEC countries in 1973.[3] In the normal course of events, these price rises in Canada would automatically have meant a sharp rise in the return to Canadian producers. But the reaction of provincial governments was to absorb much of this "windfall," or "rent," as it has been called, in the form of higher taxes or royalties. The federal government, for its part, imposed a further tax on producers who were exporting oil. (This tax, the oil export charge, amounted to the difference between the controlled Canadian price per barrel and the world price.) Proceeds from the federal tax were then used to subsidize imports of foreign oil into the eastern Canadian provinces.

In the period 1974 to 1984, both the provincial and federal governments escalated their tax effort—but especially the federal government. The National Energy Program and the subsequent Energy Agreement allowed the federal government to earn about 4 billion dollars from petroleum during 1984.

The 1985 federal budget incorporated a number of changes regarding energy taxes agreed upon in the Western Accord with the governments of Saskatchewan, Alberta, and British Columbia. Both the oil export charge and petroleum compensation charge were eliminated. Other energy taxes, such as the Petroleum and Gas Revenue Tax, were revised, reduced, and in some cases phased out. These changes, combined with the decline in world oil prices, have resulted in energy related revenues declining in both relative and absolute terms.

DIVIDING THE SPOILS

Another interesting feature of the present Canadian tax system is the extent of participation by the various levels of government—federal, provincial, and municipal. Table 3 provides a breakdown of major taxes by these different levels of government. It is clear from this table that provincial governments are rapidly becoming the dominant tax collectors. In 1961, provincial governments collected 32 percent of total taxes in Canada, while federal and municipal governments collected 68 percent. By 1986, however, provincial governments were collecting 40.5 percent and the other levels only 59.5 percent.

It must be acknowledged that the impression given by these figures is distorted somewhat by the fact that some of the revenue of municipal and provincial governments comes from other levels of government. For example, in 1961 fully 30 percent of provincial and municipal revenues were derived from other levels of government. (Provinces received transfers from the federal government, while municipalities received transfers from both levels.)

In the case of provincial revenues, the figures for 1961 reflect the tax agreement that was in effect between the federal and provincial governments. Under the agreement the federal government "rented"

TABLE 3

Taxes Collected by Federal, Provincial, and Municipal Governments

(billions of dollars)

Category of tax	Federal 1986	Federal 1961	Provincial 1986	Provincial 1961	Municipal 1986	Municipal 1961
Personal income tax	34.8	2.0	22.1	.1	0.0	0.0
Sales tax	9.4	.3	11.7	1.0	0.0	0.0
Property tax	0.0	0.0	1.3	0.0	14.6	1.3
Profits tax	9.2	1.0	4.2	.2	0.0	0.0
Resources tax	3.5	0.0	7.5	.3	0.0	0.0
Social security tax	8.8	.4	3.1	.2	0.0	0.0
Canada and Quebec Pension Plan	4.4	0.0	1.4	0.0	0.0	0.0
Import duties	4.0	.5	0.0	0.0	0.0	0.0
other taxes	6.8	.6	14.0	1.1	.4	.1
TOTAL	80.9	4.8	65.3	2.9	15.0	1.4

(percent)

Category of tax	Federal 1986	Federal 1961	Provincial 1986	Provincial 1961	Municipal 1986	Municipal 1961
Personal income tax	61.2	95.0	38.8	5.0	0.0	0.0
Sales tax	44.5	23.0	55.5	77.0	0.0	0.0
Property tax	0.0	0.0	8.2	1.0	91.8	99.0
Profits tax	68.7	83.0	31.3	17.0	0.0	0.0
Resources tax	31.8	1.0	68.2	99.0	0.0	0.0
Social security tax	73.9	67.0	26.1	33.0	0.0	0.0
Canada and Quebec Pension Plans	68.2	0.0	31.8	0.0	0.0	0.0
Import duties	100.0	100.0	0.0	0.0	0.0	0.0
Other taxes	32.1	33.0	66.0	61.0	1.9	6.0
TOTAL	50.2	53.0	40.5	32.0	9.3	1

Source: See Table 1.

the provinces' rights to tax personal incomes. In effect, the provinces relinquished their right to tax personal incomes in return for cash payments from the federal government which collected all the taxes.[4] Accordingly, the tax-collection statistics for 1961 do not reflect the division of the revenues produced but only which level of government actually collected them.

In 1986, the collection figures more closely matched the revenue divided between federal and provincial governments due to the fact that revenue-sharing agreements have been gradually modified to eliminate tax rental arrangements and shared-cost programs. In the years following 1978, the provinces have had, increasingly, to raise their own revenue. As a consequence, tax receipts by different levels of government will more closely reflect the actual sharing of tax revenues. To a considerable degree this evolution reflects the changing attitudes of the partners in Canadian confederation, and the changing tax arrangements are the harbinger of a more decentralized federation. (In the case of Quebec, separate tax collection facilities have been in existence for some time.) As a result of the Meech Lake Accord, all of the provinces will acquire even more autonomy in their program expenditures and this will lead to a more decentralized fiscal structure as time passes.

The relationship between provincial and municipal government revenues reflects a different process. Municipalities now collect much less of their total revenue in the form of taxes than they did in 1961. And, in fact, fully 49.4 percent of municipal revenue is now accounted for by transfers from federal and provincial governments—mainly the latter. In part, the emerging role of municipalities as dependencies of the provincial government is a result of decreasing reliance on property taxation as a form of finance (see Table 1). Property taxes accounted for only 9.9 percent of total taxes (of all kinds) in 1986 as opposed to 13.9 percent in 1961 (see Figure 1).

This trend toward less reliance on property taxation contrasts sharply with the situation in the United States and in California, in particular, where the sudden increase in property taxation touched off what has been called the "Proposition 13" movement. The failure of similar initiatives in Canada may be directly attributable to the different strategy of local government finance pursued in this country.

THE FIFTH COLUMN

Hidden taxation

Most people are aware of the fact that they pay income tax, sales tax and property tax, the so-called direct taxes. Many others, appropriately, regard the various social security levies like unemployment insurance contributions and Canada and Quebec Pension Plan payments, as taxes. Similarly, many families know how much of these taxes they pay, either in terms of the rate (in the case of provincial sales taxes) or the total amount (in the case of property and income taxes). There are, however, many taxes of which Canadians, by and large, are unaware. These taxes are built into the price of goods and services but are not identified to the final consumer as a tax cost. For want of a better name, we call these implicit or hidden taxes.

Indirect taxes

There are several different kinds of hidden tax. Most well known of these are the so-called indirect taxes—principally excise taxes on such items as tobacco and alcohol, manufacturers' sales taxes, and import duties. These taxes are paid by some intermediary in the production process and become incorporated in the final price of the product. The most notorious examples are tobacco, liquor and gasoline taxes. (See Figures 2 and 3 for a breakdown of taxes paid for a litre of gasoline and a bottle of liquor.) In the case of liquor, the actual indirect rate of tax is about 99.73 percent; in the case of cigarettes, it is 136.96 percent.[5] The final consumer of both of these products pays the taxes without them having been identified as such. Of course, most people are aware that alcohol and tobacco are highly taxed, even if they do not know the actual rate of tax.

During 1986, total indirect taxes of all kinds amounted to 64.1 billion dollars in Canada. This was 13 percent of total Canadian in-

Figure 2 — Government Take from a Litre of Gasoline

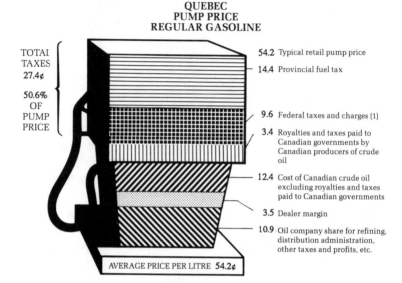

QUEBEC
PUMP PRICE
REGULAR GASOLINE

TOTAL
TAXES
27.4¢

50.6%
OF
PUMP
PRICE

54.2 Typical retail pump price

14.4 Provincial fuel tax

9.6 Federal taxes and charges (1)

3.4 Royalties and taxes paid to Canadian governments by Canadian producers of crude oil

12.4 Cost of Canadian crude oil excluding royalties and taxes paid to Canadian governments

3.5 Dealer margin

10.9 Oil company share for refining, distribution administration, other taxes and profits, etc.

AVERAGE PRICE PER LITRE 54.2¢

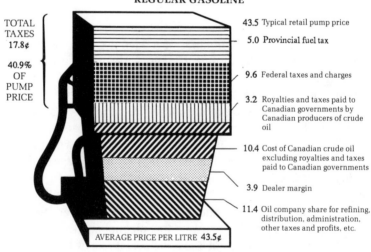

ALBERTA
PUMP PRICE
REGULAR GASOLINE

TOTAL
TAXES
17.8¢

40.9%
OF
PUMP
PRICE

43.5 Typical retail pump price

5.0 Provincial fuel tax

9.6 Federal taxes and charges

3.2 Royalties and taxes paid to Canadian governments by Canadian producers of crude oil

10.4 Cost of Canadian crude oil excluding royalties and taxes paid to Canadian governments

3.9 Dealer margin

11.4 Oil company share for refining, distribution, administration, other taxes and profits, etc.

AVERAGE PRICE PER LITRE 43.5¢

Source: Where Does Your Gasoline Dollar Go? Petroleum Resources Communication Foundation

Figure 2 — Government Take from a Litre of Gasoline

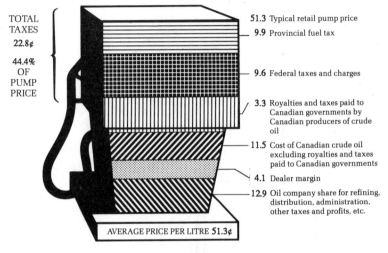

**BRITISH COLUMBIA
PUMP PRICE
REGULAR GASOLINE**

TOTAL
TAXES
22.8¢

44.4%
OF
PUMP
PRICE

51.3 Typical retail pump price

9.9 Provincial fuel tax

9.6 Federal taxes and charges

3.3 Royalties and taxes paid to
Canadian governments by
Canadian producers of crude
oil

11.5 Cost of Canadian crude oil
excluding royalties and taxes
paid to Canadian governments

4.1 Dealer margin

12.9 Oil company share for refining,
distribution, administration,
other taxes and profits, etc.

AVERAGE PRICE PER LITRE 51.3¢

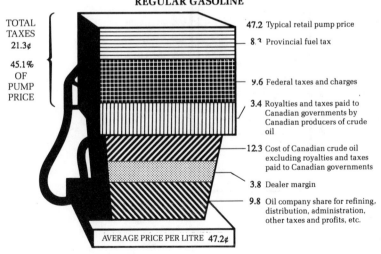

**ONTARIO
PUMP PRICE
REGULAR GASOLINE**

TOTAL
TAXES
21.3¢

45.1%
OF
PUMP
PRICE

47.2 Typical retail pump price

8.3 Provincial fuel tax

9.6 Federal taxes and charges

3.4 Royalties and taxes paid to
Canadian governments by
Canadian producers of crude
oil

12.3 Cost of Canadian crude oil
excluding royalties and taxes
paid to Canadian governments

3.8 Dealer margin

9.8 Oil company share for refining,
distribution, administration,
other taxes and profits, etc.

AVERAGE PRICE PER LITRE 47.2¢

**Source: Where Does Your Gasoline Dollar Go? Petroleum Resources
Communication Foundation**

Figure 3—Government Take from a Bottle of Liquor

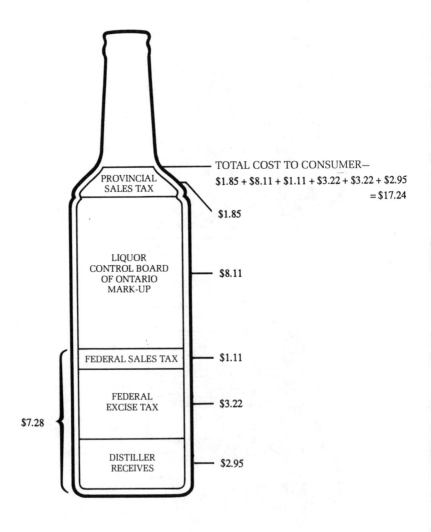

TOTAL COST TO CONSUMER—
$1.85 + $8.11 + $1.11 + $3.22 + $3.22 + $2.95
= $17.24

PROVINCIAL SALES TAX — $1.85

LIQUOR CONTROL BOARD OF ONTARIO MARK-UP — $8.11

FEDERAL SALES TAX — $1.11

FEDERAL EXCISE TAX — $3.22

$7.28

DISTILLER RECEIVES — $2.95

Source: Association of Canadian Distillers

come and accounted for 39 percent of total government revenue from taxation. In other words, quite apart from the tax they pay when they receive their incomes, Canadians pay, on average, a further 13 percent in indirect taxes when they spend their income. Furthermore, over one-third of all government revenue is collected in this indirect, hidden form.

The hot potatoes—passing tax forward

Needless to say, from the point of view of the individual, any tax that can be avoided is money in his or her pocket. As a result, people throughout the economy are constantly attempting to avoid situations in which they will have to pay taxes, and seeking to pay as little tax as possible, whatever their situation. The moonlighting tradesman who engages in "cash only" transactions; the mechanic who fixes his neighbour's truck in return for free cartage; the dentists who fix fellow dentists' families' teeth on a reciprocal basis; the tycoon whose business is incorporated in the Grand Cayman Islands: all have in common their desire to avoid taxes.

By the same token, the average Canadian employee measures his welfare in terms of after-tax dollars, and in each new wage bargain aims to get an increase in take-home pay. The fact that an increase in gross terms will imply a smaller increase in after-tax dollars motivates the employee or his union representative to demand a larger gross increase. By doing so, the employee is attempting to get the employer to bear the burden of the additional tax. For an example of this process see the box insert—Figure 4.

Expressed slightly differently, the employee who bargains in this manner is attempting to "pass the tax forward." His behaviour is not unique but, on the contrary, is a general characteristic of all employees of the Canadian economy. Corporations, for example, attempt to pass their higher profits and payroll taxes forward to the consumer in the form of higher prices (as well as backward on employees in the form of lower wages). Of course, all of these attempts may or may not be successful in any single instance, and they will be accomplished to varying degrees through time.

Figure 4 - Take Home Pay Versus Gross Pay

In 1986 an employee in Ontario with $25,001 in taxable income had to get an increase of 8.0 percent, to realize a 5 percent increase in after-tax pay. Tax rates vary by province and comparable figures for the other provinces are presented in the table below.

Percent wage increase required

(Taxable Income at $25,001)

Nfld.	P.E.I.	N.S.	N.B.	Que.
8.4	8.1	8.3	8.3	9.2
Ont.	Man.	Sask.	Alta.	B.C.
8.0	8.6	8.0	7.8	7.9

Source: Canadian Tax Foundation, The National Finances, 1986-87, Table 7.10, page 7:23

Who pays the indirect taxes?

In order to calculate the actual tax bill paid by a family, it is necessary to determine how much indirect tax it pays. But since those from whom the tax is collected attempt to pass the tax along to others, it is difficult to know where the burden of these taxes ultimately lies. For example, a general sales tax is collected by and remitted to government by retailers. It is clear, however, that in most cases the retailers do not actually bear the tax—they are merely the agents for collecting it. The actual effect of the tax is to increase the price of all goods and services affected by the tax and to cause a corresponding reduction in the purchasing power of family incomes. Accordingly, to the extent that a general sales tax causes an increase in the general level of prices, the tax is borne not by the collectors but by income earners in the economy whose incomes now buy less.

Payroll taxes such as unemployment insurance premiums and Canada and Quebec Pension Plan contributions are collected in part from the employer and in part from the employee. And, while no one would dispute the fact that the employee pays the employee portion, in most cases it is true that the employee will also pay the so-called employer's portion. This is so because the payroll tax paid by the employer reduces the total amount of money the employer has available to pay labour-related costs. In other words, payroll taxes reduce potential wage and salary payments below what they otherwise would have been. Since no corresponding reduction can be expected in the price of the products that the employee will want to purchase, the payroll tax, in effect, burdens the employee.

While both of these arguments have been framed in terms of employees and their wages and salaries, it is clear that taxes burden capital income as well. For example, a general sales tax reduces the purchasing power of all income, not just wage and salary income. As a result, it is appropriate to view the general sales tax burden as falling on all forms of income, including interest income and dividends. All of the tax burden estimates constructed in this study, therefore, allocate the burden of general sales taxes in proportion to all income received by a family. In practical terms, this means that if general sales taxes amount to 6 percent of total Canadian income in a particular year, we would add 6 percent of a family's total income to the family's tax bill when we calculate how much tax the family pays.

In computing this tax burden, income that a family receives from government is explicitly omitted. The reason for this is that the payments received from government, such as the Old Age Pension, have historically been and are currently either directly or indirectly indexed to the general level of prices (that is, increased to offset the effects of inflation). As the general price level rises, in step with the sales tax, the purchasing power of such transfers from government as Family Allowance and Old Age Security payments is not permitted to fall. As a consequence, the general sales tax does not have the effect of burdening income received from government (transfers), and it would be inappropriate to allocate any part of the burden of general sales taxes to this sort of income.[6]

While the burden of a general sales tax and payroll taxes is relatively straightforward to assign, the assignment of particular excise taxes is a little more elusive. Whereas a general sales tax increases all prices and hence reduces the purchasing power of all incomes, particular taxes on commodities usually affect only the price of that commodity. For example, excise taxes imposed on liquor, motor vehicles, and fuels affect only the prices of those products, in the first instance at least. (Ultimately, of course, they may affect a whole range of prices—fuel taxes affect the price of transportation, as do motor vehicle taxes. These taxes may therefore have an overall effect although levied only on a particular product.)

In the light of these considerations, it has been the usual practice when calculating tax burdens to allocate the burden of particular excise taxes according to the consumption of those items. The 1976 tax burden studies published by the Fraser Institute employed this methodology.[7] However, following this methodology gives rise to a variety of problems. First of all, only the first round effects of the excise tax are incorporated and, hence, the actual distribution of the tax burden may differ substantially from the estimate. Secondly, this method may not even provide good estimates of the first round effects of the tax. This is so because the relative burden of a particular tax borne by a family is determined not by the family's consumption of the taxed item but by the fraction of the family's income spent on the item relative to the national average.[8]

In view of these problems with the traditional approach, and given that the proportions of income spent on different items by various income groups do not vary widely from the average, we decided for the purposes of this study to distribute excise taxes in the same way as general sales taxes. That is to say, it is assumed that excise taxes burden total incomes—excluding government transfers to persons.

So, the answer to the question, "Who pays the indirect taxes?" is a straightforward one. Although indirect taxes appear in a variety of forms, they ultimately burden the income that the family earns.

OTHER TAXES BY OTHER NAMES

In addition to "formal" taxes levied by government, there are a variety of other government actions which, while having the same effect as taxes, are not normally identified as such. These activities are becoming an increasingly important feature of the Canadian economic landscape and must receive special mention.

Clothing and textile taxes

In November 1976, the federal government imposed a quota on imported clothing and textiles. Its purpose was to limit the importation of inexpensive clothing and textiles and so protect Canadian markets for Canadian clothing and textile manufacturers. The associated decline in competition for the Canadian consumer's clothing expenditure dollar will undoubtedly have produced a higher price for clothing than would otherwise have existed.

The difference between the price for clothing that would have prevailed in the absence of the quota and the price that actually prevails is a tax on the consumer. Proceeds from this tax go directly to producers and are, in effect, a producer subsidy. There is no difference in principle between this sort of tax and the other hidden taxes that we have been discussing. Of course, these "clothing taxes" do not show up in government revenue figures, and precise estimates of their size are difficult to make, but we cannot ignore their existence. R.J. and P. Wonnacott in their book *Free Trade Between the United States and Canada* have estimated that the total amount of tax levied in the form of tariff protection or other barriers to international competition may be as high as 10.5 percent of Canada's Gross National Product.[9] Currently, this amounts to a tax of over 40 billion dollars.

Some of the burden associated with tariffs and quotas will be eliminated as a result of the Free Trade Agreement between Canada and the United States. However, in many cases the principal source of cheaper products is not the United States but other, and in particular Third World, countries.

Marketing board taxes

At present, there are some 177 farm products' cartels in Canada. These cartels or marketing boards generally have the effect of suppressing competition in the production of the cartelized product, and they consequently cause the price of the product to be higher than it otherwise would have been. As in the case of clothing and textiles, the amount by which the marketing board price exceeds the price that would prevail in its absence—that is, in the market—is a tax on the consumer. Accordingly, marketing boards ought to be viewed as a device for transferring money from consumers to producers. And, this transfer is equivalent to a tax on consumers, the proceeds of which are given to producers.

The increasing power of marketing boards, and the seeming reluctance of government to restrain their growth suggests that these marketing board taxes will become increasingly important in Canada. Moreover, as restraint in government taxation and spending becomes a reality, it will become increasingly expedient for government to rely on hidden "regulatory" taxation of this sort. Fortunately offsetting this tendency is the pressure which free trade will exert on the political interest groups which support these developments.

Regulatory taxation

In general, a government can achieve a given objective either by taxation and subsidization or by regulation—rather than imposing import quotas, the federal government could have assisted Canadian clothing manufacturers by giving them a direct subsidy financed from general tax revenue. That the government chooses to use regulation to convey a subsidy in this fashion should not distract attention from the fact that a subsidy has been provided, and that it is the Canadian consumer who pays for it.

Deferred taxation

During his budget statement in November 1978, Mr. Chretien, former federal Minister of Finance, made much of the fact that because the personal income tax structure had been indexed to inflation, there had, in effect, been a reduction in personal income taxation compared to what would have prevailed in the absence of indexing. That is to say, exemptions had been increased by the rate of inflation and tax brackets had been shifted to ensure that incomes swollen by inflation would not be taxed more heavily on that account alone. While this change in the tax structure, first introduced in 1974, was indeed a welcome one, it would be naive to uncritically accept the move as a permanent reduction in the government's propensity to tax.

In fact, the "reduction" in personal income tax revenues was accompanied—starting in 1975—by deficits and shortfalls in the federal government's cash position which were unprecedented in peacetime.

Although this situation is not entirely attributable to the decline in personal income tax revenues, it is clearly the case that continued growth in income taxation would have meant a slightly smaller deficit and a reduction in net cash requirements to be financed by issuing debt. Accordingly, in assessing Canada's current level of taxation, it is appropriate to take into account the extent to which tax collections are merely deferred by current tax "reductions."

In other words, when calculating the total tax burden of all government operations in a given year, it is appropriate to include not only current taxes levied but also future taxes which must be levied to discharge debts acquired by the government in the current year. To the extent that government finances its operations by deficit financing or issuing bonds—deferred taxation—there is a hidden tax burden implicit in its operations. In Chapter 4, we have calculated estimates of the total tax burden which include all of these deferred taxes.

How Much Tax Should Canadians Pay?

In 1917 when he first introduced the Personal Income Tax, the Finance Minister of the day, Sir Thomas White, was of the opinion that no Canadians should pay tax on income less than $2,000 if they were single and had no dependents. Married taxpayers, he said, should pay tax on income in excess of $3,000. The tax structure that ultimately evolved provided that single Canadians pay income tax on income in excess of $1,500, while married Canadians were exempted from the tax until their incomes exceeded $3,000. However, in the very next year, this was reduced to $2,000 for a married taxpayer and $1,000 for single Canadians.*

While the tax structure has gone through many changes in the intervening years, it is interesting to ask how Canadians would be treated for tax purposes in 1987-88 if this initial view of "ability to pay" had kept pace with developments in people's incomes. To answer this question, we have adjusted the original exemption levels by the increase in average wages over the period since 1917. This adjustment yields an exemption level for 1987 of $9,425 for single taxpayers and $18,850 for married taxpayers. But actual personal exemptions for single and married taxpayers amounted to $4,220 and $7,920 in 1987—in each case less than half the level that would have been allowed if the 1917 standard had continued in force.

The reason for the disparity is that over the years from 1917 to 1974 exemption levels were not indexed to the cost-of-living or the increase in family incomes—in fact, in a few years during the depression, exemption levels were actually reduced. Since 1974, exemption levels have been indexed to the rate of inflation.

---

*House of Commons Debates, July 25, 1917, p. 3765.

CHAPTER 2

PERSONAL INCOME TAXATION IN CANADA

We alluded to the fact in Chapter 1 that income taxes are the largest single source of government revenue. It therefore follows that the largest single tax paid by the average Canadian family is the income tax. As we also noted in Chapter 1, this tax came into existence in 1917 as a "temporary" emergency measure to help finance the increasing debt associated with World War I. "Nothing," it is said, "endures like the temporary."

THE CURRENT INCOME TAX STRUCTURE

Table 4 presents the actual rates of income tax (both federal and provincial) encountered by the average single individual at various taxable income levels, for 1986 and 1987. As the figures show, the minimum rate of tax is 9.00 percent payable on taxable income of $1.00. The maximum rate is payable at income levels of $63,347 or higher and amounts to 51.00 percent of every dollar earned beyond that income level. These rates are the marginal rates of tax that a person encounters as he or she moves from one level of taxable income to the next. An equally interesting series of calculations relates to the amount of tax an individual theoretically pays on a given amount of total income (not taxable income), taking into account the standard deductions to which he or she is entitled. (Taxable income equals total income minus total deductions.) These rates are shown in Table 5.

In the case of a family, the situation can be slightly different because of deductions permitted for the dependent spouse. Support of children also eases somewhat the tax burden on the taxpayer. In perusing tax rates for the average family of four presented in Table

TABLE 4

1986 and 1987 Combined Federal and Provincial Personal Income Tax — Marginal Rates*

Taxable Income	1986	Taxable Income	1987
$ 1	8.91	$ 1	9.00
1,306	23.76	1,321	24.00
2,612	25.25	2,640	25.50
5,222	26.73	5,280	27.00
7,833	28.22	7,919	28.50
10,445	28.22	10,560	28.50
13,055	29.70	13,198	30.00
15,667	29.70	15,839	30.00
18,276	34.16	18,477	34.50
20,889	34.16	21,119	34.50
23,497	37.13	23,756	37.50
26,111	37.13	26,398	37.50
28,722	37.13	29,038	37.50
31,333	38.38	31,678	37.50
36,551	46.05	36,953	45.00
39,166	46.05	39,597	45.00
62,658	53.89	63,347	51.00
65,276	53.89	65,994	51.00
101,830	53.89	102,950	51.00
104,440	53.89	105,589	51.00
156,661	53.89	158,384	51.00
234,990	53.89	237,575	51.00
326,375	53.89	329,965	51.00
587,475	53.89	593,937	51.00
1,044,400	53.89	1,055,888	51.00

Source: Canadian Tax Foundation, *The National Finances, 1986–1987,* Table 7.5, page 7:9.
*Tax rate which comes into effect with each additional amount of income.

6, the reader should bear in mind the fact that this schedule of rates is not directly applicable for many families. In many cases, both adult members of the family declare taxable income. In this case they each file a separate return, and tax rates for individuals apply. Of course, this is to the advantage of the taxpayers. If, for example, a childless couple who are both working have the same income—say $15,000 per year—they pay total tax of about $4,644 when they file as individuals. If their total income of $30,000 were earned by

TABLE 5

Personal Income Tax Paid (Single Taxpayer—No Dependents) at Selected Levels of Income, 1986

Total Income Assessed	Total Tax Payable (Federal plus Provincial)	Tax Rate (average)
$ 7,500	$ 413	5.5%
10,000	1,017	10.2
12,500	1,654	13.2
15,000	2,322	15.5
17,500	2,999	17.1
20,000	3,697	18.5
25,000	5,167	20.7
30,000	6,888	22.9
50,000	15,089	30.2
100,000	40,621	40.6
200,000	94,511	47.3

Source: Canadian Tax Foundation, The National Finances, 1986–1987, Chapter 7, Table 7.12, page 7:25.

TABLE 6

Personal Income Tax Paid (Married Taxpayer—Two Dependent Children under Sixteen Years of Age) at Selected Levels of Income 1986

Total Income Assessed	Total Tax Payable (Federal plus Provincial)	Tax Rate (average)
$ 7,500	0	0
10,000	56	.6%
12,500	531	4.2
15,000	1,139	7.6
17,500	1,779	10.2
20,000	2,455	12.3
25,000	3,836	15.3
30,000	5,388	17.9
50,000	13,099	26.2
100,000	38,292	38.3
200,000	92,182	46.1

Source: Canadian Tax Foundation, The National Finances, 1986-1987, Chapter 7, Table 7.13, page 7:26.

TABLE 7

Tax Rates and Numbers of Earners, 1986

Total Family Income $	One Income Earner		Two Equal Income Earners	
	Total Income Tax Paid $	Tax Rate on Total Income %	Total Income Tax Paid $	Tax Rate on Total Income %
15,000	1,219	8.1	826	5.5
20,000	2,436	12.2	2,034	10.2
25,000	3,835	15.3	3,308	13.2
30,000	5,353	17.8	4,644	15.5
50,000	12,680	25.4	10,334	20.7
100,000	36,316	36.3	30,178	30.2
200,000	86,296	43.1	81,242	40.6

Source: Canadian Tax Foundation, *The National Finances 1986-1987*, Chapter 7, and calculations by the authors.

only one of them, their total tax payable would be about $5,353—a difference of $709.

In other words, if their income is earned by one family member, the family pays a gross tax rate of 17.8 percent, but if their income is composed of two salaries the tax rate is only 15.5 percent. The difference between the two tax rates rises as the family income increases until very high income levels are reached (see Table 7). This difference between the single and double income-earner family will continue to haunt the calculations in the remainder of this book. In particular, income tax payments shown in the various composite tax tables in Chapter 3 reflect the fact that, on average, tax payments are made by a mixture of single and double taxpayer families.

THE PROPOSED INCOME TAX SYSTEM

While the foregoing describes how the income tax system has been and on what basis taxpayers have had to comply during the most recent taxation year, in the future, the tax system will be different. The Canadian government has adopted a three-tiered tax system with tax rates of 17 percent on taxable income up to $27,500; 26 percent on taxable income between $27,500 and $55,000 and 29 percent on income over $55,000. Provincial tax rates will apply, as at the present time, to the basic federal tax. The distribution of the tax burden under the new tax system will be the subject of analysis in *Tax Facts 7,* the next book in this series. For the present, the analysis must focus on the known impact of the present system.

WHO PAYS THE INCOME TAX BILL?

While it is possible to calculate tax rates and amounts of tax payable on an "up-to-date" basis, analysis of the income tax system as a whole has to be based on two-year-old statistics. This arises because Revenue Canada processes its data with a two-year lag. Accordingly, our analysis of who pays the income tax—and of other related questions—must be based on 1986 data and in some cases, 1985 data. For the most part, however, we can rest assured that the relative magnitudes involved will be stable over time and, hence, that conclusions reached are reliable for 1988.

In 1985, a total of $48.1 billion was paid by individuals in income taxes and, as Table 8 shows, more than half of it was paid by individuals with incomes below $40,000. Individuals with incomes below $45,000 paid nearly 65 percent of the total income tax bill. In fact, 51 percent of all income taxes were paid by individuals with incomes in the relatively narrow range, $20,000 to $40,000.

As column 4 of Table 8 shows, half of all taxable returns were filed by individuals with incomes less than $15,000. This proportion reflects the large number of part-time workers, students employed during the summer, and other intermittent workers earning modest low incomes. These taxpayers generated only 5.3 percent of total tax revenue, while the top 13.8 percent of taxpayers—those declaring income of $35,000 or more—contributed 54.3 percent of the total income tax bill.

An interesting aspect of the information in Table 8 is the relationship between taxes paid and income declared. For example, as noted above, 45.7 percent of the total income tax bill was paid by individuals with incomes below $35,000. From column 6 we discover that this group of individuals earned 61.3 percent of all the income declared. So, income earners below $35,000 paid a smaller proportion of the total tax bill than their share of total earned income might

TABLE 8

An Analysis of Income, Taxes, and Tax Returns by Income Class, 1985

Total Income Assessed	Col. 1 Percentage of Total Tax Paid by Income Class	Col. 2 Percentage of Total Tax Paid by All Classes at or below this Class Level	Col. 3 Percentage of Total Returns Filed by this Income Class	Col. 4 Percentage of Total Returns Filed by All Classes at or below this Class Level	Col. 5 Percentage of Total Income Declared by this Income Class	Col. 6 Percentage of Total Income Declared by All Classes at or below this Class Level
Less than 5,000	0.0	0.0	19.2	19.2	1.7	1.7
5,000– 9,999	0.9	0.9	16.4	35.6	6.3	8.0
10,000– 14,999	4.4	5.3	14.2	49.8	9.1	17.1
15,000– 19,999	8.0	13.3	12.2	62.0	11.0	28.1
20,000– 24,999	9.9	23.2	9.9	71.9	11.4	39.5
25,000– 29,999	11.1	34.3	8.0	79.9	11.3	50.8
30,000– 34,999	11.4	45.7	6.3	86.2	10.5	61.3
35,000– 39,999	10.1	55.8	4.4	90.6	8.6	69.9
40,000– 44,999	8.4	64.2	3.1	93.7	6.8	76.7
45,000– 49,999	6.1	70.3	1.9	95.6	4.7	81.4
50,000– 99,999	17.5	87.8	3.7	99.3	12.1	93.5
100,000–199,999	6.1	93.9	0.5	99.8	3.5	97.0
200,000 and over	6.0	100.0	0.1	100.0	3.0	100.0

Source: Taxation Statistics, Revenue Canada Taxation, Ottawa, 1987.

suggest. On the other hand, the top 13.8 percent of taxpayers, who had incomes in excess of $35,000, paid about 54.3 percent of the total tax bill while receiving only 38.7 percent of total income earned.

The reason for this, of course, is the fact that the income tax structure is "progressive." That is, it takes a larger fraction from high incomes than it does from low incomes, as is clear from the tax rates presented in Table 4.

GET IT FROM THE RICH

It is often said, and more often believed, that the key to "social welfare" or "social justice" is the redistribution of income. That is, take income from those who have much and give it to those who have little. The extreme form of this prescription is the formula "from each according to his ability [to pay?] and to each according to his need"—the rule advanced in the *Communist Manifesto.*[1]

Our analysis in the preceding section of who pays the income tax reveals that Canada as a country already engages in significant taxation of those whose incomes are above the average. However, a recent publication has suggested that Canada has not been successful in redistributing income from the rich to the poor—that ours is not a "Robin Hood" society.[2] It, therefore, remains interesting to ask whether or not we could achieve a more equal distribution of the benefits of the Canadian good-life by taxing more of the income of the richest Canadians.

How rich is rich?

The question that immediately arises is "How rich is rich?" At what level of income should the government tax away all increases in the interest of "equitable" income distribution? In view of the fact that Members of Parliament earn in excess of $50,000 per year, it is unlikely that "Canadians" would find it equitable to confiscate earnings less than that level. Let us, then, for the sake of illustration, select $50,000 as the maximum income that Canadians should be allowed to earn. Under this rule, all incomes above that level would be subject to a 100 percent rate of income tax, and the proceeds would be distributed to all income earners with incomes less than $50,000.

Counting the rich

In 1985, 690,753 persons filed tax returns reporting income of $50,000 or more. Total income reported by these people was $57 billion. If the government had really taxed away all income beyond $49,999, total tax revenue in 1985 would have been $8.5 billion higher than it actually was. Redistribution of this increased tax revenue to those (15 million people) with incomes less than $50,000 would yield an average annual payment of $566.67 for each person submitting a tax return.

Taxing the "rich" not the source of wealth

This calculation is an important one because it reveals the practical impossibility of "getting it from the rich and redistributing it to the poor." Those who are impatient with the speed at which the economic process improves the condition of the poorest members of society ought to reflect on the fact that the same (or larger) total increase in the incomes of those earning less than $50,000 would be achieved by about 5.6 percent growth in total incomes even if it were distributed in exactly the same way as it is currently.

CHAPTER 3

HOW MUCH TAX
DO YOU REALLY PAY?

The issues discussed in Chapter 2 focus on the income tax bill that Canadians pay. But income tax represents less than half of the total taxes paid by the average Canadian family. The purpose of this chapter is to expand the analysis of taxation to include all taxes that Canadians pay. Tables 13 and 14 at the end of this chapter enable the reader to calculate his or her own total income and total tax bill for 1987. (Complete income and tax tables for each of the provinces are included as an appendix.)

HOW MUCH INCOME DO YOU REALLY EARN?

Cash income

In order to properly calculate how much tax a person (or a group) pays, it is necessary first to determine their income. While this process may seem simple, what a person's income seems to be is very different from what it actually is. This section of the chapter, therefore, explains the method for deriving the income figures used in subsequent sections.

The ultimate goal of income calculations is to determine the total income a Canadian citizen would have if there were no taxes of any sort and other factors remained unchanged. To arrive at such a figure, it is necessary to discover all the income sources a person might have to determine the taxes that might have been paid on this income before the person received it, and finally to add up all of the income including the taxes.

The first layer of income items is easily discovered: wages, salaries, interest from savings bonds, rent from the in-law suite in the basement, or even rent on "the back forty." These sorts of items comprise what in this study is called cash income.

Full cash income and underreporting

In its regular surveys of household income, Statistics Canada finds that people typically omit some income items when they estimate their cash income—that is they underreport their income. The particular items omitted vary from family to family, but, on average, families tend to underestimate their total income by from 4 to 12 percent. Items that might be omitted include miscellaneous interest income, income from "moonlighting," and so on. Fortunately, Statistics Canada does have a comprehensive measure of income in the National Accounts framework, and it is, therefore, possible not only to know that the survey information is incorrect but also to adjust that information to make it more accurate.[1] Accordingly, the full cash income estimates used in this study have been adjusted to make them consistent with the comprehensive income figures contained in the National Accounts. In interpreting the results, in light of his or her own circumstances, the reader should use the cash income figure as the key income figure. The full cash income corresponding to it has been calculated and is displayed in all of the relevant tables.

It may be useful at this stage to provide an example based on a fictitious individual. In order to make the example as comprehensive as possible, it is assumed that the individual involved in the example has income from all of the sources identified in the study—an unlikely circumstance for any real individual. The example is presented in Table 9.

Total income

In addition to cash income, most families also have various forms of non-cash income that must be included in a comprehensive income figure. For example, most wage and salary earners receive fringe benefits as a condition of their employment. Also part of an employee's income is the investment accumulated by his or her pension plan and the interest accumulated—though not paid—on his or her insurance policy.

TABLE 9

Full Cash Income, 1987

Category	$
Wages and salaries	26,598
Income from farm operations	409
Unincorporated non-farm income	2,556
Interest	3,060
Dividends	872
Private Pension Payments	1,617
Family Allowance*	298
Old Age Pension Payments	1,698
Other transfers from government	3,460

Equals

Full Cash Income	40,568

Source: Fraser Institute Canadian Tax Simulator (CANTASIM).
*Income from government is commonly referred to as a "negative tax" or a "transfer payment."

At a higher level of subtlety, a comprehensive income total should also include a number of other income sources. For example, a homeowner is, in effect, his or her own landlord. Therefore, the homeowner receives rental income. Because this implicit income is not paid in cash, its existence must be "imputed" or assigned to the homeowner.

The reason for including such income in a comprehensive income measure is that the homeowner could actually earn that income by renting the premises to somebody else. On the same basis, income is imputed for the rental of farm properties. Income is also imputed because of interest-free loans that people make. The interest foregone is in fact implicit income in the form of a gift.

Profits not paid out as dividends by corporations but held in the form of retained earnings are, in fact, income of the shareholders of the corporation, even though they do not receive it in the year in which it is reported. Also, bad debts which are written off by corporations are, in fact, a source of net income to the debtor and are

TABLE 10

Total Income, 1987

Category	$
Full Cash Income	40,568

Plus

Fringe benefits from employment	2,817
Investment income of insurance companies	697
Investment income of trusteed pension plans	865
Imputed interest	422
Value of food from farms	33
Corporate retained earnings	1,234
Bad debts	82

Equals

Total Income	46,718

Source: Fraser Institute Canadian Tax Simulator (CANTASIM).

treated as such. Finally, food consumed by farm operators is evaluated at market price and attributed to farm operators as income.

Again to make the calculation clear, the total income figure is accumulated in Table 10 for a fictitious individual who is assumed to have income from all sources.

Total income before tax

Some of the income earned by Canadians is taxed before they receive it. For example, shareholders receive dividends on corporate profits after corporate profit taxes have been paid. In the absence of taxes, the dividends (or retained earnings) of the shareholder would have been higher. Therefore, in order to arrive at a total income before tax, it is necessary to add back the corporate profits collected from corporations. Similarly, if there were no property taxes, net after-tax rental income would be higher than it actually is. Therefore, before-tax income must be augmented by the amount of property taxes paid.

In the discussion of indirect and hidden taxes in Chapter 1, it was noted that these taxes reduce the effective income available to Canadians because they increase the price of items that people buy with their incomes. In effect, income after tax is less, in terms of the things it will buy, than it was before tax. In order to arrive at an estimate of before-tax income it is necessary, therefore, to add back to incomes the reduction brought about by indirect taxes.

Finally, payroll taxes levied on firms are, as noted earlier, effectively paid by employees, because the taxes reduce the amount of money available to pay wages and salaries. Accordingly, it is necessary to add back the amount of payroll taxes to employees' incomes to arrive at a before-tax total income estimate.

Table 11 presents an example of a complete income calculation for a fictitious individual who is assumed to have income from all of the income sources identified in the study and to have paid all of the identified taxes.

CALCULATING THE TOTAL TAX BILL

Basically, the tax calculation for the average Canadian family consists of adding up the various taxes that the family pays. Hidden taxes such as taxes on tobacco and alcohol are allocated according to the method indicated in Chapter 1. To preserve consistency, the family used, by way of example, in the tax calculation in Table 12 is the same family used in the income calculation. Readers who have an interest in their own income and tax situation (or that of their neighbour) for 1987 can refer to Tables 13 and 14. An appendix at the end of the book contains income and tax tables for each of the provinces.

TABLE 11

Total Income Before Tax, 1987

Category	$
Wages and salaries	26,598
Income from farm operations	409
Unincorporated non-farm income	2,556
Interest	3,060
Dividends	872
Private Pension Payments	1,617
Family Allowance	298
Old Age Pension	1,371
Government Pension Payments	327
Other transfers from government	3,460

Equals

Full Cash Income	40,568

Plus

Fringe benefits from employment	2,817
Investment income of insurance companies	697
Investment income of trusteed pension plans	865
Imputed interest	422
Value of food from farms	33
Corporate retained earnings	1,234
Bad debts	82

Equals

Total Income	46,718

Plus

Payroll taxes	2,453
Property taxes	1,493
Profit taxes	1,645
Indirect taxes	5,349

Equals

Total income before tax	57,658

Source: Tables 9-11, Fraser Institute Canadian Tax Simulator (CANTASIM).

TABLE 12

Tax Bill of the Average Canadian Family, 1987

Category	$
Family cash income	37,118
Full cash income	40,568
Total income	46,718
Total income before tax	57,658
Taxes	
Income taxes	6,677
Profit taxes	1,537
Sales taxes	2,732
Liquor, tobacco, amusement, and other excise taxes	1,258
Auto, fuel,and motor vehicle license taxes	509
Social security, medical, and hospital taxes	2,966
Property tax	1,395
Natural resources taxes	424
Import duties	452
Other taxes	560
Total taxes	18,510

Taxes as a percentage of: Family cash income 50%
Total income before tax 32%

Source: Fraser Institute Canadian Tax Simulator (CANTASIM).

TABLE A-13
1987 Income Table for Canada

Your Cash Income	Your Full Cash Income	Income from Government	Hidden Income	Hidden Purchasing Power Loss	Total Income Before Tax
		(Dollars per family)			
5000	5302	3708	472	594	6368
5500	5888	4065	510	670	7068
6000	6475	4421	547	746	7769
6500	7062	4777	585	823	8469
7000	7649	5133	623	899	9170
7500	8235	5489	660	975	9870
8000	8822	5846	698	1051	10571
8500	9320	6288	726	1113	11159
9000	9818	6730	753	1175	11747
9500	10317	7172	781	1237	12334
10000	10815	7614	809	1299	12922
10500	11313	8056	836	1361	13510
11000	11863	8071	906	1593	14363
11500	12413	8086	976	1825	15215
12000	12964	8101	1046	2058	16067
12500	13514	8116	1116	2290	16920
13000	14064	8130	1186	2522	17772
13500	14614	8145	1256	2754	18625
14000	15165	8160	1326	2986	19477
14500	15715	8175	1396	3219	20330
15000	16265	8190	1466	3451	21182
15500	16812	8174	1556	3643	22012
16000	17359	8159	1646	3836	22842
16500	17906	8144	1737	4028	23671
17000	18454	8129	1827	4221	24501
17500	19001	8114	1917	4413	25331
18000	19548	8099	2007	4606	26161
18500	20095	8084	2098	4798	26991
19000	20642	8069	2188	4991	27820
19500	21189	8053	2278	5183	28650
20000	21736	8038	2368	5376	29480
20500	22283	8023	2459	5568	30310
21000	22831	7830	2563	5759	31153
21500	23380	7637	2667	5951	31997
22000	23928	7444	2771	6142	32841
22500	24476	7251	2875	6334	33684
23000	25024	7058	2979	6525	34528
23500	25572	6865	3083	6717	35372
24000	26121	6672	3187	6908	36215
24500	26669	6479	3291	7099	37059
25000	27217	6286	3395	7291	37903
25500	27765	6093	3499	7482	38746
26000	28308	6055	3605	7638	39550
26500	28850	6016	3711	7793	40354
27000	29393	5977	3817	7949	41158
27500	29936	5939	3923	8104	41962
28000	30478	5900	4029	8259	42766
28500	31021	5861	4135	8415	43570
29000	31563	5823	4241	8570	44374
29500	32106	5784	4347	8726	45179
30000	32649	5745	4453	8881	45983
30500	33191	5707	4559	9036	46787
31000	33734	5668	4665	9192	47591
31500	34300	5584	4774	9331	48405
32000	34867	5501	4882	9470	49219
32500	35434	5417	4991	9609	50034

TABLE A-13 continued
1987 Income Table for Canada

Your Cash Income	Your Full Cash Income	Income from Government	Hidden Income	Hidden Purchasing Power Loss	Total Income Before Tax
		(Dollars per family)			
33000	36000	5333	5100	9748	50848
33500	36567	5250	5209	9887	51662
34000	37134	5166	5317	10026	52477
34500	37700	5082	5426	10164	53291
35000	38267	4999	5535	10303	54105
35500	38834	4915	5644	10442	54920
36000	39369	4869	5713	10589	55670
36500	39904	4822	5783	10735	56421
37000	40438	4776	5852	10881	57172
37500	40973	4729	5922	11027	57922
38000	41508	4683	5991	11173	58673
38500	42043	4636	6061	11319	59423
39000	42578	4590	6130	11466	60174
39500	43113	4544	6200	11612	60925
40000	43648	4497	6269	11758	61675
40500	44183	4451	6339	11904	62426
41000	44718	4404	6408	12050	63177
41500	45250	4384	6494	12154	63898
42000	45781	4364	6580	12258	64619
42500	46313	4344	6665	12362	65340
43000	46845	4323	6751	12466	66062
43500	47377	4303	6836	12570	66783
44000	47908	4283	6922	12674	67504
44500	48440	4263	7008	12778	68225
45000	48972	4243	7093	12881	68947
45500	49504	4222	7179	12985	69668
46000	50077	4181	7280	13206	70563
46500	50650	4140	7382	13426	71458
47000	51224	4099	7483	13647	72353
47500	51797	4057	7584	13867	73248
48000	52370	4016	7685	14087	74143
48500	52944	3975	7787	14308	75038
49000	53517	3934	7888	14528	75933
49500	54091	3892	7989	14748	76828
50000	54664	3851	8091	14969	77724
50500	55237	3810	8192	15189	78619
51000	55778	3807	8318	15358	79454
51500	56319	3803	8443	15527	80289
52000	56860	3800	8569	15696	81125
52500	57401	3797	8694	15865	81960
53000	57942	3793	8820	16033	82796
53500	58483	3790	8946	16202	83631
54000	59024	3787	9071	16371	84467
54500	59565	3783	9197	16540	85302
55000	60106	3780	9322	16709	86137
55500	60647	3777	9448	16878	86973
56000	61188	3773	9573	17046	87808
56500	61729	3770	9699	17215	88644
57000	62270	3767	9825	17384	89479
57500	62811	3764	9950	17553	90315
58000	63352	3760	10076	17722	91150
58500	63893	3757	10201	17891	91985
59000	64434	3754	10327	18060	92821
59500	64975	3750	10453	18228	93656
60000	65516	3747	10578	18397	94492

TABLE A-14
1987 Tax Table for Canada

Your Cash Income	Profits Tax	Income Tax	Sales Tax	Liquor, Tobacco, Amusement and Other Excise Taxes	Auto, Fuel & Motor Vehicle Licence Taxes	Social Security, Pension, Medical & Hospital Taxes	Property Tax	Natural Resources Taxes	Import Duties	Other Taxes	Total Taxes
					(Dollars per family)						
5000	105	66	133	61	25	551	95	29	22	31	1117
5500	119	73	150	69	28	566	108	33	25	35	1204
6000	132	80	167	77	31	581	120	36	28	39	1290
6500	146	86	184	85	34	595	132	40	30	43	1376
7000	160	93	201	92	37	610	145	44	33	46	1462
7500	173	100	218	100	41	625	157	48	36	50	1549
8000	187	107	234	108	44	640	170	52	39	54	1635
8500	214	129	236	109	44	637	194	59	39	58	1718
9000	241	150	237	109	44	634	219	66	39	61	1802
9500	268	171	239	110	45	631	243	74	40	64	1886
10000	295	193	241	111	45	628	268	81	40	68	1969
10500	322	214	242	111	45	625	293	89	40	71	2053
11000	384	266	278	128	52	652	349	106	46	83	2344
11500	446	318	314	145	59	678	405	123	52	95	2636
12000	508	371	350	161	65	705	461	140	58	108	2927
12500	570	423	386	178	72	731	517	157	64	120	3218
13000	632	475	422	194	79	757	574	174	70	132	3509
13500	694	527	458	211	85	784	630	191	76	144	3801
14000	756	579	494	227	92	810	686	208	82	156	4092
14500	818	632	530	244	99	836	742	225	88	168	4383
15000	880	684	566	261	106	863	798	243	94	181	4674
15500	915	792	608	280	113	900	830	252	101	191	4983
16000	950	901	651	300	121	937	862	262	108	201	5292
16500	985	1009	693	319	129	975	894	272	115	211	5601
17000	1020	1118	735	338	137	1012	926	281	122	221	5910
17500	1056	1227	777	358	145	1049	958	291	129	230	6219
18000	1091	1335	820	377	153	1086	990	301	136	240	6528
18500	1126	1444	862	397	161	1124	1022	310	143	250	6838
19000	1161	1552	904	416	169	1161	1054	320	150	260	7147

7456	270	156	330	1086	1198	176	436	946	1661	1196	19500
7765	280	163	339	1118	1235	184	455	989	1769	1231	20000
8074	290	170	349	1149	1273	192	474	1031	1878	1267	20500
8422	300	180	352	1160	1332	203	502	1090	2023	1278	21000
8770	310	190	356	1171	1391	214	529	1150	2169	1290	21500
9119	319	200	359	1182	1450	226	557	1210	2315	1302	22000
9467	329	210	362	1192	1509	237	584	1270	2460	1314	22500
9816	339	220	365	1203	1568	248	612	1329	2606	1326	23000
10164	349	230	369	1214	1627	259	639	1389	2752	1338	23500
10513	358	240	372	1225	1686	270	667	1449	2897	1349	24000
10861	368	249	375	1235	1745	281	694	1508	3043	1361	24500
11209	378	259	379	1246	1804	292	722	1568	3189	1373	25000
11558	387	269	382	1257	1863	303	749	1628	3334	1385	25500
11856	395	276	386	1272	1904	312	769	1671	3469	1401	26000
12155	403	283	391	1286	1946	320	789	1714	3604	1418	26500
12454	411	291	395	1301	1987	328	809	1758	3739	1434	27000
12752	419	298	400	1316	2029	336	829	1801	3874	1450	27500
13051	427	305	404	1331	2070	344	849	1844	4009	1467	28000
13349	435	312	409	1346	2112	352	869	1888	4144	1483	28500
13648	443	319	413	1361	2154	360	889	1931	4279	1499	29000
13946	451	326	418	1375	2195	368	909	1974	4414	1516	29500
14245	459	334	422	1390	2237	376	929	2018	4549	1532	30000
14543	467	341	427	1405	2278	384	949	2061	4684	1548	30500
14842	475	348	431	1420	2320	392	969	2104	4819	1565	31000
15154	482	357	430	1414	2377	403	994	2159	4981	1558	31500
15465	489	366	428	1408	2434	414	1019	2214	5143	1552	32000
15777	496	375	426	1403	2491	423	1044	2269	5305	1546	32500
16088	503	384	424	1397	2548	433	1069	2323	5468	1539	33000
16400	510	393	423	1391	2605	443	1095	2378	5630	1533	33500
16712	517	402	421	1385	2662	454	1120	2433	5792	1526	34000
17023	523	411	419	1379	2719	464	1145	2488	5954	1520	34500
17335	530	420	417	1374	2776	474	1170	2543	6117	1514	35000
17646	537	429	416	1368	2833	484	1195	2597	6279	1507	35500
17934	545	437	418	1377	2878	493	1216	2642	6411	1517	36000
18221	552	444	421	1386	2922	501	1237	2687	6544	1527	36500
18509	560	452	424	1395	2966	509	1258	2732	6677	1537	37000
18796	567	459	426	1404	3011	518	1278	2777	6810	1547	37500
19084	574	467	429	1412	3055	526	1299	2822	6942	1556	38000
19371	582	474	432	1421	3099	535	1320	2867	7075	1566	38500
19659	589	482	434	1430	3144	543	1340	2912	7208	1576	39000
19946	597	489	437	1439	3188	551	1361	2957	7341	1586	39500

40000	1596	7473	3002	1382	560	3232	1448	440	496	604	20233
40500	1605	7606	3047	1403	568	3277	1457	443	504	612	20521
41000	1615	7739	3092	1423	576	3321	1466	445	511	619	20808
41500	1600	7875	3141	1446	586	3373	1452	441	519	624	21057
42000	1585	8011	3190	1468	595	3426	1439	437	527	629	21307
42500	1570	8147	3239	1491	604	3478	1425	433	536	634	21556
43000	1555	8283	3287	1513	613	3531	1411	429	544	639	21805
43500	1540	8419	3336	1536	622	3583	1398	425	552	645	22054
44000	1525	8554	3385	1558	631	3635	1384	420	560	650	22303
44500	1510	8690	3434	1581	640	3688	1370	416	568	655	22552
45000	1495	8826	3483	1603	649	3740	1357	412	576	660	22801
45500	1480	8962	3531	1625	658	3793	1343	408	584	665	23050
46000	1521	9126	3579	1647	667	3835	1380	419	592	676	23443
46500	1562	9289	3627	1670	676	3877	1417	431	600	688	23836
47000	1603	9452	3675	1692	685	3919	1454	442	608	699	24228
47500	1643	9615	3723	1714	694	3961	1491	453	616	711	24621
48000	1684	9778	3771	1736	703	4003	1528	464	624	722	25014
48500	1725	9942	3819	1758	712	4045	1565	476	632	733	25407
49000	1766	10105	3867	1780	721	4087	1602	487	639	745	25799
49500	1807	10268	3915	1802	730	4130	1640	498	647	756	26192
50000	1847	10431	3963	1824	739	4172	1677	509	655	768	26585
50500	1888	10594	4011	1846	748	4214	1714	521	663	779	26977
51000	1916	10733	4050	1864	755	4250	1739	528	670	788	27292
51500	1943	10872	4090	1883	763	4286	1763	536	676	797	27607
52000	1971	11010	4130	1901	770	4321	1788	543	683	805	27922
52500	1998	11149	4169	1919	777	4357	1813	551	689	814	28237
53000	2025	11288	4209	1937	785	4393	1838	558	696	823	28552
53500	2053	11426	4249	1955	792	4429	1863	566	703	831	28867
54000	2080	11565	4288	1974	799	4465	1888	574	709	840	29182
54500	2108	11703	4328	1992	807	4501	1913	581	716	849	29497
55000	2135	11842	4367	2010	814	4537	1938	589	722	858	29812
55500	2163	11981	4407	2028	822	4573	1963	596	729	866	30127
56000	2190	12119	4447	2047	829	4609	1988	604	735	875	30442
56500	2218	12258	4486	2065	836	4644	2013	611	742	884	30757
57000	2245	12397	4526	2083	844	4680	2038	619	748	892	31072
57500	2273	12535	4566	2101	851	4716	2062	626	755	901	31387
58000	2300	12674	4605	2120	859	4752	2087	634	762	910	31702
58500	2327	12812	4645	2138	866	4788	2112	642	768	919	32017
59000	2355	12951	4684	2156	873	4824	2137	649	775	927	32332
59500	2382	13090	4724	2174	881	4860	2162	657	781	936	32647
60000	2410	13228	4764	2193	888	4896	2187	664	788	945	32962

CHAPTER 4

THE CANADIAN
CONSUMER TAX INDEX

INTRODUCTION

As noted in preceding chapters, Canada's system of taxation is enormously complex. This complexity makes it extremely difficult to describe the tax system in a simple way—difficult to provide a few concise numbers or words to characterize it at a given point in time. Any discussion of the tax system—even a simplified one—is likely to be complicated because the system has so many different aspects. As shown in Chapter 1, even counting the number of taxes is a difficult business. Also complicated is the pattern of tax rates—who pays what—and, of course, the changes in these factors over a period of time. In fact, this book attempts to provide a simplified description of how the tax system is evolving—and, natural pride of authorship notwithstanding, this is not a simple book.

Why construct a Consumer Tax Index?

For individual taxpayers, the most interesting variable for Canadians is how much tax they actually have to pay. In 1976, when we wrote the Fraser Institute's first tax study, *How Much Tax Do You Really Pay?*, we devised an index which we called the Consumer Tax Index. Its purpose was to provide a summary-at-a-glance indicator of what has been happening to the tax bill faced by the average Canadian family over the years since 1961.

Some readers of that book found the tax index too simple—it failed to take into account how the tax money was spent by governments and, therefore, showed only one side of the ledger.[1] On the other hand, the index in that first study and in all subsequent studies has been widely used by financial and consumer affairs columnists across the country to describe how the Canadian tax system has evolved. Moreover, it has been in continuous use ever since its release and has been described as the most up-to-date measure of the extent of Canadian taxation. It was particularly widely cited during the summer of 1978 in the wake of the California tax revolt—the so-called "Proposition 13" movement.

While it is easy to acknowledge that any single measure of something as complex as the Canadian tax system is bound to be incomplete, it is our view that the Canadian Consumer Tax Index is a useful and important indicator of a very important economic burden. Moreover, it remains the only widely available measurement of its kind. In this spirit, we shall continue to calculate and publish the Consumer Tax Index and other associated statistics, in our ongoing assessment of the Canadian tax system.

What is the Canadian Consumer Tax Index?

The Consumer Tax Index is an index of the total dollar tax bill paid by the average Canadian family. It is constructed by calculating the tax bill of an average Canadian family for each of the years included in the index. The index below, therefore, shows the tax bill for a family with an income of $5,000 in 1961, for a family with an income of $8,000 in 1969, and so on. Now, while each of these families was average, in an income sense, in each year selected, it is not necessarily the same family. The objective is not to trace the tax experience of a particular family but rather to plot the experience of a family which was average in each year.

The index thus answers the question, "How has the tax burden of the average family changed since 1961, bearing in mind the fact that the average family has changed in that period?" To be clear about some of the questions the index will not answer, we can note that the average family in 1987 was headed by a younger person, who was more likely to own a car, less likely to own a house, and had fewer members than the average family in 1961. Most important, the family's earned income increased by more than 600 percent over the period.

TABLE 15

Taxes Paid by the Average Canadian Family, 1961–1987

Year	Your Cash Income $	Full Cash Income $	Total Income before Tax $	Taxes Paid $	Increase in Taxes Paid over Base Year %
1961	5,000	5,643	7,582	1,675	—
1969	8,000	8,448	11,323	3,117	86.1
1972	10,000	10,690	14,154	4,203	150.9
1974	12,500	13,353	17,976	5,429	224.1
1976	16,500	17,607	21,872	5,979	257.0
1978	18,500	20,298	27,627	8,343	398.1
1981	26,000	28,343	39,236	12,475	644.8
1984	29,500	34,373	47,484	15,066	799.5
1987	37,118	40,568	57,658	18,510	1,005.1

Source: Data for the years 1961–1987 were calculated from the Fraser Institute tax tables.

The basis of the tax index is the total tax calculation presented in Table 15. Income and tax calculations were made for a selection of years beginning in 1961 and culminating in 1987. (As information becomes available in the future, we shall publish the index to include the later years. We hope to be able to provide the reader with the Consumer Tax Index every two years.) The tax bill of the average family yielded by this process was then converted to index form. The results are reported in Table 16 and Figure 5. They show that the tax bill of the average Canadian family has increased by 1005.1 percent over the period since 1961, and that the index had a value of 1105.1 in 1987.

At least part of that increase reflects the effects of inflation. In order to eliminate the effect of the declining value of the dollar, we have also calculated the tax index in real dollars—that is, dollars of 1971 purchasing power. While this adjustment has the effect of reducing the steepness of the index's path over time, the real-dollar tax index, nevertheless, increased by 153.2 percent over the period (see Table 17).

TABLE 16

The Canadian Consumer Tax Index
1961 = 100

Year	Index*
1961	100.0
1969	186.1
1972	250.9
1974	324.1
1976	357.0
1978	498.1
1981	744.8
1984	899.5
1987	1,105.1

Source: Table 15.

*The Index is constructed from the "Taxes Paid" column in Table 15. To calculate the Index, the taxes in each year are divided by the figure in the base year, in this case 1961, and then multiplied by 100.

TABLE 17

The Consumer Tax Index Based on 1971 Dollars of Purchasing Power

Year	Real Value of Taxes Paid	Percent Increase in Taxes Paid over Base Year
1961	$2,233.3	—
1969	3,312.4	48.3
1972	4,010.5	79.6
1974	4,343.2	94.5
1976	4,015.4	79.8
1978	4,762.0	113.2
1981	5,264.4	135.7
1984	5,198.6	132.8
1987	5,653.8	153.2

Source: See Table 15 and Statistics Canada, The Consumer Price Index, Catalogue No. 62-001, Table 2.

Figure 5—The Canadian Consumer Tax Index
1961–1987

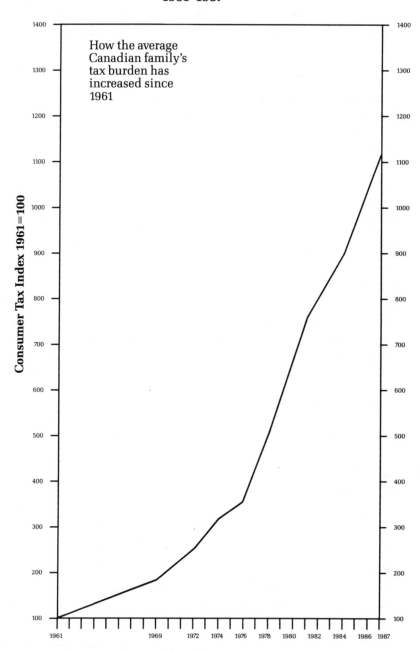

How the average
Canadian family's
tax burden has
increased since
1961

Consumer Tax Index 1961=100

Source: Table 16

What the Consumer Tax Index shows

The dramatic increase in the Consumer Tax Index over the period 1961-1987 was produced by the interaction of a number of factors. First, there was a dramatic increase in incomes over the period, and even with no change in tax rates the family's tax bill would have increased substantially. In the absence of a change in the tax rate, growth in family income alone would have produced an increase in the tax bill from $1,675 in 1961 to $12,435 in 1987. The second contributing factor was a 55 percent increase in the tax rate faced by the average family.

In recent years, commencing in 1975, the rate of increase in the tax bill has slowed appreciably, reflecting a decline in the overall rate of taxation and an increase in the extent to which all governments are resorting to issuing debt—that is, bonds—to finance their expenditures. This phenomenon shows up most clearly in a comparison of the Consumer Tax Index and the Fraser Institute's new Balanced Budget Tax Index. The latter includes the debt that is being acquired by the various levels of government on the grounds that, if the governments' budgets were, in fact, balanced and no debt were issued, the tax bill would have been higher by the amount of the debt issued. The debt issued by such Crown corporations as electric power authorities is not included in this calculation since, in a case of this kind, future electricity rates or other prices—rather than tax rates—will reflect the cost of the debt.

This comparison of the two indices in Table 18 and Figure 6 shows that if governments were to balance their budgets, the tax bill of the average family would be very much higher than it actually is. To the extent that Canadians are made to feel better off by the apparent decline in tax rates, ignoring the accumulating debt acquired by government, they are being subjected to a colossal fiscal illusion.

TAXES VERSUS THE NECESSITIES OF LIFE

While the Consumer Tax Index does show the way in which the average family's tax bill has changed over the past twenty-six years, that information becomes even more significant when it is compared

TABLE 18

**The Consumer Tax Index Versus
the Balanced Budget Tax Index**

Year	Consumer Tax Index	Balanced Budget Tax Index
1961	100.0	100.0
1969	186.1	204.3
1972	250.9	281.1
1974	324.1	368.5
1976	357.0	398.4
1978	498.1	581.9
1981	744.8	828.4
1984	899.5	1,080.1
1987	1,105.1	1,379.5

Source: Table 19.

with other major expenditures of the average Canadian family—for food, shelter, and clothing.

Table 19 and Figure 7 compare the average dollar amount of family cash income, total income before tax, and total taxes paid with family expenditures on other items such as food, shelter, and clothing. It is clear from these figures not only that taxation has become the most significant item that consumers face in their budgets but also that it is growing more rapidly than any other single item. This is made more evident in Table 20 and Figure 8, which show the various items as indices based on 1961 to 1986 values. While incomes rose during the period from 1961 to 1986 by 615.8 percent, prices rose 313.6 percent, food expenditures rose 294.5 percent, shelter by 479.3 percent, and clothing 302.3 percent, the tax bill of the average family grew by 938.4 percent. The balanced budget tax rate grew even more rapidly, rising by 1,083.0 percent over the same period.

Table 21 and Figure 9 present the same information but expressed as percentages of total income before tax. In this form, the data reveal some interesting comparisons. For example:

• In 1961 the average family had to use 35.2 percent of its income to provide itself with food, shelter, and clothing. In the same year, 22.1 percent of the family's income went to government in the form of taxes.

Figure 6 —The Canadian Consumer Tax Index
Versus the Balanced Budget Tax Index 1961–1987

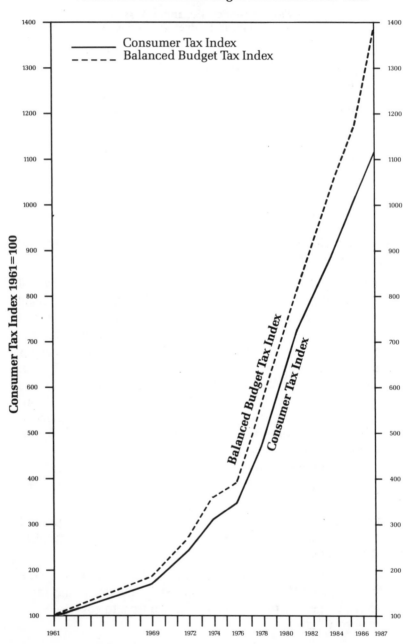

TABLE 19

Income, Taxes, and Selected Expenditures of the Average Canadian Family
(dollars)

	Income		Taxes		Selected Expenditures*		
Year	Average cash income	Total income before tax	Average taxes paid	Average taxes paid (including deficits)	Average shelter expenditures	Average food expenditures	Average clothing expenditures
1961	5,000	7,582	1,675	1,675	977	1,259	435
1969	8,000	11,323	3,117	3,422	1,294	1,634	654
1972	10,000	14,154	4,203	4,708	1,778	1,791	739
1974	12,500	17,976	5,429	6,172	1,983	2,320	886
1976	16,500	21,872	5,979	6,673	2,709	2,838	1,119
1978	18,500	27,627	8,343	9,746	3,283	3,319	1,250
1981	26,000	39,236	12,475	13,876	4,009	3,690	1,486
1984	29,000	47,484	15,066	18,092	5,355	4,722	1,659
1986**	33,500	54,272	17,393	19,816	5,660	4,967	1,750

Source: Statistics Canada, *Urban Family Expenditure, 1978-1981,* Catalogue Nos. 62-549, 62-547, 62-544, 62-541, 62-537, 62-535, 62-525, 62-555, 62-001, *Prices and Price Indices.*

*All selected expenditure items include indirect taxes.

**Estimates for 1986 are based on separate estimates of the 1986 income, tax, and family distribution.

Figure 7—Taxes and Selected Expenditures of the Average Canadian Family, 1961-1986

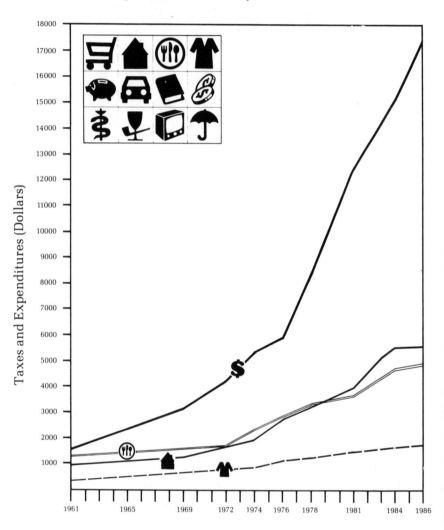

Source: Table 19

TABLE 20

Indices of Income, Taxes, and Selected Expenditures of the Average Canadian Family
1961 = 100

	Taxes		Income	Consumer Prices	Selected Expenditures*		
Year	Consumer tax index	Consumer tax index (including deficits)	Total income before tax index	Consumer price index	Average shelter expenditure index	Average food expenditure index	Average clothing expenditure index
1961	100.0	100.0	100.0	100.0	100.0	100.0	100.0
1969	186.1	204.3	149.3	125.5	132.4	129.8	150.3
1972	250.9	281.1	186.7	139.8	182.0	142.3	169.9
1974	324.1	368.5	237.1	166.8	203.0	184.3	203.7
1976	357.0	398.4	288.5	198.7	277.3	225.4	257.2
1978	498.1	581.9	364.4	233.7	336.0	263.6	287.4
1981	744.8	828.4	517.5	316.0	410.3	293.1	341.6
1984	899.5	1,080.1	626.3	386.5	548.1	375.1	381.4
1986**	1,038.4	1,183.0	715.8	413.6	579.3	394.5	402.3
Percent Increase 1961–1986	938.4	1,083.0	615.8	313.6	479.3	294.5	302.3

Source: The figures in this table are converted to indices by dividing each series in Table 19 by its value in 1961 and then multiplying that figure by 100.

Consumer Price Index data from Statistics Canada, No. 62-001.

*All expenditure items include indirect taxes.

**Expenditure data for 1986 are trend estimates.

Figure 8—How the Canadian Consumer Tax Index (CTI) Has Increased, Relative to Other Selected Indices, 1961-1986

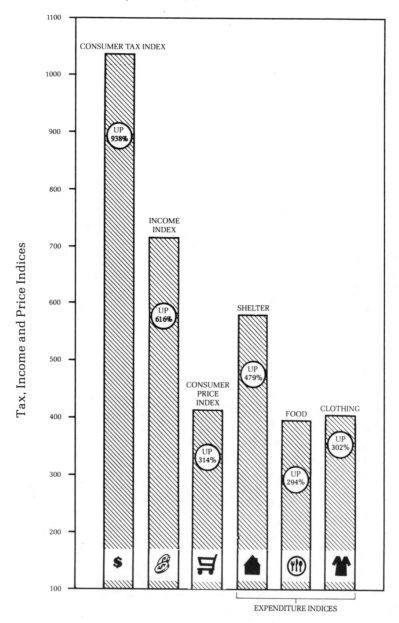

Source: Table 20

TABLE 21

Taxes and Selected Expenditures of the Average Canadian Family Expressed as a Percentage of Total Income Before Tax (percent)

Year	Taxes	Selected Expenditure*		
		Shelter	Food	Clothing
1961	22.1	12.9	16.6	5.7
1969	27.5	11.4	14.4	5.8
1972	29.7	12.6	12.7	5.2
1974	30.2	11.0	12.9	4.9
1976	27.3	12.4	13.0	5.1
1978	30.2	11.9	12.0	4.5
1981	31.8	10.2	9.4	3.9
1984	31.7	11.3	9.9	3.5
1986**	32.0	10.5	9.2	3.2

Source: Table 19.
*All selected expenditure items include indirect taxes.
**Expenditure data for 1986 are trend estimates.

- By 1974 the situation had been reversed, and 30.2 percent of income went to satisfy the taxman, while only 29 percent was required to provide the family with food, shelter, and clothing.
- By 1986 the situation had worsened significantly. Whereas the proportion of income consumed by taxes continued to increase, the fraction of income spent on necessities (food, shelter, and clothing) dropped dramatically. The average family spent just over 23 percent of its income on the necessities of life while 32 percent of its income went to the taxman.

The average burden of tax versus the average family's tax burden

This chapter has dealt exclusively with the tax position of the "average" family. To some extent the conclusions of such an analysis can be misleading, because of the exclusive focus on the average family. In the next chapter this weakness is corrected by discussing the tax position of "unaverage" Canadians. Similarly, it is possible to mistake the average family's burden for another measure which is sometimes used, that of the average tax burden of all Canadian families. Before leaving this discussion of the average

Figure 9—Taxes and Selected Expenditures* of the Average Canadian Family Expressed as a Percentage of Total Income Before Tax

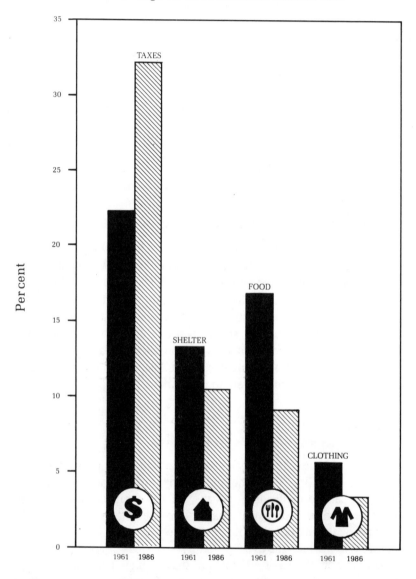

* All selected expenditure items include indirect taxes.

Source: Table 21

TABLE 22

**Average Tax Rates for All Canadian Families Versus
Tax Rates of the Average Canadian Family
(percent)**

Year	*Average Canadian Family's Tax Rate*		*Average Tax Rate for All Canadian Families*	
	Excluding deficit	*Including deficit*	*Excluding deficit*	*Including deficit*
1961	22.1	22.1	25.2	25.2
1969	27.5	30.2	31.1	34.3
1972	29.7	33.3	31.6	35.3
1974	30.2	34.3	33.3	37.8
1976	27.3	30.5	31.8	35.9
1978	30.2	35.3	31.0	35.0
1981	31.8	35.4	32.9	35.7
1984	31.7	36.3	32.3	36.8
1987	32.1	40.1	32.7	40.8

Source: Fraser Institute Canadian Tax Simulator (CANTASIM).

family's tax burden, therefore, it is important to establish and understand the differences between these two measures.

In this chapter, the tax burden of the average family has been calculated by selecting an average-income family and calculating that family's theoretical tax burden from the tax tables. In this regard, it is interesting to note that the average family in 1987 had an income of $37,118 and that the family paid $6,677 in income tax or 36.1 percent of its total tax bill. The remaining $11,833 or 63.9 percent was made up of other taxes such as sales and property taxes. Another way of calculating an average tax burden would be to add up all the taxes in the economy and simply divide that total tax figure by total incomes in the economy. This would produce an average tax rate for all Canadian families. Such a calculation is displayed in Table 22 along with the average family's tax rate. This table also shows what the tax rates would have been if the deficits incurred by governments were included.

It is quite clear from the table that the average family's tax rate is below that faced by all Canadians in the economy as a whole. Moreover, as the analysis in the next chapter shows, the tax rate faced by the average family is considerably lower than the tax rates faced by families whose incomes are above average. Similarly, much of the total tax bill is collected from families whose incomes are above the average. For example, in 1986, 68 percent of the tax bill was collected from families with incomes above the income of the average family ($33,500).

It is this "progressivity" of the tax structure which produces the difference between the two average tax calculations—the more progressive the tax system the greater the difference. This "progressivity" is the subject of discussion in the next chapter.

CHAPTER 5

THE RELATIVE
BURDEN OF TAX

In Chapter 4 we investigated the tax burden of the average Canadian family and how that burden has changed through time. While that view of the tax system has some inherent interest, it represents a very particular aspect of a much larger picture. The purpose of this chapter is to examine this larger picture—to examine all income groups and how their relative income and tax positions have changed over the time span between 1961 and 1987.

THE DISTRIBUTION OF INCOME

In order to analyze the relative income and tax positions of Canadians, we have divided all Canadian families into ten groups or deciles. This was accomplished by arranging families according to total income before tax from lowest to highest and then selecting the first 10 percent (lowest incomes), the second 10 percent, and so on. The resulting grouping of families is presented in Table 23.

The table reveals that the relative shares of the different income groups have been remarkably constant over the period since 1961. In evaluating this result, the reader should bear in mind that the data have a variety of aspects that make them susceptible to misinterpretation. First of all, the data fail to make any allowance for the age of the individuals. This is an important fact, since age is a principal determinant of income. Young people first entering the labour market typically earn wages or salaries considerably below the national or provincial average and considerably below their own lifetime average. Similarly, elderly people who have passed the age of retirement are typically in a phase of their life when their incomes

TABLE 23

Decile Distribution of Income
(percent)

Year	Lower Income Groups			Middle Income Groups				Upper Income Groups		
	1st	*2nd*	*3rd*	*4th*	*5th*	*6th*	*7th*	*8th*	*9th*	*10th*
1961	2.6	2.6	5.6	7.0	8.1	9.1	11.3	11.5	14.9	27.2
1969	1.6	2.9	4.9	6.2	7.7	8.7	10.3	12.3	15.2	30.0
1972	1.0	3.3	4.7	6.2	7.5	8.9	10.4	12.7	15.8	29.4
1974	1.0	2.8	4.6	6.2	7.5	9.2	10.3	13.3	15.6	29.8
1976	1.2	3.0	4.6	5.9	7.1	8.9	9.8	13.2	16.5	29.8
1978	1.3	3.0	4.9	6.6	8.0	9.1	10.9	12.7	15.7	28.0
1981	1.4	3.2	5.1	6.5	7.8	9.3	11.0	13.1	15.9	26.8
1984	1.4	3.0	4.5	6.1	7.8	9.1	10.9	12.9	19.2	25.1
1987	1.4	3.1	4.4	6.0	7.7	9.2	11.2	13.4	21.8	21.8

Source: Fraser Institute Canadian Tax Simulator (CANTASIM).

TABLE 24

Income in Age Groups as a Percentage of Average for All Groups, Male Canadian, 1985

Age	Taxation Statistics Data	Statistics Canada Income Survey Data	Average Profile
under 25	0.553	0.537	0.545
25–34	1.227	1.362	1.295
35–44	1.674	1.744	1.709
45–54	1.728	1.733	1.731
55–64	1.542	1.437	1.489
65 & over	1.110	0.906	1.008

Source: Statistics Canada, *Income Distribution by Size in Canada, 1987,* Catalogue No. 13-207; Revenue Canada, *Taxation Statistics,* 1987 Edition, Analyzing Returns for the 1985 Taxation Year and Miscellaneous Statistics, Summary Table 4.

are considerably below their lifetime average and when they are spending the savings and pensions of their working lifetime.

For example, Table 24 displays the "life-cycle average expected wage" for a Canadian male in 1985. Two sources of data on the earnings profile are available—information from taxation statistics and Statistics Canada's income surveys. While the two sources yield different estimates, they both show the expected age-related movement in wages relative to the average.

Failure to account for the age of income earners can lead to a considerably distorted impression of how income distribution is changing—particularly if there are dramatic changes in the age structure of the population as there have been in Canada. In future years, as the number of people in or near retirement grows, it can be expected that the distribution of income will be affected. More of the population will be elderly and more of the population will have lower incomes as a result. Evidently, this will not mean that the population is, in any sense, worse off.

A second important warning for those who would draw from these data conclusions about the "equity" of the income distribution is that they ignore income-in-kind that people receive from government. Housing, medical care, education, and other services which are received as direct benefits from government, rather than in the form of cash payments, are not reflected in the income distribution table. And the public provision of these services potentially represents one of the most significant redistributive aspects of Canadian society.

For these reasons it would be inappropriate to infer from the data in Table 23 that there had been no change in the effective distribution of income since 1961. The data in its present form is incapable of providing meaningful answers to that question. What the data does provide is a yardstick against which to measure the distribution of taxes. It will allow us to infer whether, for example, groups of people with low incomes bear a disproportionate share of the tax burden. It will also permit us to construct tax rates for families, ranging from those with the lowest incomes to those with the highest incomes. This will provide an indication of the progressivity or regressivity of the Canadian tax burden. In order to arrive at these results, it is necessary to combine income results with those on tax distribution which are the subject of the next section.

TAX DISTRIBUTION AND TAX RATES

Our measurements of the distribution of the tax burden provide some interesting and, indeed, puzzling results for the tax distribution. Whereas up until 1978 there had been a more or less steady increase in the tax burden borne by the upper third of income groups (that is to say, the top three income deciles), during the interval 1976 to 1978, the share of the top group fell markedly. As can be seen from Table 25, during 1976 the top three income deciles accounted for fully 66.5 percent of the total tax payments. By 1978, this had fallen to 59.6 percent of the total. Of course, the decline in the tax burden borne by the top three income deciles was matched by a corresponding increase in the tax burden faced by the middle income deciles. For example, the fourth to seventh income deciles which had borne 27.3 percent of the total tax burden in 1976, by 1978 were bearing 33.5 percent—an increase of 6.2 percentage points. This almost completely matches the 6.9 percentage point reduction in the tax burden borne by the upper income group.

Some, but not all, of the shift in incidence had reversed by 1981 when the top three deciles paid 61 percent of the total tax bill. This trend continued to 1984 as the tax paid by the top three deciles

TABLE 25
Decile Distribution of Taxes
(percent)

Year	Lower Income Groups			Middle Income Groups				Upper Income Groups		
	1st	2nd	3rd	4th	5th	6th	7th	8th	9th	10th
1961	2.1	2.1	4.5	5.7	6.7	7.7	10.5	10.7	14.6	35.6
1969	1.1	2.0	4.0	5.3	6.9	7.7	9.4	11.8	15.0	36.9
1972	.6	1.9	3.5	5.1	6.7	8.4	9.8	12.4	16.1	35.5
1974	.6	1.8	3.7	5.1	6.7	8.4	9.6	13.0	15.9	35.5
1976	.6	1.9	3.6	5.1	6.0	7.6	8.6	12.9	17.3	36.3
1978	.7	2.2	4.2	6.2	7.7	8.8	10.8	13.0	16.6	30.0
1981	.6	1.9	3.8	5.5	7.1	8.9	11.0	13.4	16.8	31.1
1984	.6	1.6	3.0	5.1	7.2	8.9	10.9	13.2	21.0	28.5
1987	.7	1.9	3.3	5.2	7.3	9.1	11.2	13.9	23.7	23.7

Source: Fraser Institute Canadian Tax Simulator (CANTASIM).

TABLE 26
Decile Distribution of the Personal Income Tax
(percent)

Year	Lower Income Groups			Middle Income Groups				Upper Income Groups		
	1st	2nd	3rd	4th	5th	6th	7th	8th	9th	10th
1976	.05	.60	2.1	3.7	6.0	9.5	10.3	13.7	17.1	37.3
1978	.03	.30	1.5	4.1	6.5	8.6	11.7	14.7	19.5	33.2
1981	.11	.35	1.5	3.7	5.8	8.4	11.5	14.6	19.1	35.1
1984	.12	.42	1.2	3.2	5.7	8.5	11.5	14.5	23.3	31.6
1987	.14	.72	1.8	3.8	6.1	8.6	11.4	14.8	26.3	26.3

Source: Fraser Institute Canadian Tax Simulator (CANTASIM).

reached nearly 63 percent. Both the lower and middle income groups experienced relative declines in their share of taxes paid.

The reasons for the fluctuations in the tax burden are somewhat difficult to isolate. Tables 26, 27 and 28 help to illuminate the various determining elements. The first of these tables is the distribution of the personal income tax and it shows that personal income taxes have offset the decline in the overall tax burden of upper income groups, albeit very slightly.

As Table 26 shows, there had been a very modest shift in the incidence of the personal income tax system away from the lower income deciles and toward the upper income deciles. The top three income groups accounted for 69.4 percent of total income tax payments in 1984 up from 68.1 percent in 1976. In 1987, the top three income groups accounted for 67.4 percent of total income tax payments. This modest shift was accompanied by a dramatic change within the upper three deciles. Whereas in 1976 the highest income decile paid 37.3 percent of the total personal income tax burden, by 1987 this decile's share had dropped to only 26.3 percent.

A major factor explaining variations in the share of taxes paid by the top three deciles has been the change in the incidence of the capital related taxes in the interval between 1976 and 1984. The "capital related taxes," are chiefly property taxes and corporate profit taxes. As Table 27 shows, the change in the pattern of these taxes has been truly astounding. A dramatic shift took place between 1976 and 1978 when the burden of property taxes for the top three deciles dropped from 72.2 to 51.8 percent. Since that time, however, the burden has been creeping up so that by 1987 the top three deciles accounted for 53.3 percent of property taxes.

Analysis of the underlying factors reveals that the reason for the dramatic shift in the incidence of the capital taxes has been the change in the distribution of capital income amongst Canadians. The procedure for allocating the burden of capital taxes, such as the Corporate Profits Tax, property taxation, and so on, is to allocate them to individuals on the basis of the individual's receipt of income from capital. (This is done because economic analysis suggests that taxes on capital reduce all capital income.) Between 1976 and 1978 there was a significant change in the distribution of capital income especially between high- and middle-income earners. The extent of this

TABLE 27
Decile Distribution of Profit Taxes and Property Taxes
Profit Taxes
(percent)

	Lower Income Groups				Middle Income Groups			Upper Income Groups		
Year	1st	2nd	3rd	4th	5th	6th	7th	8th	9th	10th
1976	1.3	3.5	5.5	6.6	4.1	3.3	3.8	10.7	18.1	43.4
1978	1.7	4.6	8.3	9.1	8.5	7.5	8.0	9.2	11.8	31.2
1981	1.0	4.2	7.0	7.5	7.5	7.9	8.9	10.4	12.6	33.0
1984	.8	3.2	5.5	7.4	8.8	7.9	8.1	9.3	19.0	30.0
1987	.9	3.9	6.3	7.8	9.2	9.2	9.3	10.9	21.3	21.3

Property Taxes

	Lower Income Groups				Middle Income Groups			Upper Income Groups		
	1st	2nd	3rd	4th	5th	6th	7th	8th	9th	10th
1976	1.3	3.5	5.5	6.6	4.1	3.3	3.8	10.7	18.1	43.4
1978	1.7	4.7	8.3	9.5	8.6	7.4	8.0	8.9	11.2	31.7
1981	1.1	4.4	7.5	7.9	7.8	8.2	9.2	10.6	12.6	30.8
1984	.9	3.5	6.3	8.0	9.3	7.6	8.3	9.2	18.4	28.5
1987	.9	3.9	6.3	7.8	9.2	9.2	9.4	11.1	21.1	21.1

Source: Fraser Institute Canadian Tax Simulator (CANTASIM).

TABLE 28
Decile Distribution of Capital Income
(percent)

	Lower Income Groups				Middle Income Groups			Upper Income Groups		
Year	1st	2nd	3rd	4th	5th	6th	7th	8th	9th	10th
1976	1.3	3.5	5.5	6.6	4.1	3.3	3.8	10.7	18.1	43.4
1978	1.7	4.6	8.3	9.1	8.5	7.4	8.0	9.1	11.8	31.2
1981	1.1	4.4	7.5	7.9	7.8	8.2	9.2	10.6	12.6	30.8
1984	.9	3.7	6.6	8.3	9.4	7.6	8.3	9.2	18.3	27.7
1987	.9	3.9	6.3	7.8	9.2	9.2	9.4	11.1	21.1	21.1

Source: Fraser Institute Canadian Tax Simulator (CANTASIM).

change can be seen in Table 28 which displays the distribution of total capital income in the two years. As can also be seen, the shift has persisted through to 1984.

One factor which underlies all of the distribution series is the massive surge in the number of individuals in the upper income classes. In 1978, for example, only 10.0 percent of the population had an income of $35,000 or more. By 1987, 39.6 percent of the population enjoyed an income at least as large as that. Much of this increase in the number of families in the higher income groups is a result of the fact that an increasing number of families contains two income earners whose joint income pushes the family into the higher bracket. The implication of this for the distribution of taxation amongst families is that the upper-income deciles seem to be paying less and less tax because they are composed increasingly of individuals with lower incomes.

As noted in Chapter 2, two incomes totalling, say, $30,000 are taxed less in total (by the income tax structure) than one income of $30,000. Since upper income families are increasingly composed of two income earners, the average tax rate in this income range has been falling. And, during the 1974-1984 period the number of two income earner families included in the top income brackets has increased.

In 1974, 80.6 percent of the families in the top quintile had two or more income earners: by 1987 this figure had risen to 89 percent. The upper income group is disproportionately affected by this phenomenon because if two income earners are earning the average national income, their family falls into the highest income group.

There is also, however, some evidence that the rates of taxation have been declining, particularly those experienced by the upper income groups. Thus, for example, in 1976 the top decile of income tax filers in Canada paid an average tax rate of 22.2 percent. However, by 1983 the average income tax rate of the top income group had dropped to 21.6 percent. To some considerable extent this drop in the average tax rate has been due to the increasing extent to which Canadians have taken advantage of the tax preferences which the government has inserted in the tax system to encourage the development of various sectors of the economy such as oil exploration, scientific research, rental housing, and Canadian films.

One feature of the income distribution developments has been the reversal of trends established in 1976. Until 1984 the percent of income of the upper income groups had been steadily decreasing with the middle income groups gaining ground. This is quite clearly reflected in Table 23 which shows the distribution of income by population decile. Whereas in 1976 nearly 60 percent of all income was earned by the top three deciles, this had dropped to 56.4 percent by 1978 and to 55.8 percent by 1981. However, by 1987, the upper three deciles had rebounded to claim 57 percent of income. Whether or not this is the start of a new trend is too early to tell. One trend that did continue though was the decline of the top income decile. From 1976 to 1987, the percent of income claimed by the top decile dropped from 29.8 to 21.8.

Two further implications of the total tax distribution (as opposed to the distribution of income taxes which will have been examined) are interesting to note. The flatness in the tax distribution which began to emerge in the late 1970s was reversed in 1981 and 1984 as a sharper progressivity developed. The difference between the tax rate of the top decile and that experienced by the bottom decile has risen from 13.0 percent in 1961 to 18.9 percent in 1987.

However, as Table 29 shows, the difference between the tax rate experienced by the top decile and the middle income deciles has collapsed. Whereas the tax rate in the tenth decile was 12 percentage points higher than the fifth decile in 1961, by 1987 the difference had shrunk to 4.7 percentage points.

The reason for this development can be seen in Table 30 which shows the change in tax rates by decile since 1961. Evidently, the increase in tax rates has been concentrated on the middle and upper middle income decile families. The lowest income deciles have experienced a reduction in their tax rates while the top decile has had to bear an increase in rates less than a third the rate increase experienced by the ninth decile, for example. On the average, middle income deciles have faced an increase in tax rates greater than 8 percent.

The natural flattening of the tax system means that there will not be dramatic changes in the incidence of tax once the three-tiered system of income tax is fully in effect.

TABLE 29

Decile Distribution of Tax Rates

(percent)

Year	Lower Income Groups			Middle Income Groups				Upper Income Groups		
	1st	2nd	3rd	4th	5th	6th	7th	8th	9th	10th
1961	19.9	19.9	19.9	20.4	20.9	21.3	23.2	23.3	24.6	32.9
1969	20.6	21.5	25.1	26.4	27.8	27.4	28.2	29.7	30.6	38.2
1972	17.0	18.7	23.8	26.2	28.0	29.6	29.7	31.0	32.2	38.1
1974	21.4	21.5	26.8	27.6	29.7	30.2	30.9	32.5	33.9	39.6
1976	15.7	20.9	25.2	27.4	27.0	27.3	27.9	31.0	33.4	38.8
1978	16.3	22.7	26.4	29.1	29.9	30.0	30.7	31.7	32.8	33.2
1981	13.6	19.5	24.4	28.1	29.9	31.4	32.8	33.7	34.7	38.2
1984	12.7	17.3	21.3	26.6	29.4	30.9	31.9	32.5	34.9	36.2
1987	16.7	19.9	24.5	28.4	30.9	32.1	32.9	34.0	35.6	35.6

Source: Fraser Institute Canadian Tax Simulator (CANTASIM).

TABLE 30

Increase in Tax Rates by Decile Since 1961

(percent)

Year	Lower Income Groups			Middle Income Groups				Upper Income Groups		
	1st	2nd	3rd	4th	5th	6th	7th	8th	9th	10th
to 1978	-3.6	2.8	6.5	8.7	9.0	8.7	7.5	8.4	8.2	.3
to 1981	-6.3	-.4	4.5	7.7	9.0	10.1	9.5	10.5	10.1	5.3
to 1984	-7.2	-2.6	1.4	6.2	8.5	9.6	8.7	9.2	10.3	3.3
to 1987	-3.2	0	4.6	8.0	10.0	10.8	9.7	10.7	11.0	2.7

Source: Fraser Institute Canadian Tax Simulator (CANTASIM).

WHO PAYS THE TAX BILL?

As can be seen from Table 25, the largest portion of the tax burden ultimately settles on the highest income group. In 1987, the top 10 percent of Canadian families paid 23.7 percent of all taxes paid. The top 30 percent of families paid just over 61 percent of all taxes paid. Of course, while the tax burden fell disproportionately on the top 30 percent of families, that group also received a substantial fraction of the income. In 1987, the top 30 percent earned 57 percent. While this was down from the 59.5 percent of the total earned in 1976, it is larger than the 53.6 percent share this group received in 1961.

In 1984, the top 30 percent of income earners had an average cash income of $55,101 and included all families whose incomes were above $36,370. (This compares to an average income of $32,615 in 1976 and an entry income of $21,494 in that year.)

THE RAGS-TO-RICHES TAX BURDEN

The notion that a tax system may discourage people from improving their income situation suggests the value of calculating the extent to which Canadians' individual tax situations would have changed during the 1961 to 1987 period if their incomes had increased. Table 31 presents the results of a tax analysis for a hypothetical Canadian individual whose cash income grew at a constant rate from half the average in 1961 to twice the average in 1987. This "Horatio Alger's" income grew from $2,750 in 1961 to $74,240 in 1987.

In 1961, a total income of $4,776 attracted a tax bill of $960, or an average tax rate of total income of 20.1 percent. By 1972, the hypothetical income earner had a total income of $17,518 and paid taxes of $4,382, or a tax rate of 25.0 percent. Finally, in 1987, when cash income was $74,240, total income was $116,000, and taxes paid amounted to $40,847. Thus, the average tax rate on total income had risen to 35.2 percent. In each case, the tax calculation does not include the amount of debt accumulated by government on behalf of the taxpayer. Including debt, the increase in tax burden is even more dramatic, as can be seen in Table 31.

TABLE 31

The Rags-To-Riches Tax Burden

	1961	1969	1972	1976	1981	1984	1987	% Increase 1961–87
Cash income (assumed)*$	$2,750	$7,302	$10,531	$17,159	$31,591	$45,561	$74,240	2,600
Total income $	4,776	12,290	17,518	28,101	50,732	72,313	116,000	2,329
Taxes paid (excluding deficit)** $	960	2,900	4,382	6,184	15,196	24,299	40,847	4,155
Taxes paid (including deficit)** $	960	3,232	4,993	7,081	17,046	27,551	51,007	5,213
Tax rate on total income (excluding deficit)	20.1%	23.6%	25.0%	22.0%	30.0%	33.6%	35.2%	75
Tax rate on total income (including deficit)	20.1%	26.3%	28.5%	25.2%	33.6%	38.1%	44.0%	118

Source: Fraser Institute Canadian Tax Simulator (CANTASIM).

*Assumed income was arrived at by assuming that income increased smoothly in equal percentage increases from the poverty level in 1961 to high income in 1987.

**Taxes are calculated for 1961,1969,1972,1976,1981,1984,and 1987 using the tax tables in the study. The figures are shown in two ways, one including deficit and one excluding the government deficit.

Over the twenty-six-year period 1961-1987, the hypothetical Horatio experienced a 2,328.8 percent increase in total income. Over the same period, taxes paid increased by 4,154.9 percent excluding debt. Including debt they increased 5,213.2 percent.

Meanwhile, the tax rate faced by the individual increased 75.1 percent. In improving their circumstances, Canadian Horatio Algers would have earned a total income over the period of $583,110 and paid total taxes of $288,280.

CHAPTER 6

TAXES ACROSS CANADA

In this chapter, we extend the analysis of the preceding sections to focus on particular provinces.

Table 32 presents the tax situation for the average family by province of residence. Average family in this context is taken to mean a family unit which had an average income for the province of residence. Thus, for example, the average family in Newfoundland had an income of $28,605 in 1987 whereas the average family in Ontario had an income of $41,415 and so on. It is very interesting to survey the results for each of these families and to see just how the tax bill varies from province to province and from category to category. It is particularly interesting to see which provinces have the highest propensity to tax in each of the tax categories. In this regard, there are some real surprises. The most obvious surprise in the table is that the most heavily taxed family in the country is an Albertan family. The average Albertan family, according to the table, pays a total of $22,151 in tax on an income of $39,138. This seems astonishing indeed and requires some explanation—particularly in light of the popular notion that Albertans are the least taxed Canadians because of the revenue from the petroleum in that province.

In allocating the tax burden in the Province of Alberta, it became obvious at an early stage of the analysis that there was a problem. The source of the difficulty was that the tax collected in the Province of Alberta from the petroleum industry totally swamped the other sources of taxation in Alberta and, indeed, in any of the other provinces. In the case of Alberta, our estimates suggest that some $3,876 of natural resource revenues were extracted for each family resident in Alberta in 1987. This was composed of $2,052 in direct natural resource taxes and some $1,824 in estimated corporate profit taxes associated with petroleum development. Of course, these

TABLE 32

Taxes of the Average Family by Province, 1987
(dollars)

Prov.	Average Cash Income	Full Income	Total Income Before Tax	Profits Tax	Income Tax	Sales Tax	Liquor Tobacco, Amusement, and Other Excise Taxes	Auto Fuel, & Motor Vehicle Licence Taxes	Social Security Pension, Medical & Hospital Taxes	Property Tax	Natural Resources Taxes	Import Duties	Other Taxes	Total Taxes
Nfld.	28,605	34,353	45,499	813	3,633	2,199	636	437	1,886	311	159	52	592	10,718
PEI	30,967	31,029	40,751	686	3,545	1,610	606	466	1,973	840	12	29	142	9,909
N.S.	33,118	34,161	48,433	678	4,928	2,653	1,637	529	3,086	726	52	239	375	14,903
N.B.	32,175	33,211	46,575	817	4,284	2,809	1,264	573	2,198	949	107	138	799	13,938
Que.	34,618	37,294	52,223	960	6,477	2,804	1,031	595	2,960	939	43	396	962	17,167
Ont.	41,415	45,561	65,506	1,455	7,377	3,656	1,306	539	3,312	1,592	68	651	482	20,438
Man.	33,754	38,059	51,423	1,248	5,078	2,047	635	390	2,288	1,466	204	243	1,107	14,706
Sask.	32,065	35,686	51,204	1,746	5,013	1,416	1,333	263	1,847	1,895	3,002	93	-157	16,451
Alta.	39,138	41,541	61,872	3,596	8,168	983	1,904	325	3,291	1,437	2,052	258	137	22,151
B.C.	36,053	37,931	53,068	1,156	6,376	1,974	1,303	466	2,647	1,141	719	531	102	16,415
Canada	37,118	40,568	57,658	1,537	6,677	2,732	1,258	509	2,966	1,395	424	452	560	18,510

Source: Statistics Canada data on taxes and income; and Fraser Institute Canadian Tax Simulator (CANTASIM).

petroleum, related taxes are not collected directly from the tax-paying public in Alberta, rather they are collected, indirectly, from the corporations who recover the oil and gas from the ground. It is nevertheless the case, that the gas and oil in the ground in Alberta belongs to the people of Alberta. It is appropriate, therefore, to regard the taxes which are paid as a result of the exploitation of these petroleum resources, as the income of Albertans and, hence, a tax on Albertans.

While this is the appropriate technical treatment of petroleum resource taxes it does confuse somewhat the inter-provincial comparison of tax burdens. Many Canadians, for example, would like nothing better than to live in Alberta and be subject to what looks like the heaviest tax burden in the country. That, of course, is because of the high incomes which are available to those fortunate enough to work in the petroleum industry in Alberta and because of the relatively high level of services provided by government and the low level of direct tax which Albertans are compelled to pay. If we subtract from the $22,151 total tax bill that the average Albertan family faced in 1987, the $3,876 per family which was collected on their behalf from the petroleum industry, we find that the total tax bill of Albertans is reduced very significantly to $18,275 for the average family. The implications of this for the gross tax rate faced by Albertans can be seen in Table 33 wherein the bracketed figures represent the tax rate calculated on a basis which excludes the natural resource taxes. Thus, for example, in the case of the tax rate on cash income, the rate is reduced from an unbelievable 56.6 percent down to 46.7 percent which is in line with other provinces.

A similar adjustment for natural resource taxes has been made for both Saskatchewan and British Columbia. Adjusted tax rates are also shown for these provinces in Table 33. As can be seen from that table the fraction of income paid in taxes by the average Canadian family varies very significantly from province to province. Excluding for the moment the unusual case of Alberta, we find that the average rate of taxation on total income before tax varies from a low of 23.6 percent in Newfoundland to a high of 32.9 percent in Quebec. It is also interesting to note that the relatively high income provinces of British Columbia, Saskatchewan, and Ontario all have

TABLE 33

Provincial Tax Rates* as a Percentage of Cash Income, Full Income, and Total Income Before Tax, 1987

Province	Cash Income		Full Income		Total Income Before Tax	
	Excluding Deficit	Including Deficit	Excluding Deficit	Including Deficit	Excluding Deficit	Including Deficit
Newfoundland	37.5	45.1	32.1	37.6	23.6	28.4
Prince Edward Island	32.0	36.6	32.0	36.5	24.3	27.8
Nova Scotia	45.0	53.1	43.6	51.4	30.8	36.3
New Brunswick	43.3	49.6	42.0	48.0	29.9	34.2
Quebec	49.6	58.6	46.0	54.3	32.9	38.8
Ontario	49.3	56.7	44.9	51.6	31.2	35.9
Manitoba	43.6	52.6	38.6	46.7	28.6	34.6
Saskatchewan**	51.3	61.7	46.1	55.4	32.1	38.6
	(41.9)	(50.4)	(37.7)	(45.3)	(26.3)	(31.5)
Alberta**	56.6	70.8	53.3	66.7	35.8	44.8
	(46.7)	(58.3)	(44.0)	(54.9)	(29.5)	(36.9)
British Columbia**	45.5	54.0	43.3	51.4	30.9	36.7
	(43.5)	(51.8)	(41.4)	(49.2)	(29.6)	(35.2)
Canada	49.9	62.3	45.6	57.0	32.1	40.1

Source: Fraser Institute Canadian Tax Simulator (CANTASIM).
*For the average family in 1987 in each of the provinces.
**Bracketed figures are the tax rates resulting when natural resources taxes are removed from the average family's tax bill.

tax rates in the 30 percent range—very close to the national average tax rate.

As Table 32 reveals, there are also some interesting variations within the various tax categories—for example, the relative dependence on property taxation and income taxation as revenue sources. Outstanding in this regard is the reliance of the prairie provinces on property taxation and Newfoundland's almost complete lack of this form of taxation. In the case of Saskatchewan, 11.5 cents out of every tax dollar paid by Saskatchewan taxpayers is collected in the form of property taxes. In the case of Newfoundland, only 2.9 cents of the taxpayers' dollar is collected in the form of property tax. Newfoundland's lack of activity on the property tax front is more than compensated for by sales tax activity. In fact, Newfoundland pays 20.5 cents out of every tax dollar in the form of sales tax, followed by New Brunswick which pays 20.1. Of course, this is made up of both the provincial retail sales tax, which is obvious to every taxpayer, as well as the federal and provincial sales taxes which are paid for at the wholesale level and are not evident to retail customers.

Income tax is most heavily relied upon in British Columbia which collects 38.8 percent of its total revenue in that form. However, Alberta had the highest rate of income taxation in that the average income earner in Alberta faced a 20.9 percent rate of income tax on cash income. By comparison, the average Prince Edward Islander faced an income tax rate of only 11.4 percent.

In comparing these tax results for the various provinces, it is important to remember that the standard of comparison is the average family. That is to say, the family in each province whose income was average. It is, therefore, the case that the individuals in different provinces will have different incomes since the average income in each province varies considerably. And, some of the differences in tax burden between the provinces is due to nothing more than the differences in income.

Table 34 provides a distribution of taxes by province according to population decile. The great benefit of this table is that it is independent of the incomes within each province and makes possible a comparison of the provinces according to how the tax burden is spread within that province amongst the various income groups. The

TABLE 34
Decile Distribution of Taxes by Province, 1987
(percent)

Province	Lower Income Groups			Middle Income Groups				Upper Income Groups		
	1st	2nd	3rd	4th	5th	6th	7th	8th	9th	10th
Newfoundland	0.4	1.4	2.2	4.8	6.2	8.1	10.9	14.3	18.8	32.7
Prince Edward Island	0.6	1.6	2.7	4.9	6.3	8.9	11.2	13.7	17.6	32.5
Nova Scotia	0.4	1.4	2.4	4.4	6.5	8.6	11.1	14.1	22.5	28.7
New Brunswick	0.4	1.5	2.8	4.9	7.1	8.9	11.9	14.2	20.0	28.4
Quebec	0.8	1.6	2.8	4.9	6.8	9.0	11.4	13.8	23.1	25.8
Ontario	0.8	2.2	3.7	6.1	7.9	9.1	11.1	17.2	21.0	21.0
Manitoba	0.5	1.8	3.2	5.0	6.8	9.1	11.3	13.5	22.6	26.3
Saskatchewan	0.6	1.6	2.9	5.2	7.0	9.2	11.0	12.8	22.4	27.2
Alberta	0.7	2.6	3.9	5.8	7.4	9.4	10.6	15.3	22.2	22.2
British Columbia	0.7	1.9	3.1	5.1	7.1	9.2	11.5	13.5	23.4	24.5
Canada	0.7	1.9	3.3	5.2	7.3	9.1	11.2	13.9	23.7	23.7

Source: Fraser Institute Canadian Tax Simulator (CANTASIM).

outcome of this analysis as reflected in the table is simply astounding in that there seems to be very little variation amongst the provinces in the extent of the progressivity or regressivity of the tax systems in the various provinces. That is to say, the upper income groups tend to absorb a little over 60 percent of the total tax bill with some minor variations around that. The Maritimes and Quebec have a tendency to tax the upper income groups a little heavier than the other provinces but the differences are not dramatic.

The stability of the distribution series in each of the provinces is made the more remarkable by the fact that there is such a different reliance on the different forms of taxation in the various provinces. This fact, which was pointed out above in the discussion of Table 32, ought to provide some variation in the tax rates unless, of course, the differences in the progressivity and regressivity of the various tax rates are offsetting. From Table 34 it appears that the various tax measures are offsetting in their effect on the rate of progressivity of the provincial tax systems.

However, as Table 35 shows, there are some important differences between the tax systems in the various provinces. Table 35 highlights these differences in the form of the average tax rates which are payable by the various income deciles in the different provinces. Thus, for example, in Newfoundland the lowest income decile paid a tax rate of 6.4 percent on average, whereas the top decile paid a tax rate of 37.1 percent. In Quebec, on the other hand, the top decile paid 38.1 percent, whereas the bottom decile paid 18.0 percent.

ACCOUNTING FOR THE FUTURE TAX BURDEN

During the last year, it has become increasingly obvious that the tax comparison between provinces has a major defect. Namely, those provinces which relied less on taxes and more on borrowing to finance their expenditures, even though expenditures had not fallen, would appear to have a less intrusive taxation system. The reason, as we have discussed in previous chapters, is because deficits force the burden of the taxes needed to finance current expenditures onto future generations of taxpayers. A measure of taxation which ignores this shifting of the tax burden cannot provide an accurate picture of

TABLE 35

Tax Rates by Decile by Province, 1987
(percent)
(Income Measure = Total Income Before Tax)

Province	Lower Income Groups			Middle Income Groups				Upper Income Groups		
	1st	*2nd*	*3rd*	*4th*	*5th*	*6th*	*7th*	*8th*	*9th*	*10th*
Newfoundland	6.4	10.8	13.9	20.8	22.2	24.3	27.7	30.2	32.3	37.1
Prince Edward Island	6.9	10.9	14.1	18.4	20.6	23.7	25.4	26.1	27.9	30.6
Nova Scotia	8.7	13.9	18.1	24.0	28.2	30.0	32.1	32.9	34.8	35.4
New Brunswick	9.1	14.6	18.9	23.7	27.7	29.8	32.9	33.3	35.3	37.2
Quebec	18.0	18.3	22.2	27.5	30.5	32.5	34.1	34.7	37.6	38.1
Ontario	17.8	22.7	26.6	30.5	31.6	32.4	33.6	33.7	33.7	33.7
Manitoba	10.5	15.5	20.2	24.2	26.0	28.2	29.4	30.0	32.4	33.1
Saskatchewan	13.8	16.4	21.3	27.5	30.1	31.1	32.3	32.1	35.9	36.8
Alberta	19.5	27.6	30.2	34.3	35.2	36.9	36.7	38.0	39.5	39.5
British Columbia	15.3	18.6	22.4	26.0	28.9	30.5	31.6	33.0	35.2	35.3
Canada	16.7	19.9	24.5	28.4	30.9	32.1	32.9	34.0	35.6	35.6

Source: Fraser Institute Canadian Tax Simulator (CANTASIM).

the true fiscal stance of a government. Therefore, we have created a provincial distribution of tax burdens based on the total tax consequences of the current expenditures of government—that is, including the deficits which governments incur. The data are presented in Table 36.

It is clear from this data, and the compilations included in Table 33, which show tax rates by province including the deficit levels, that there is significant reliance on taxing future generations by all jurisdictions. But, some are more enthusiastic about this form of taxation. The result is to change the ranking of tax burdens to some extent. On the total income before tax basis, the inclusion of future taxes pushes Alberta from fifth to first in total tax burden—excluding the resource taxation in which that and other provinces engage. On the other hand, New Brunswick moves from fourth to seventh once deficits have been included.

Underlying this pattern of taxation, is a pattern of expenditures. That is, the reason for raising revenues is to pay for government spending. Accordingly, an alternative, and perhaps more direct measure of the level of government activity is the level of government spending. Table 37 presents provincial government spending levels in each of the provinces both in total dollar terms and per capita. These figures do not include the amount of federal government spending by province and the impression given by the figures may be misleading to the extent that there is a differential in the level of spending activity by the federal government in the various provinces.

Even though there may be some difficulties with the calculations, they reveal a very interesting pattern of spending and suggest interesting comparisons with the taxation data. As in the case of the tax data, Quebec emerges as the top spender with $4,528 per capita. It is followed closely by Alberta, which spends $4,355 per head and Newfoundland and Prince Edward Island at $4,296 and $4,157 respectively.

TABLE 36

Taxes of the Average Family Including Deficits by Province, 1987
(dollars)

Prov.	Average Cash Income	Full Income	Total Income Before Tax	Profits Tax	Income Tax	Sales Tax	Liquor, Tobacco, Amusement, and Other Excise Taxes	Auto Fuel, & Motor Vehicle Licence Taxes	Social Security Pension, Medical & Hospital Taxes	Property Tax	Natural Resources Taxes	Import Duties	Other Taxes	Total Taxes
Nfld.	28,605	34,353	45,499	986	4,434	2,551	743	507	2,358	371	184	65	703	12,902
PEI	30,967	31,029	40,751	793	4,146	1,680	638	486	2,467	909	12	36	170	11,337
N.S.	33,118	34,161	48,433	811	5,871	2,919	1,983	582	3,858	769	58	299	425	17,575
N.B.	32,175	33,211	46,575	966	5,034	2,954	1,468	603	2,748	1,027	113	173	865	15,949
Que.	34,618	37,294	52,223	1,141	7,641	3,105	1,233	659	3,595	1,181	48	496	1,172	20,271
Ont.	41,415	45,561	65,506	1,673	8,718	3,896	1,544	575	4,052	1,627	72	814	528	23,499
Man.	33,754	38,059	51,423	1,516	6,347	2,413	716	460	2,930	1,512	237	310	1,290	17,731
Sask.	32,065	35,686	51,204	2,154	6,198	1,713	1,631	318	2,309	1,929	3,631	116	-219	19,780
Alta.	39,138	41,541	61,872	4,518	10,307	1,271	2,406	420	4,125	1,595	2,652	322	111	27,727
B.C.	36,053	37,931	53,068	1,405	7,700	2,195	1,553	518	3,264	1,252	800	663	130	19,480
Canada	37,118	40,568	57,658	1,950	8,469	3,546	1,596	661	3,729	1,413	549	565	629	23,107

Source: Statistics Canada data on taxes and income; and Fraser Institute Canadian Tax Simulator (CANTASIM).

TABLE 37

Total Spending and Spending Per Capita by Province, 1987

Province	Total Spending (millions of $)	Spending Per Capita ($)
Newfoundland	2,488.0	4,296
Prince Edward Island	533.3	4,157
Nova Scotia	3,289.7	3,702
New Brunswick	2,821.0	3,901
Quebec	30,080.0	4,528
Ontario	34,846.0	3,745
Manitoba	4,188.0	3,868
Saskatchewan	3,779.7	3,694
Alberta	10,416.1	4,355
British Columbia	10,220.0	3,483

Source: Provicial Government Budget Addresses, 1987.

Even though there may be some difficulties with the calculations, they reveal a very interesting pattern of spending and suggest interesting comparisons with the taxation data. As in the case of the tax data, Quebec emerges as the top spender with $4,528 per capita. It is followed closely by Alberta, which spends $4,355 per head and Newfoundland and Prince Edward Island at $4,296 and $4,157 respectively.

Appendix

HOW TO USE THE INCOME TABLES

Tables A-1 to A-11 are the 1987 Income Tables for each of the ten provinces and Canada as a whole. You will be able to locate within $500 your cash income in the first column of each Income Table. You will then be able to establish for the province in which you reside, your full cash income, income from government, hidden income, hidden purchasing power loss, and total income before tax.

Step 1. Make a rough calculation of your family's cash income from all sources for the year 1987.

			$
	eg. Alberta		
Example:	Husband's income in 1987	=	10,500
	Wife's income in 1987	=	10,500
	Dependent daughter's income in 1987	=	200
	Total cash income	=	21,200

Step 2. Since the table is calculated to the nearest $500, round off your cash income to the nearest $500.
Example: $21,200
Round to nearest $500   = $21,000

Step 3. If your income exceeded $60,000, skip to step 5. If not, proceed through steps 3 and 4.
Locate the line in the 1987 Income Table for your province of residence that has the entry $21,000 in the first column. (The column headed "Your Cash Income".)
Example: See the line in the 1987 Income Table.

Step 4. Read off Full Cash Income, Income from Government, Hidden Income, Hidden Purchasing Power Loss, and Total Income Before Tax.
Example:

Your Cash Income	Your Full Cash Income	Income from Government	Hidden Income	Hidden Purchasing Power Loss	Total Income Before Tax
$	$	$	$	$	$
21000	22164	8284	2196	7142	31502

Step 5. If your cash income exceeded $60,000 you will have to use the Detailed Income Calculation Schedules which accompany each Income Table.

There may be a discrepancy in the totals across the columns in both the Income and the Tax Tables, and the given totals. Any discrepancy is due to rounding

TABLE A-1
1987 Income Table for the Province of Alberta

Your Cash Income	Your Full Cash Income	Income from Government	Hidden Income	Hidden Purchasing Power Loss	Total Income Before Tax
		(Dollars per family)			
5000	4834	2785	503	1174	6512
5500	5522	3181	547	1213	7281
6000	6210	3578	590	1251	8051
6500	6897	3974	634	1289	8821
7000	7585	4370	677	1328	9590
7500	8273	4767	721	1366	10360
8000	8961	5163	764	1404	11129
8500	9410	5772	767	1451	11628
9000	9859	6381	770	1498	12128
9500	10308	6989	774	1545	12627
10000	10757	7598	777	1592	13126
10500	11205	8207	780	1639	13625
11000	11749	8116	867	2126	14741
11500	12292	8024	954	2612	15858
12000	12835	7933	1041	3098	16975
12500	13378	7841	1128	3585	18091
13000	13921	7750	1215	4071	19208
13500	14465	7658	1302	4557	20324
14000	15008	7567	1390	5044	21441
14500	15551	7475	1477	5530	22558
15000	16094	7384	1564	6016	23674
15500	16646	7465	1621	6119	24386
16000	17198	7547	1679	6221	25097
16500	17750	7629	1736	6323	25809
17000	18302	7711	1793	6426	26521
17500	18853	7793	1851	6528	27232
18000	19405	7875	1908	6630	27944
18500	19957	7956	1966	6733	28655
19000	20509	8038	2023	6835	29367
19500	21061	8120	2081	6937	30079
20000	21613	8202	2138	7039	30790
20500	22164	8284	2196	7142	31502
21000	22685	8063	2293	7459	32436
21500	23205	7843	2389	7776	33370
22000	23725	7623	2486	8093	34304
22500	24245	7402	2583	8410	35238
23000	24765	7182	2680	8727	36172
23500	25285	6962	2777	9044	37105
24000	25805	6741	2873	9361	38039
24500	26325	6521	2970	9678	38973
25000	26845	6301	3067	9995	39907
25500	27365	6080	3164	10312	40841
26000	27901	6047	3293	10435	41630
26500	28438	6014	3423	10558	42419
27000	28974	5981	3552	10681	43207
27500	29510	5948	3682	10804	43996
28000	30046	5915	3812	10927	44785
28500	30582	5881	3941	11050	45573
29000	31118	5848	4071	11173	46362
29500	31654	5815	4200	11296	47151
30000	32190	5782	4330	11419	47940
30500	32727	5749	4459	11542	48728
31000	33263	5716	4589	11665	49517
31500	33841	5633	4671	11911	50422
32000	34419	5550	4753	12156	51328
32500	34997	5468	4834	12402	52233

TABLE A-1 continued
1987 Income Table for the Province of Alberta

Your Cash Income	Your Full Cash Income	Income from Government	Hidden Income	Hidden Purchasing Power Loss	Total Income Before Tax
		(Dollars per family)			
33000	35575	5385	4916	12648	53139
33500	36153	5303	4998	12893	54044
34000	36731	5220	5080	13139	54950
34500	37309	5138	5162	13385	55856
35000	37887	5055	5243	13630	56761
35500	38465	4973	5325	13876	57667
36000	38884	4933	5339	13841	58065
36500	39302	4893	5354	13807	58463
37000	39720	4853	5368	13772	58861
37500	40139	4813	5382	13738	59259
38000	40557	4774	5396	13703	59657
38500	40976	4734	5410	13669	60055
39000	41394	4694	5425	13634	60453
39500	41812	4654	5439	13600	60851
40000	42231	4614	5453	13565	61249
40500	42649	4574	5467	13531	61647
41000	43067	4535	5481	13496	62045
41500	43621	4429	5578	13683	62881
42000	44174	4324	5675	13869	63717
42500	44727	4218	5771	14056	64554
43000	45280	4112	5868	14242	65390
43500	45833	4007	5964	14429	66226
44000	46386	3901	6061	14615	67062
44500	46939	3796	6158	14802	67898
45000	47492	3690	6254	14988	68735
45500	48045	3585	6351	15175	69571
46000	48626	3584	6509	15321	70457
46500	49207	3584	6668	15468	71343
47000	49788	3584	6826	15615	72229
47500	50368	3583	6985	15762	73115
48000	50949	3583	7143	15909	74001
48500	51530	3583	7302	16056	74887
49000	52110	3582	7460	16203	75773
49500	52691	3582	7619	16350	76659
50000	53272	3581	7777	16496	77546
50500	53853	3581	7936	16643	78432
51000	54391	3583	8060	16872	79322
51500	54928	3584	8184	17100	80212
52000	55466	3586	8308	17328	81103
52500	56004	3587	8433	17556	81993
53000	56542	3589	8557	17785	82883
53500	57080	3590	8681	18013	83774
54000	57617	3592	8806	18241	84664
54500	58155	3593	8930	18469	85555
55000	58693	3595	9054	18698	86445
55500	59231	3596	9178	18926	87335
56000	59769	3598	9303	19154	88226
56500	60307	3599	9427	19382	89116
57000	60844	3601	9551	19611	90006
57500	61382	3602	9675	19839	90897
58000	61920	3604	9800	20067	91787
58500	62458	3606	9924	20296	92677
59000	62996	3607	10048	20524	93568
59500	63533	3609	10173	20752	94458
60000	64071	3610	10297	20980	95348

SCHEDULE A-1

1987 Detailed Income Calculation for the Province of Alberta

Your Cash Income

1. Full Cash Income	$= \text{Cash Income} \times 1.068$	= _____
2. Of which Income from Government	$= \$ \ 3610$	= _____
3. Hidden Income	$= \text{Cash Income} \times 0.172$	= _____
4. Hidden Purchasing Power Loss	$= \text{Cash Income} \times 0.350$	= _____
Total Income before Tax	$= 1 + 3 + 4$	= _____

EXAMPLE:

Your Cash Income

1. Full Cash Income	$= \$ \ 70,000 \times 1.068$	$= \$ \ 70,000$
2. Of which Income from Government	$= \$ \ 3,610$	$= \$ \ 74,760$
3. Hidden Income	$= \$ \ 70,000 \times 0.172$	$= \$ \ 3,610$
4. Hidden Purchasing Power Loss	$= \$ \ 70,000 \times 0.350$	$= \$ \ 12,040$
		$= \$ \ 24,500$
Total Income before Tax		$= \$ 111,300$

TABLE A-2
1987 Income Table for the Province of British Columbia

Your Cash Income	Your Full Cash Income	Income from Government	Hidden Income	Hidden Purchasing Power Loss	Total Income Before Tax
		(Dollars per family)			
5000	4518	3444	505	522	5545
5500	5259	3752	549	610	6418
6000	6001	4059	592	698	7291
6500	6742	4367	636	785	8164
7000	7484	4675	680	873	9036
7500	8225	4983	723	960	9909
8000	8966	5290	767	1048	10782
8500	9372	5678	795	1102	11269
9000	9777	6065	824	1155	11756
9500	10182	6452	852	1209	12243
10000	10588	6840	880	1263	12730
10500	10993	7227	909	1316	13218
11000	11460	7263	958	1501	13918
11500	11927	7299	1007	1685	14619
12000	12394	7334	1056	1869	15320
12500	12861	7370	1105	2054	16020
13000	13329	7406	1154	2238	16721
13500	13796	7442	1204	2422	17422
14000	14263	7478	1253	2607	18122
14500	14730	7513	1302	2791	18823
15000	15197	7549	1351	2975	19524
15500	15833	7608	1483	3162	20477
16000	16469	7666	1614	3348	21431
16500	17105	7725	1746	3534	22385
17000	17741	7783	1877	3720	23339
17500	18377	7842	2009	3907	24292
18000	19012	7901	2141	4093	25246
18500	19648	7959	2272	4279	26200
19000	20284	8018	2404	4466	27154
19500	20920	8076	2536	4652	28108
20000	21556	8135	2667	4838	29061
20500	22192	8193	2799	5025	30015
21000	22678	7957	2873	5209	30759
21500	23163	7720	2946	5394	31504
22000	23649	7483	3020	5579	32248
22500	24135	7247	3094	5763	32992
23000	24621	7010	3168	5948	33737
23500	25107	6773	3241	6133	34481
24000	25593	6537	3315	6317	35225
24500	26079	6300	3389	6502	35970
25000	26564	6063	3463	6687	36714
25500	27050	5827	3536	6871	37458
26000	27537	5768	3591	6943	38071
26500	28023	5709	3646	7016	38684
27000	28509	5650	3701	7088	39297
27500	28995	5591	3755	7160	39910
28000	29481	5532	3810	7232	40523
28500	29968	5473	3865	7304	41136
29000	30454	5415	3920	7376	41749
29500	30940	5356	3974	7448	42362
30000	31426	5297	4029	7520	42975
30500	31912	5238	4084	7592	43588
31000	32398	5179	4139	7664	44201
31500	32945	5155	4321	7855	45121
32000	33492	5130	4504	8045	46041
32500	34039	5106	4687	8236	46962

TABLE A-2 continued
1987 Income Table for the Province of British Columbia

Your Cash Income	Your Full Cash Income	Income from Government	Hidden Income	Hidden Purchasing Power Loss	Total Income Before Tax
		(Dollars per family)			
33000	34586	5082	4870	8427	47882
33500	35132	5057	5053	8617	48802
34000	35679	5033	5235	8808	49723
34500	36226	5009	5418	8999	50643
35000	36773	4984	5601	9190	51563
35500	37320	4960	5784	9380	52484
36000	37876	4922	5830	9516	53222
36500	38432	4883	5876	9651	53959
37000	38988	4845	5923	9787	54697
37500	39544	4806	5969	9922	55435
38000	40100	4768	6015	10058	56173
38500	40656	4729	6062	10193	56911
39000	41212	4691	6108	10329	57649
39500	41768	4653	6154	10464	58387
40000	42325	4614	6200	10600	59125
40500	42881	4576	6247	10735	59863
41000	43437	4537	6293	10871	60601
41500	43792	4389	6333	10895	61020
42000	44147	4240	6373	10920	61440
42500	44502	4091	6413	10944	61860
43000	44857	3942	6454	10968	62279
43500	45212	3793	6494	10993	62699
44000	45567	3644	6534	11017	63118
44500	45922	3496	6574	11042	63538
45000	46277	3347	6614	11066	63958
45500	46632	3198	6654	11090	64377
46000	47225	3329	6768	11413	65406
46500	47818	3460	6881	11736	66435
47000	48411	3591	6994	12059	67464
47500	49004	3722	7107	12382	68493
48000	49596	3853	7220	12705	69522
48500	50189	3984	7333	13028	70551
49000	50782	4115	7447	13351	71580
49500	51375	4246	7560	13674	72609
50000	51967	4377	7673	13997	73638
50500	52560	4508	7786	14320	74667
51000	53063	4498	7891	14457	75411
51500	53567	4488	7995	14594	76156
52000	54070	4478	8100	14730	76900
52500	54573	4468	8204	14867	77645
53000	55077	4458	8309	15004	78389
53500	55580	4448	8413	15141	79134
54000	56084	4438	8518	15277	79879
54500	56587	4428	8622	15414	80623
55000	57090	4418	8727	15551	81368
55500	57594	4408	8831	15688	82112
56000	58097	4398	8936	15824	82857
56500	58600	4388	9040	15961	83601
57000	59104	4378	9144	16098	84346
57500	59607	4368	9249	16235	85091
58000	60110	4358	9353	16371	85835
58500	60614	4348	9458	16508	86580
59000	61117	4338	9562	16645	87324
59500	61620	4328	9667	16782	88069
60000	62124	4318	9771	16918	88813

SCHEDULE A-2

1987 Detailed Income Calculation for the Province of British Columbia

Your Cash Income

1. Full Cash Income = Cash Income × 1.035 = _____

2. Of which Income from Government = $ 4,318 = _____

3. Hidden Income = Cash Income × 0.163 = _____

4. Hidden Purchasing Power Loss = Cash Income × 0.282 = _____

Total Income before Tax = 1 + 3 + 4 = _____

EXAMPLE:

Your Cash Income

1. Full Cash Income = $ 70,000 × 1.035 = $ 70,000

2. Of which Income from Government = $ 4,318 = $ 72,450

3. Hidden Income = $ 70,000 × 0.163 = $ 4,318

4. Hidden Purchasing Power Loss = $ 70,000 × 0.282 = $ 11,410

= $ 19,740

Total Income before Tax = $ 103,600

TABLE A-3
1987 Income Table for the Province of Manitoba

Your Cash Income	Your Full Cash Income	Income from Government	Hidden Income	Hidden Purchasing Power Loss	Total Income Before Tax
		(Dollars per family)			
5000	4467	3048	414	411	5293
5500	5022	3406	457	479	5958
6000	5577	3764	500	546	6623
6500	6131	4123	544	614	7289
7000	6686	4481	587	682	7954
7500	7241	4839	623	749	8620
8000	7796	5198	673	817	9285
8500	8407	5638	720	878	10005
9000	9018	6078	768	939	10724
9500	9629	6519	815	1000	11444
10000	10240	6959	862	1062	12164
10500	10851	7400	910	1123	12883
11000	11421	7356	996	1290	13707
11500	11992	7312	1082	1458	14531
12000	12562	7269	1168	1625	15355
12500	13133	7225	1254	1792	16179
13000	13704	7181	1340	1960	17003
13500	14274	7138	1426	2127	17827
14000	14845	7094	1512	2294	18651
14500	15415	7050	1598	2462	19475
15000	15986	7006	1684	2629	20299
15500	16525	6973	1743	2813	21081
16000	17064	6939	1802	2996	21863
16500	17604	6906	1861	3180	22645
17000	18143	6872	1920	3363	23426
17500	18682	6839	1979	3547	24208
18000	19222	6805	2038	3730	24990
18500	19761	6771	2097	3914	25772
19000	20300	6738	2156	4097	26553
19500	20839	6704	2215	4281	27335
20000	21379	6671	2274	4464	28117
20500	21918	6637	2333	4648	28899
21000	22596	6509	2441	4782	29819
21500	23275	6382	2548	4917	30740
22000	23953	6254	2656	5051	31661
22500	24632	6126	2764	5185	32581
23000	25310	5998	2872	5320	33502
23500	25989	5871	2980	5454	34423
24000	26667	5743	3088	5589	35343
24500	27345	5615	3196	5723	36264
25000	28024	5487	3304	5857	37185
25500	28702	5359	3411	5991	38105
26000	29223	5277	3537	6158	38917
26500	29743	5195	3662	6324	39729
27000	30264	5112	3787	6490	40541
27500	30784	5030	3912	6656	41353
28000	31305	4948	4038	6822	42165
28500	31825	4865	4163	6989	42977
29000	32345	4783	4288	7155	43788
29500	32866	4700	4413	7321	44600
30000	33386	4618	4539	7487	45412
30500	33907	4536	4664	7653	46224
31000	34427	4453	4789	7819	47036
31500	35096	4430	4843	7957	47897
32000	35766	4406	4897	8095	48758
32500	36435	4382	4951	8233	49619

TABLE A-3 continued
1987 Income Table for the Province of Manitoba

Your Cash Income	Your Full Cash Income	Income from Government	Hidden Income	Hidden Purchasing Power Loss	Total Income Before Tax
		(Dollars per family)			
33000	37104	4359	5005	8371	50480
33500	37773	4335	5059	8509	51341
34000	38442	4311	5113	8647	52202
34500	39112	4287	5167	8785	53063
35000	39781	4264	5221	8923	53924
35500	40450	4240	5275	9061	54785
36000	40972	4205	5382	9184	55538
36500	41495	4169	5490	9306	56291
37000	42017	4134	5598	9429	57044
37500	42539	4098	5706	9552	57797
38000	43061	4063	5813	9675	58550
38500	43584	4027	5921	9798	59302
39000	44106	3992	6029	9921	60055
39500	44628	3956	6136	10044	60808
40000	45150	3921	6244	10166	61561
40500	45673	3885	6352	10289	62314
41000	46195	3850	6460	10412	63067
41500	46799	3858	6466	10469	63734
42000	47404	3867	6472	10526	64402
42500	48008	3876	6478	10583	65069
43000	48612	3885	6484	10640	65737
43500	49217	3894	6490	10698	66404
44000	49821	3902	6496	10755	67072
44500	50426	3911	6502	10812	67739
45000	51030	3920	6508	10869	68406
45500	51634	3929	6514	10926	69074
46000	52274	3920	6674	11115	70063
46500	52913	3911	6835	11304	71052
47000	53552	3902	6995	11493	72041
47500	54192	3893	7156	11683	73030
48000	54831	3884	7316	11872	74019
48500	55470	3875	7477	12061	75008
49000	56109	3866	7637	12250	75997
49500	56749	3857	7797	12440	76986
50000	57388	3848	7958	12629	77975
50500	58027	3839	8118	12818	78964
51000	58532	3829	8201	12946	79678
51500	59036	3819	8283	13073	80392
52000	59540	3808	8365	13201	81106
52500	60044	3798	8447	13329	81820
53000	60549	3788	8529	13457	82534
53500	61053	3778	8611	13584	83248
54000	61557	3768	8694	13712	83963
54500	62061	3758	8776	13840	84677
55000	62565	3748	8858	13967	85391
55500	63070	3738	8940	14095	86105
56000	63574	3728	9022	14223	86819
56500	64078	3718	9104	14351	87533
57000	64582	3708	9187	14478	88247
57500	65087	3698	9269	14606	88961
58000	65591	3688	9351	14734	89676
58500	66095	3678	9433	14862	90390
59000	66599	3668	9515	14989	91104
59500	67104	3658	9597	15117	91818
60000	67608	3648	9680	15245	92532

SCHEDULE A-3

1987 Detailed Income Calculation for the Province of Manitoba

Your Cash Income

1. Full Cash Income = Cash Income × 1.127 = _____

2. Of which Income from Government = $ 3,648 = _____

3. Hidden Income = Cash Income × 0.161 = _____

4. Hidden Purchasing Power Loss = Cash Income × 0.254 = _____

Total Income before Tax = 1 + 3 + 4 = _____

EXAMPLE:

Your Cash Income

1. Full Cash Income = $ 70,000 × 1.127 = $ 70,000

2. Of which Income from Government = $ 3,648 = $ 78,890

3. Hidden Income = $ 70,000 × 0.161 = $ 3,648

4. Hidden Purchasing Power Loss = $ 70,000 × 0.254 = $ 11,270

= $ 17,780

Total Income before Tax = $ 107,940

TABLE A-4
1987 Income Table for the Province of New Brunswick

Your Cash Income	Your Full Cash Income	Income from Government	Hidden Income	Hidden Purchasing Power Loss	Total Income Before Tax
		(Dollars per family)			
5000	4077	3990	377	449	4903
5500	4889	4581	408	469	5766
6000	5700	5171	439	489	6628
6500	6512	5761	469	509	7490
7000	7323	6352	500	529	8353
7500	8135	6942	531	549	9215
8000	8946	7532	562	569	10077
8500	9367	7597	601	715	10683
9000	9788	7662	641	860	11288
9500	10208	7727	680	1005	11894
10000	10629	7792	720	1150	12499
10500	11049	7857	760	1296	13105
11000	11564	7997	818	1448	13830
11500	12079	8137	876	1600	14555
12000	12594	8276	934	1752	15280
12500	13109	8416	993	1904	16006
13000	13624	8556	1051	2056	16731
13500	14139	8696	1109	2208	17456
14000	14654	8835	1167	2360	18181
14500	15169	8975	1226	2513	18907
15000	15684	9115	1284	2665	19632
15500	16277	9143	1385	2864	20526
16000	16870	9172	1487	3063	21420
16500	17463	9200	1589	3263	22314
17000	18056	9229	1690	3462	23209
17500	18649	9257	1792	3661	24103
18000	19242	9286	1894	3861	24997
18500	19835	9314	1995	4060	25891
19000	20428	9343	2097	4260	26785
19500	21022	9371	2199	4459	27679
20000	21615	9400	2300	4658	28573
20500	22208	9428	2402	4858	29467
21000	22730	9355	2446	5049	30226
21500	23253	9282	2491	5240	30984
22000	23775	9209	2535	5431	31742
22500	24298	9136	2580	5623	32500
23000	24820	9063	2624	5814	33258
23500	25342	8990	2668	6005	34016
24000	25865	8917	2713	6196	34774
24500	26387	8844	2757	6388	35532
25000	26910	8770	2801	6579	36290
25500	27432	8697	2846	6770	37048
26000	27841	8642	2936	6894	37671
26500	28249	8587	3027	7017	38293
27000	28657	8531	3117	7141	38915
27500	29066	8476	3208	7265	39538
28000	29474	8421	3298	7388	40160
28500	29882	8365	3389	7512	40783
29000	30291	8310	3479	7635	41405
29500	30699	8255	3569	7759	42028
30000	31108	8199	3660	7883	42650
30500	31516	8144	3750	8006	43273
31000	31924	8089	3841	8130	43895
31500	32465	7932	3921	8415	44801
32000	33006	7776	4002	8700	45707
32500	33546	7620	4082	8985	46613

TABLE A-4 continued
1987 Income Table for the Province of New Brunswick

Your Cash Income	Your Full Cash Income	Income from Government	Hidden Income	Hidden Purchasing Power Loss	Total Income Before Tax
		(Dollars per family)			
33000	34087	7463	4163	9270	47519
33500	34628	7307	4243	9555	48425
34000	35168	7151	4324	9840	49332
34500	35709	6994	4404	10124	50238
35000	36250	6838	4485	10409	51144
35500	36791	6681	4565	10694	52050
36000	37275	6572	4638	10819	52731
36500	37759	6463	4711	10943	53413
37000	38243	6354	4784	11067	54094
37500	38728	6245	4857	11192	54776
38000	39212	6135	4930	11316	55457
38500	39696	6026	5003	11440	56139
39000	40180	5917	5076	11564	56820
39500	40665	5808	5149	11689	57502
40000	41149	5699	5222	11813	58184
40500	41633	5589	5294	11937	58865
41000	42118	5480	5367	12062	59547
41500	42799	5569	5506	12238	60543
42000	43480	5657	5645	12414	61539
42500	44162	5745	5784	12590	62535
43000	44843	5833	5923	12766	63532
43500	45524	5922	6062	12942	64528
44000	46206	6010	6201	13118	65524
44500	46887	6098	6340	13294	66521
45000	47568	6186	6479	13470	67517
45500	48250	6275	6617	13646	68513
46000	48707	6252	6631	13853	69191
46500	49163	6230	6645	14060	69869
47000	49620	6208	6659	14267	70546
47500	50077	6186	6673	14474	71224
48000	50534	6164	6687	14681	71902
48500	50991	6142	6701	14888	72579
49000	51447	6120	6715	15095	73257
49500	51904	6098	6729	15302	73935
50000	52361	6075	6743	15509	74612
50500	52818	6053	6756	15716	75290
51000	53224	6032	6867	15861	75951
51500	53630	6011	6977	16006	76612
52000	54036	5990	7087	16151	77273
52500	54442	5969	7197	16296	77934
53000	54848	5949	7307	16441	78596
53500	55254	5928	7417	16586	79257
54000	55660	5907	7527	16731	79918
54500	56066	5886	7637	16876	80579
55000	56472	5865	7747	17021	81240
55500	56878	5844	7857	17166	81901
56000	57284	5823	7967	17311	82562
56500	57690	5802	8077	17456	83223
57000	58096	5781	8188	17601	83884
57500	58501	5760	8298	17746	84545
58000	58907	5739	8408	17891	85207
58500	59313	5718	8518	18036	85868
59000	59719	5697	8628	18181	86529
59500	60125	5676	8738	18327	87190
60000	60531	5655	8848	18472	87851

SCHEDULE A-4

1987 Detailed Income Calculation for the Province of New Brunswick

Your Cash Income

1. Full Cash Income = Cash Income × 1.009 = _____

2. Of which Income from Government = $ 5,655 = _____

3. Hidden Income = Cash Income × 0.147 = _____

4. Hidden Purchasing Power Loss = Cash Income × 0.308 = _____

Total Income before Tax = 1 + 3 + 4 = _____

EXAMPLE:

Your Cash Income

1. Full Cash Income = $ 70,000 × 1.009 = $ 70,000

2. Of which Income from Government = $ 5,655 = $ 70,630

3. Hidden Income = $ 70,000 × 0.147 = $ 5,655

4. Hidden Purchasing Power Loss = $ 70,000 × 0.308 = $ 10,290

 = $ 21,560

Total Income before Tax = $ 102,480

TABLE A-5
1987 Income Table for the Province of Newfoundland

Your Cash Income	Your Full Cash Income	Income from Government	Hidden Income	Hidden Purchasing Power Loss	Total Income Before Tax
		(Dollars per family)			
5000	6084	4727	341	434	6859
5500	6633	5317	357	411	7401
6000	7181	5906	373	389	7943
6500	7730	6496	389	367	8485
7000	8278	7085	404	345	9028
7500	8827	7675	420	323	9570
8000	9375	8265	436	300	10112
8500	9972	8604	472	380	10824
9000	10568	8942	508	460	11536
9500	11164	9281	544	540	12248
10000	11761	9620	580	620	12960
10500	12357	9959	616	700	13672
11000	12915	10162	655	844	14414
11500	13472	10366	695	989	15156
12000	14030	10569	734	1134	15898
12500	14588	10772	773	1279	16640
13000	15145	10976	813	1424	17382
13500	15703	11179	852	1569	18124
14000	16261	11382	892	1714	18866
14500	16819	11586	931	1859	19608
15000	17376	11789	970	2003	20350
15500	17964	11843	1048	2207	21219
16000	18552	11897	1125	2411	22088
16500	19140	11951	1202	2615	22957
17000	19727	12005	1280	2819	23826
17500	20315	12060	1357	3023	24695
18000	20903	12114	1434	3226	25564
18500	21491	12168	1511	3430	26432
19000	22079	12222	1589	3634	27301
19500	22666	12276	1666	3838	28170
20000	23254	12330	1743	4042	29039
20500	23842	12384	1821	4246	29908
21000	24534	12441	1878	4346	30759
21500	25226	12497	1936	4447	31609
22000	25918	12554	1993	4548	32460
22500	26610	12611	2051	4649	33310
23000	27302	12667	2108	4750	34161
23500	27994	12724	2166	4851	35011
24000	28686	12780	2223	4952	35862
24500	29379	12837	2281	5053	36712
25000	30071	12894	2338	5153	37563
25500	30763	12950	2396	5254	38413
26000	31340	13031	2457	5461	39258
26500	31917	13111	2518	5668	40103
27000	32495	13192	2579	5875	40949
27500	33072	13272	2640	6082	41794
28000	33649	13353	2701	6289	42639
28500	34227	13434	2762	6496	43484
29000	34804	13514	2823	6703	44329
29500	35381	13595	2884	6910	45175
30000	35959	13675	2945	7117	46020
30500	36536	13756	3006	7324	46865
31000	37113	13836	3067	7530	47710
31500	37478	13540	3179	7698	48356
32000	37842	13243	3292	7866	49001
32500	38207	12947	3405	8034	49646

TABLE A-5 continued
1987 Income Table for the Province of Newfoundland

Your Cash Income	Your Full Cash Income	Income from Government	Hidden Income	Hidden Purchasing Power Loss	Total Income Before Tax
		(Dollars per family)			
33000	38571	12651	3518	8202	50291
33500	38936	12354	3630	8370	50936
34000	39300	12058	3743	8538	51582
34500	39665	11761	3856	8706	52227
35000	40030	11465	3969	8874	52872
35500	40394	11168	4082	9042	53517
36000	40975	10939	4161	9244	54380
36500	41556	10710	4241	9446	55242
37000	42136	10482	4321	9648	56105
37500	42717	10253	4400	9850	56967
38000	43298	10024	4480	10052	57830
38500	43879	9795	4560	10254	58692
39000	44459	9566	4639	10456	59555
39500	45040	9337	4719	10658	60417
40000	45621	9108	4799	10861	61280
40500	46202	8879	4878	11063	62142
41000	46782	8650	4958	11265	63005
41500	47298	8558	5049	11439	63785
42000	47813	8466	5140	11612	64565
42500	48329	8373	5230	11786	65346
43000	48844	8281	5321	11960	66126
43500	49360	8189	5412	12134	66906
44000	49875	8097	5503	12308	67686
44500	50391	8004	5594	12482	68467
45000	50906	7912	5685	12655	69247
45500	51422	7820	5776	12829	70027
46000	51863	7687	5863	12958	70684
46500	52304	7554	5950	13086	71340
47000	52744	7421	6038	13215	71997
47500	53185	7288	6125	13343	72654
48000	53626	7155	6213	13471	73310
48500	54067	7022	6300	13600	73967
49000	54508	6889	6387	13728	74623
49500	54949	6756	6475	13857	75280
50000	55389	6623	6562	13985	75937
50500	55830	6490	6649	14114	76593
51000	56237	6508	6732	14290	77258
51500	56643	6525	6814	14466	77923
52000	57050	6543	6897	14642	78588
52500	57456	6561	6979	14818	79253
53000	57863	6579	7061	14993	79918
53500	58270	6597	7144	15169	80583
54000	58676	6614	7226	15345	81248
54500	59083	6632	7309	15521	81913
55000	59489	6650	7391	15697	82578
55500	59896	6668	7473	15873	83243
56000	60302	6686	7556	16049	83908
56500	60709	6703	7638	16225	84572
57000	61115	6721	7721	16401	85237
57500	61522	6739	7803	16577	85902
58000	61928	6757	7886	16753	86567
58500	62335	6775	7968	16929	87232
59000	62742	6792	8050	17105	87897
59500	63148	6810	8133	17281	88562
60000	63555	6828	8215	17457	89227

SCHEDULE A-5

1987 Detailed Income Calculation for the Province of Newfoundland

Your Cash Income

1. Full Cash Income	= Cash Income × 1.059	= _____
2. Of which Income from Government	= $ 6,828	= _____
3. Hidden Income	= Cash Income × 0.137	= _____
4. Hidden Purchasing Power Loss	= Cash Income × 0.291	= _____
Total Income before Tax	= 1 + 3 + 4	= _____

EXAMPLE:

Your Cash Income

1. Full Cash Income	= $ 70,000 × 1.059	= $ 70,000
2. Of which Income from Government	= $ 6,828	= $ 74,130
3. Hidden Income	= $ 70,000 × 0.137	= $ 6,828
4. Hidden Purchasing Power Loss	= $ 70,000 × 0.291	= $ 9,590
		= $ 20,370
Total Income before Tax		= $ 104,090

TABLE A-6
1987 Income Table for the Province of Nova Scotia

Your Cash Income	Your Full Cash Income	Income from Government	Hidden Income	Hidden Purchasing Power Loss	Total Income Before Tax
		(Dollars per family)			
5000	4994	3822	411	507	5912
5500	5536	4298	433	518	6487
6000	6077	4774	456	529	7062
6500	6619	5250	478	539	7637
7000	7161	5725	500	550	8212
7500	7703	6201	523	561	8786
8000	8245	6677	545	572	9361
8500	8694	6780	587	690	9971
9000	9144	6883	628	808	10580
9500	9593	6986	670	927	11190
10000	10043	7089	712	1045	11799
10500	10492	7192	753	1164	12409
11000	11012	7378	801	1307	13119
11500	11532	7564	848	1449	13829
12000	12052	7750	895	1592	14539
12500	12572	7936	942	1735	15249
13000	13092	8123	989	1878	15958
13500	13612	8309	1036	2021	16668
14000	14131	8495	1083	2163	17378
14500	14651	8681	1131	2306	18088
15000	15171	8867	1178	2449	18798
15500	15671	8781	1268	2659	19598
16000	16170	8694	1359	2868	20398
16500	16670	8607	1449	3078	21197
17000	17169	8521	1540	3288	21997
17500	17669	8434	1630	3497	22797
18000	18168	8347	1721	3707	23597
18500	18668	8261	1812	3917	24396
19000	19167	8174	1902	4127	25196
19500	19667	8087	1993	4336	25996
20000	20166	8001	2083	4546	26796
20500	20666	7914	2174	4756	27595
21000	21189	7787	2264	4981	28434
21500	21713	7660	2354	5206	29273
22000	22236	7533	2444	5431	30112
22500	22760	7406	2535	5657	30951
23000	23283	7279	2625	5882	31790
23500	23807	7152	2715	6107	32629
24000	24330	7025	2805	6332	33468
24500	24853	6898	2896	6557	34307
25000	25377	6771	2986	6783	35146
25500	25900	6644	3076	7008	35984
26000	26446	6545	3158	7161	36766
26500	26991	6447	3241	7315	37547
27000	27537	6348	3323	7468	38328
27500	28083	6250	3405	7622	39110
28000	28628	6151	3487	7775	39891
28500	29174	6053	3570	7929	40672
29000	29719	5954	3652	8082	41454
29500	30265	5856	3734	8236	42235
30000	30810	5757	3816	8389	43016
30500	31356	5659	3899	8543	43798
31000	31901	5560	3981	8696	44579
31500	32436	5482	4073	8915	45425
32000	32970	5404	4166	9134	46270
32500	33505	5326	4258	9353	47116

TABLE A-6 continued
1987 Income Table for the Province of Nova Scotia

Your Cash Income	Your Full Cash Income	Income from Government	Hidden Income	Hidden Purchasing Power Loss	Total Income Before Tax
		(Dollars per family)			
33000	34039	5248	4351	9572	47962
33500	34574	5169	4443	9791	48808
34000	35108	5091	4536	10009	49653
34500	35642	5013	4628	10228	50499
35000	36177	4935	4721	10447	51345
35500	36711	4857	4813	10666	52190
36000	37315	4969	4866	10871	53053
36500	37919	5081	4920	11076	53915
37000	38523	5193	4973	11280	54777
37500	39128	5305	5026	11485	55639
38000	39732	5417	5079	11690	56501
38500	40336	5529	5132	11895	57363
39000	40940	5641	5185	12100	58225
39500	41544	5753	5238	12305	59087
40000	42148	5865	5291	12510	59949
40500	42752	5977	5345	12715	60811
41000	43356	6089	5398	12920	61673
41500	44021	6040	5575	13068	62664
42000	44686	5990	5751	13216	63654
42500	45351	5941	5928	13364	64644
43000	46016	5892	6105	13513	65634
43500	46681	5842	6282	13661	66624
44000	47346	5793	6459	13809	67614
44500	48011	5743	6636	13958	68605
45000	48676	5694	6813	14106	69595
45500	49341	5645	6990	14254	70585
46000	49676	5556	7054	14425	71154
46500	50010	5467	7118	14596	71724
47000	50345	5378	7182	14766	72293
47500	50679	5289	7246	14937	72862
48000	51014	5201	7310	15108	73431
48500	51349	5112	7373	15279	74001
49000	51683	5023	7437	15449	74570
49500	52018	4934	7501	15620	75139
50000	52352	4845	7565	15791	75708
50500	52687	4757	7629	15962	76278
51000	53212	4749	7754	16134	77100
51500	53737	4741	7879	16307	77923
52000	54262	4733	8004	16479	78745
52500	54786	4725	8129	16652	79567
53000	55311	4718	8254	16825	80390
53500	55836	4710	8379	16997	81212
54000	56361	4702	8504	17170	82035
54500	56886	4694	8628	17343	82857
55000	57411	4686	8753	17515	83679
55500	57936	4679	8878	17688	84502
56000	58460	4671	9003	17861	85324
56500	58985	4663	9128	18033	86147
57000	59510	4655	9253	18206	86969
57500	60035	4647	9378	18379	87792
58000	60560	4640	9503	18551	88614
58500	61085	4632	9628	18724	89436
59000	61610	4624	9753	18897	90259
59500	62134	4616	9878	19069	91081
60000	62659	4608	10003	19242	91904

SCHEDULE A-6

1987 Detailed Income Calculation for the Province of Nova Scotia

Your Cash Income = _____

1. Full Cash Income = Cash Income × 1.044 = _____

2. Of which Income from Government = $ 4,608 = _____

3. Hidden Income = Cash Income × 0.167 = _____

4. Hidden Purchasing Power Loss = Cash Income × 0.321 = _____

Total Income before Tax = 1 + 3 + 4 = _____

EXAMPLE:

Your Cash Income = $ 70,000

1. Full Cash Income = $ 70,000 × 1.044 = $ 73,080

2. Of which Income from Government = $ 4,608 = $ 4,608

3. Hidden Income = $ 70,000 × 0.167 = $ 11,690

4. Hidden Purchasing Power Loss = $ 70,000 × 0.321 = $ 22,470

Total Income before Tax = $ 107,240

TABLE A-7
1987 Income Table for the Province of Ontario

Your Cash Income	Your Full Cash Income	Income from Government	Hidden Income	Hidden Purchasing Power Loss	Total Income Before Tax
		(Dollars per family)			
5000	5039	3046	484	784	6307
5500	5672	3365	538	892	7103
6000	6305	3685	593	1001	7898
6500	6938	4004	647	1109	8694
7000	7571	4323	701	1217	9489
7500	8204	4643	756	1325	10285
8000	8837	4962	810	1433	11080
8500	9295	5541	807	1401	11503
9000	9753	6119	804	1369	11926
9500	10211	6698	800	1337	12349
10000	10669	7277	797	1305	12772
10500	11127	7856	794	1273	13195
11000	11717	7800	878	1571	14166
11500	12306	7745	962	1869	15137
12000	12896	7690	1046	2166	16108
12500	13486	7635	1130	2464	17079
13000	14075	7579	1214	2761	18050
13500	14665	7524	1297	3059	19021
14000	15255	7469	1381	3356	19992
14500	15844	7414	1465	3654	20963
15000	16434	7358	1549	3951	21934
15500	16944	7373	1613	4112	22669
16000	17454	7387	1677	4273	23403
16500	17963	7401	1741	4434	24138
17000	18473	7416	1805	4594	24873
17500	18983	7430	1869	4755	25607
18000	19493	7444	1933	4916	26342
18500	20003	7459	1997	5076	27076
19000	20513	7473	2061	5237	27811
19500	21023	7488	2125	5398	28545
20000	21532	7502	2189	5558	29280
20500	22042	7516	2253	5719	30014
21000	22652	7287	2396	5973	31021
21500	23261	7058	2539	6227	32028
22000	23870	6829	2682	6482	33034
22500	24480	6600	2825	6736	34041
23000	25089	6371	2969	6990	35048
23500	25699	6142	3112	7244	36054
24000	26308	5913	3255	7498	37061
24500	26918	5684	3398	7752	38068
25000	27527	5455	3541	8006	39074
25500	28136	5226	3684	8260	40081
26000	28736	5225	3770	8471	40977
26500	29335	5224	3856	8682	41874
27000	29935	5223	3942	8893	42770
27500	30534	5223	4028	9104	43666
28000	31134	5222	4114	9314	44562
28500	31733	5221	4200	9525	45459
29000	32333	5220	4286	9736	46355
29500	32932	5220	4372	9947	47251
30000	33532	5219	4458	10158	48148
30500	34131	5218	4545	10368	49044
31000	34731	5217	4631	10579	49940
31500	35243	5071	4778	10617	50638
32000	35756	4924	4925	10655	51336

TABLE A-7 continued
1987 Income Table for the Province of Ontario

Your Cash Income	Your Full Cash Income	Income from Government	Hidden Income	Hidden Purchasing Power Loss	Total Income Before Tax
		(Dollars per family)			
32500	36269	4778	5072	10693	52033
33000	36782	4631	5219	10730	52731
33500	37295	4485	5366	10768	53429
34000	37808	4338	5513	10806	54126
34500	38321	4192	5660	10843	54824
35000	38834	4045	5807	10881	55522
35500	39347	3899	5954	10919	56220
36000	39870	3869	5981	11013	56864
36500	40393	3840	6008	11106	57508
37000	40917	3810	6035	11200	58152
37500	41440	3780	6061	11294	58796
38000	41964	3751	6088	11388	59440
38500	42487	3721	6115	11481	60084
39000	43010	3692	6142	11575	60728
39500	43534	3662	6169	11669	61372
40000	44057	3633	6196	11763	62016
40500	44581	3603	6223	11857	62660
41000	45104	3574	6249	11950	63304
41500	45733	3596	6389	12194	64316
42000	46362	3618	6528	12438	65328
42500	46991	3641	6668	12683	66341
43000	47619	3663	6807	12927	67353
43500	48248	3685	6946	13171	68365
44000	48877	3708	7086	13415	69377
44500	49506	3730	7225	13659	70390
45000	50134	3752	7364	13903	71402
45500	50763	3774	7504	14147	72414
46000	51321	3694	7560	14342	73222
46500	51878	3613	7616	14537	74030
47000	52435	3533	7672	14731	74838
47500	52992	3452	7727	14926	75646
48000	53549	3372	7783	15121	76454
48500	54107	3291	7839	15316	77262
49000	54664	3210	7895	15511	78069
49500	55221	3130	7951	15705	78877
50000	55778	3049	8007	15900	79685
50500	56336	2969	8063	16095	80493
51000	56917	2969	8211	16264	81393
51500	57499	2969	8359	16434	82293
52000	58081	2969	8508	16603	83192
52500	58663	2969	8656	16773	84092
53000	59245	2969	8804	16942	84992
53500	59827	2969	8953	17112	85892
54000	60409	2969	9101	17281	86791
54500	60991	2969	9249	17451	87691
55000	61573	2968	9397	17620	88591
55500	62155	2968	9546	17790	89490
56000	62737	2968	9694	17959	90390
56500	63319	2968	9842	18129	91290
57000	63901	2968	9991	18298	92190
57500	64483	2968	10139	18467	93089
58000	65065	2968	10287	18637	93989
58500	65647	2968	10436	18806	94889
59000	66229	2968	10584	18976	95789
59500	66811	2968	10732	19145	96688
60000	67393	2968	10880	19315	97588

SCHEDULE A-7

1987 Detailed Income Calculation for the Province of Ontario

Your Cash Income

1. Full Cash Income	= Cash Income × 1.123	= _____
2. Of which Income from Government	= $ 2,968	= _____
3. Hidden Income	= Cash Income × 0.181	= _____
4. Hidden Purchasing Power Loss	= Cash Income × 0.322	= _____
Total Income before Tax	= 1 + 3 + 4	= _____

EXAMPLE:

Your Cash Income

1. Full Cash Income	= $ 70,000 × 1.123	= $ 70,000
2. Of which Income from Government	= $ 2,968	= $ 78,610
3. Hidden Income	= $ 70,000 × 0.181	= $ 2,968
4. Hidden Purchasing Power Loss	= $ 70,000 × 0.322	= $ 12,670
		= $ 22,540
Total Income before Tax		= $ 113,820

TABLE A-8
1987 Income Table for the Province of Prince Edward Island

Your Cash Income	Your Full Cash Income	Income from Government	Hidden Income	Hidden Purchasing Power Loss	Total Income Before Tax
		(Dollars per family)			
5000	6026	4301	407	493	6926
5500	6498	4816	424	490	7412
6000	6970	5331	442	486	7898
6500	7442	5846	459	483	8384
7000	7914	6361	477	480	8870
7500	8386	6876	494	477	9356
8000	8857	7391	512	473	9842
8500	9366	7462	565	591	10521
9000	9874	7532	618	708	11200
9500	10382	7602	672	826	11879
10000	10890	7673	725	943	12559
10500	11398	7743	778	1061	13238
11000	11803	7921	822	1140	13766
11500	12208	8099	866	1219	14294
12000	12613	8278	910	1299	14822
12500	13018	8456	955	1378	15350
13000	13423	8634	999	1457	15878
13500	13827	8812	1043	1536	16406
14000	14232	8991	1087	1615	16934
14500	14637	9169	1131	1695	17462
15000	15042	9347	1175	1774	17991
15500	15602	9367	1271	1925	18798
16000	16161	9386	1368	2077	19606
16500	16721	9406	1464	2228	20414
17000	17281	9426	1561	2380	21222
17500	17841	9445	1657	2531	22029
18000	18400	9465	1754	2683	22837
18500	18960	9484	1850	2834	23645
19000	19520	9504	1947	2986	24452
19500	20080	9524	2043	3137	25260
20000	20639	9543	2140	3289	26068
20500	21199	9563	2237	3440	26876
21000	21592	9544	2287	3504	27384
21500	21984	9524	2338	3568	27891
22000	22377	9505	2389	3633	28399
22500	22770	9485	2440	3697	28907
23000	23163	9466	2491	3761	29415
23500	23555	9446	2542	3825	29923
24000	23948	9427	2593	3889	30430
24500	24341	9407	2644	3953	30938
25000	24733	9388	2695	4018	31446
25500	25126	9368	2746	4082	31954
26000	25666	9373	2779	4269	32713
26500	26205	9377	2812	4455	33472
27000	26745	9381	2844	4642	34231
27500	27285	9386	2877	4829	34990
28000	27824	9390	2910	5015	35750
28500	28364	9394	2943	5202	36509
29000	28904	9399	2975	5389	37268
29500	29443	9403	3008	5576	38027
30000	29983	9407	3041	5762	38786
30500	30522	9412	3074	5949	39545
31000	31062	9416	3107	6136	40304
31500	31622	9352	3180	6265	41067
32000	32182	9288	3254	6393	41829
32500	32742	9224	3327	6522	42592

TABLE A-8 continued
1987 Income Table for the Province of Prince Edward Island

Your Cash Income	Your Full Cash Income	Income from Government	Hidden Income	Hidden Purchasing Power Loss	Total Income Before Tax
		(Dollars per family)			
33000	33302	9159	3401	6651	43354
33500	33862	9095	3475	6780	44117
34000	34423	9031	3548	6909	44879
34500	34983	8967	3622	7037	45642
35000	35543	8903	3695	7166	46404
35500	36103	8839	3769	7295	47167
36000	36615	8718	3981	7431	48027
36500	37126	8596	4193	7568	48887
37000	37638	8475	4405	7704	49747
37500	38150	8354	4618	7840	50608
38000	38661	8233	4830	7977	51468
38500	39173	8112	5042	8113	52328
39000	39685	7991	5254	8249	53188
39500	40197	7870	5466	8385	54048
40000	40708	7749	5678	8522	54909
40500	41220	7628	5891	8658	55769
41000	41732	7507	6103	8794	56629
41500	42029	7281	6000	8814	56843
42000	42326	7055	5897	8835	57058
42500	42624	6829	5794	8855	57272
43000	42921	6603	5691	8875	57487
43500	43218	6377	5588	8895	57701
44000	43515	6150	5485	8915	57916
44500	43812	5924	5383	8936	58130
45000	44110	5698	5280	8956	58345
45500	44407	5472	5177	8976	58559
46000	45074	5621	5316	9211	59600
46500	45741	5769	5455	9445	60641
47000	46408	5918	5594	9680	61682
47500	47075	6067	5733	9915	62723
48000	47742	6216	5872	10149	63764
48500	48410	6364	6011	10384	64805
49000	49077	6513	6150	10619	65846
49500	49744	6662	6289	10854	66887
50000	50411	6810	6428	11088	67927
50500	51078	6959	6567	11323	68968
51000	51557	6962	6648	11457	69661
51500	52035	6964	6728	11591	70354
52000	52514	6966	6808	11725	71048
52500	52992	6969	6889	11859	71741
53000	53471	6971	6969	11993	72434
53500	53950	6974	7050	12128	73127
54000	54428	6976	7130	12262	73820
54500	54907	6979	7210	12396	74513
55000	55385	6981	7291	12530	75206
55500	55864	6984	7371	12664	75899
56000	56342	6986	7451	12798	76592
56500	56821	6989	7532	12932	77285
57000	57300	6991	7612	13066	77978
57500	57778	6994	7693	13200	78671
58000	58257	6996	7773	13334	79364
58500	58735	6999	7853	13469	80057
59000	59214	7001	7934	13603	80750
59500	59693	7003	8014	13737	81443
60000	60171	7006	8095	13871	82136

SCHEDULE A-8

1987 Detailed Income Calculation for the Province of Prince Edward Island

Your Cash Income

1. Full Cash Income	= Cash Income × 1.003	= _____
2. Of which Income from Government	= $ 7,006	= _____
3. Hidden Income	= Cash Income × 0.135	= _____
4. Hidden Purchasing Power Loss	= Cash Income × 0.231	= _____
Total Income before Tax	= 1 + 3 + 4	= _____

EXAMPLE:

Your Cash Income

1. Full Cash Income	= $ 70,000 × 1.003	= $ 70,210
2. Of which Income from Government	= $ 7,006	= $ 7,006
3. Hidden Income	= $ 70,000 × 0.135	= $ 9,450
4. Hidden Purchasing Power Loss	= $ 70,000 × 0.231	= $ 13,860
Total Income before Tax		= $ 93,520

TABLE A-9
1987 Income Table for the Province of Quebec

Your Cash Income	Your Full Cash Income	Income from Government	Hidden Income	Hidden Purchasing Power Loss	Total Income Before Tax
		(Dollars per family)			
5000	5958	4495	460	400	6818
5500	6439	4801	493	468	7400
6000	6919	5108	527	537	7983
6500	7400	5414	560	605	8565
7000	7881	5720	593	673	9147
7500	8361	6027	627	741	9729
8000	8842	6333	660	810	10311
8500	9366	6775	690	879	10934
9000	9890	7216	720	948	11557
9500	10414	7657	750	1016	12180
10000	10937	8098	780	1085	12803
10500	11461	8540	810	1154	13426
11000	12027	8603	879	1314	14220
11500	12593	8667	948	1475	15015
12000	13159	8730	1017	1635	15810
12500	13725	8794	1086	1795	16605
13000	14291	8858	1155	1955	17400
13500	14857	8921	1223	2115	18195
14000	15423	8985	1292	2275	18990
14500	15988	9049	1361	2435	19785
15000	16554	9112	1430	2595	20580
15500	17090	9013	1544	2797	21430
16000	17626	8913	1657	2998	22281
16500	18161	8814	1771	3199	23131
17000	18697	8714	1884	3401	23982
17500	19233	8615	1997	3602	24832
18000	19769	8516	2111	3803	25683
18500	20304	8416	2224	4005	26533
19000	20840	8317	2338	4206	27384
19500	21376	8217	2451	4407	28234
20000	21911	8118	2565	4609	29085
20500	22447	8018	2678	4810	29935
21000	22972	7821	2781	4966	30720
21500	23497	7623	2885	5122	31504
22000	24023	7425	2988	5278	32289
22500	24548	7228	3092	5434	33074
23000	25073	7030	3195	5590	33858
23500	25598	6832	3298	5746	34643
24000	26123	6635	3402	5902	35427
24500	26648	6437	3505	6058	36212
25000	27174	6239	3609	6214	36997
25500	27699	6041	3712	6370	37781
26000	28170	5997	3840	6498	38509
26500	28641	5952	3968	6626	39236
27000	29113	5907	4097	6754	39963
27500	29584	5862	4225	6882	40691
28000	30055	5817	4353	7010	41418
28500	30526	5772	4481	7138	42145
29000	30998	5727	4610	7265	42873
29500	31469	5682	4738	7393	43600
30000	31940	5637	4866	7521	44327
30500	32412	5592	4994	7649	45055
31000	32883	5547	5123	7777	45782
31500	33495	5531	5202	7953	46650
32000	34107	5515	5281	8129	47517
32500	34719	5499	5361	8305	48384

TABLE A-9 continued
1987 Income Table for the Province of Quebec

Your Cash Income	Your Full Cash Income	Income from Government	Hidden Income	Hidden Purchasing Power Loss	Total Income Before Tax
		(Dollars per family)			
33000	35330	5483	5440	8481	49252
33500	35942	5468	5519	8658	50119
34000	36554	5452	5598	8834	50987
34500	37166	5436	5678	9010	51854
35000	37778	5420	5757	9186	52721
35500	38390	5404	5836	9362	53589
36000	38995	5346	5967	9582	54544
36500	39600	5289	6097	9802	55499
37000	40205	5232	6227	10022	56454
37500	40809	5174	6358	10241	57408
38000	41414	5117	6488	10461	58363
38500	42019	5060	6619	10681	59318
39000	42624	5002	6749	10900	60273
39500	43229	4945	6879	11120	61228
40000	43834	4888	7010	11340	62183
40500	44438	4831	7140	11560	63138
41000	45043	4773	7270	11779	64093
41500	45518	4791	7320	11782	64620
42000	45992	4810	7369	11785	65146
42500	46467	4828	7418	11788	65673
43000	46941	4846	7467	11791	66199
43500	47416	4864	7516	11794	66726
44000	47890	4883	7566	11797	67253
44500	48365	4901	7615	11800	67779
45000	48839	4919	7664	11803	68306
45500	49314	4937	7713	11806	68833
46000	49841	4861	7846	11993	69681
46500	50369	4784	7979	12180	70528
47000	50897	4708	8112	12367	71376
47500	51424	4631	8245	12554	72224
48000	51952	4555	8379	12741	73072
48500	52480	4478	8512	12928	73920
49000	53008	4402	8645	13115	74768
49500	53535	4325	8778	13302	75615
50000	54063	4249	8911	13489	76463
50500	54591	4172	9044	13676	77311
51000	55080	4175	9151	13833	78064
51500	55568	4178	9258	13990	78816
52000	56057	4181	9365	14147	79569
52500	56546	4184	9472	14304	80321
53000	57035	4187	9579	14460	81074
53500	57523	4191	9686	14617	81826
54000	58012	4194	9793	14774	82579
54500	58501	4197	9900	14931	83331
55000	58990	4200	10006	15088	84084
55500	59478	4203	10113	15245	84836
56000	59967	4206	10220	15401	85589
56500	60456	4209	10327	15558	86342
57000	60945	4212	10434	15715	87094
57500	61433	4215	10541	15872	87847
58000	61922	4218	10648	16029	88599
58500	62411	4221	10755	16186	89352
59000	62900	4224	10862	16342	90104
59500	63388	4227	10969	16499	90857
60000	63877	4231	11076	16656	91609

SCHEDULE A-9

1987 Detailed Income Calculation for the Province of Quebec

Your Cash Income

1. Full Cash Income	= Cash Income × 1.065	= ___
2. Of which Income from Government	= $ 4,231	= ___
3. Hidden Income	= Cash Income × 0.185	= ___
4. Hidden Purchasing Power Loss	= Cash Income × 0.278	= ___
Total Income before Tax	= 1 + 3 + 4	= ___

EXAMPLE:

Your Cash Income

1. Full Cash Income	= $ 70,000 × 1.065	= $ 70,000
2. Of which Income from Government	= $ 4,231	= $ 74,550
3. Hidden Income	= $ 70,000 × 0.185	= $ 4,231
4. Hidden Purchasing Power Loss	= $ 70,000 × 0.278	= $ 12,950
		= $ 19,460
Total Income before Tax		= $ 106,960

TABLE A-10
1987 Income Table for the Province of Saskatchewan

Your Cash Income	Your Full Cash Income	Income from Government	Hidden Income	Hidden Purchasing Power Loss	Total Income Before Tax
		(Dollars per family)			
5000	5320	3588	553	915	6788
5500	5921	3947	585	959	7465
6000	6522	4306	617	1002	8141
6500	7123	4666	649	1046	8818
7000	7723	5025	682	1089	9494
7500	8324	5384	714	1133	10171
8000	8925	5743	746	1176	10847
8500	9605	6219	800	1370	11776
9000	10286	6694	854	1565	12704
9500	10966	7170	908	1759	13633
10000	11647	7645	962	1953	14562
10500	12327	8121	1016	2147	15491
11000	12854	8218	1076	2377	16307
11500	13381	8315	1135	2607	17124
12000	13909	8412	1195	2837	17940
12500	14436	8509	1254	3067	18756
13000	14963	8606	1313	3297	19573
13500	15490	8703	1373	3527	20389
14000	16017	8800	1432	3757	21206
14500	16545	8898	1491	3987	22022
15000	17072	8995	1551	4217	22839
15500	17590	8885	1621	4497	23708
16000	18107	8774	1692	4778	24577
16500	18625	8664	1762	5059	25446
17000	19143	8554	1833	5339	26315
17500	19661	8444	1903	5620	27184
18000	20179	8334	1974	5901	28053
18500	20697	8224	2044	6181	28922
19000	21215	8114	2115	6462	29791
19500	21733	8004	2185	6743	30660
20000	22250	7894	2256	7023	31529
20500	22768	7784	2326	7304	32398
21000	23286	7706	2402	7493	33181
21500	23803	7627	2478	7682	33963
22000	24321	7549	2554	7871	34745
22500	24838	7471	2629	8060	35528
23000	25356	7392	2705	8249	36310
23500	25873	7314	2781	8438	37092
24000	26391	7236	2857	8627	37875
24500	26909	7157	2933	8815	38657
25000	27426	7079	3009	9004	39439
25500	27944	7001	3085	9193	40222
26000	28569	6932	3284	9399	41252
26500	29195	6864	3483	9604	42282
27000	29820	6795	3682	9809	43312
27500	30446	6727	3881	10015	44341
28000	31071	6659	4080	10220	45371
28500	31697	6590	4279	10425	46401
29000	32323	6522	4478	10631	47431
29500	32948	6454	4677	10836	48461
30000	33574	6385	4876	11041	49491
30500	34199	6317	5075	11247	50521
31000	34825	6248	5274	11452	51551
31500	35219	6156	5228	11494	51941
32000	35613	6064	5182	11536	52331
32500	36007	5971	5135	11578	52721

TABLE A-10 continued
1987 Income Table for the Province of Saskatchewan

Your Cash Income	Your Full Cash Income	Income from Government	Hidden Income	Hidden Purchasing Power Loss	Total Income Before Tax
		(Dollars per family)			
33000	36402	5879	5089	11620	53110
33500	36796	5787	5043	11662	53500
34000	37190	5694	4996	11704	53890
34500	37584	5602	4950	11746	54280
35000	37978	5510	4903	11788	54669
35500	38372	5417	4857	11830	55059
36000	38880	5390	4912	11874	55666
36500	39388	5362	4966	11918	56272
37000	39896	5334	5020	11963	56879
37500	40403	5306	5075	12007	57485
38000	40911	5279	5129	12051	58092
38500	41419	5251	5183	12096	58698
39000	41927	5223	5238	12140	59305
39500	42435	5196	5292	12184	59911
40000	42942	5168	5347	12229	60518
40500	43450	5140	5401	12273	61124
41000	43958	5112	5455	12317	61731
41500	44487	5055	5511	12403	62401
42000	45016	4997	5567	12488	63071
42500	45546	4939	5622	12573	63741
43000	46075	4881	5678	12658	64411
43500	46604	4823	5734	12744	65082
44000	47133	4766	5790	12829	65752
44500	47663	4708	5845	12914	66422
45000	48192	4650	5901	13000	67092
45500	48721	4592	5957	13085	67763
46000	49086	4592	6056	13278	68419
46500	49450	4591	6156	13470	69076
47000	49815	4591	6255	13663	69733
47500	50180	4590	6354	13856	70390
48000	50544	4589	6454	14048	71047
48500	50909	4589	6553	14241	71704
49000	51274	4588	6653	14434	72360
49500	51638	4588	6752	14627	73017
50000	52003	4587	6852	14819	73674
50500	52367	4587	6951	15012	74331
51000	52906	4572	7049	15232	75186
51500	53444	4557	7146	15452	76042
52000	53982	4542	7243	15671	76897
52500	54521	4527	7341	15891	77752
53000	55059	4512	7438	16111	78608
53500	55597	4497	7535	16331	79463
54000	56135	4482	7633	16550	80318
54500	56674	4467	7730	16770	81174
55000	57212	4452	7827	16990	82029
55500	57750	4437	7925	17210	82885
56000	58289	4422	8022	17429	83740
56500	58827	4407	8119	17649	84595
57000	59365	4392	8217	17869	85451
57500	59904	4377	8314	18089	86306
58000	60442	4361	8411	18308	87162
58500	60980	4346	8509	18528	88017
59000	61518	4331	8606	18748	88872
59500	62057	4316	8703	18968	89728
60000	62595	4301	8801	19187	90583

SCHEDULE A-10

1987 Detailed Income Calculation for the Province of Saskatchewan

Your Cash Income = _____

1. Full Cash Income	= Cash Income × 1.043	= _____
2. Of which Income from Government	= $ 4,301	= _____
3. Hidden Income	= Cash Income × 0.147	= _____
4. Hidden Purchasing Power Loss	= Cash Income × 0.320	= _____
Total Income before Tax	= 1 + 3 + 4	= _____

EXAMPLE:

Your Cash Income = $ 70,000

1. Full Cash Income	= $ 70,000 × 1.043	= $ 73,010
2. Of which Income from Government	= $ 4,301	= $ 4,301
3. Hidden Income	= $ 70,000 × 0.147	= $ 10,290
4. Hidden Purchasing Power Loss	= $ 70,000 × 0.320	= $ 22,400
Total Income before Tax		= $ 105,700

TABLE A-11
1987 Income Table for Canada

Your Cash Income	Your Full Cash Income	Income from Government	Hidden Income	Hidden Purchasing Power Loss	Total Income Before Tax
		(Dollars per family)			
5000	5302	3708	472	594	6368
5500	5888	4065	510	670	7068
6000	6475	4421	547	746	7769
6500	7062	4777	585	823	8469
7000	7649	5133	623	899	9170
7500	8235	5489	660	975	9870
8000	8822	5846	698	1051	10571
8500	9320	6288	726	1113	11159
9000	9818	6730	753	1175	11747
9500	10317	7172	781	1237	12334
10000	10815	7614	809	1299	12922
10500	11313	8056	836	1361	13510
11000	11863	8071	906	1593	14363
11500	12413	8086	976	1825	15215
12000	12964	8101	1046	2058	16067
12500	13514	8116	1116	2290	16920
13000	14064	8130	1186	2522	17772
13500	14614	8145	1256	2754	18625
14000	15165	8160	1326	2986	19477
14500	15715	8175	1396	3219	20330
15000	16265	8190	1466	3451	21182
15500	16812	8174	1556	3643	22012
16000	17359	8159	1646	3836	22842
16500	17906	8144	1737	4028	23671
17000	18454	8129	1827	4221	24501
17500	19001	8114	1917	4413	25331
18000	19548	8099	2007	4606	26161
18500	20095	8084	2098	4798	26991
19000	20642	8069	2188	4991	27820
19500	21189	8053	2278	5183	28650
20000	21736	8038	2368	5376	29480
20500	22283	8023	2459	5568	30310
21000	22831	7830	2563	5759	31153
21500	23380	7637	2667	5951	31997
22000	23928	7444	2771	6142	32841
22500	24476	7251	2875	6334	33684
23000	25024	7058	2979	6525	34528
23500	25572	6865	3083	6717	35372
24000	26121	6672	3187	6908	36215
24500	26669	6479	3291	7099	37059
25000	27217	6286	3395	7291	37903
25500	27765	6093	3499	7482	38746
26000	28308	6055	3605	7638	39550
26500	28850	6016	3711	7793	40354
27000	29393	5977	3817	7949	41158
27500	29936	5939	3923	8104	41962
28000	30478	5900	4029	8259	42766
28500	31021	5861	4135	8415	43570
29000	31563	5823	4241	8570	44374
29500	32106	5784	4347	8726	45179
30000	32649	5745	4453	8881	45983
30500	33191	5707	4559	9036	46787
31000	33734	5668	4665	9192	47591
31500	34300	5584	4774	9331	48405
32000	34867	5501	4882	9470	49219
32500	35434	5417	4991	9609	50034

TABLE A-11 continued
1987 Income Table for Canada

Your Cash Income	Your Full Cash Income	Income from Government	Hidden Income	Hidden Purchasing Power Loss	Total Income Before Tax
		(Dollars per family)			
33000	36000	5333	5100	9748	50848
33500	36567	5250	5209	9887	51662
34000	37134	5166	5317	10026	52477
34500	37700	5082	5426	10164	53291
35000	38267	4999	5535	10303	54105
35500	38834	4915	5644	10442	54920
36000	39369	4869	5713	10589	55670
36500	39904	4822	5783	10735	56421
37000	40438	4776	5852	10881	57172
37500	40973	4729	5922	11027	57922
38000	41508	4683	5991	11173	58673
38500	42043	4636	6061	11319	59423
39000	42578	4590	6130	11466	60174
39500	43113	4544	6200	11612	60925
40000	43648	4497	6269	11758	61675
40500	44183	4451	6339	11904	62426
41000	44718	4404	6408	12050	63177
41500	45250	4384	6494	12154	63898
42000	45781	4364	6580	12258	64619
42500	46313	4344	6665	12362	65340
43000	46845	4323	6751	12466	66062
43500	47377	4303	6836	12570	66783
44000	47908	4283	6922	12674	67504
44500	48440	4263	7008	12778	68225
45000	48972	4243	7093	12881	68947
45500	49504	4222	7179	12985	69668
46000	50077	4181	7280	13206	70563
46500	50650	4140	7382	13426	71458
47000	51224	4099	7483	13647	72353
47500	51797	4057	7584	13867	73248
48000	52370	4016	7685	14087	74143
48500	52944	3975	7787	14308	75038
49000	53517	3934	7888	14528	75933
49500	54091	3892	7989	14748	76828
50000	54664	3851	8091	14969	77724
50500	55237	3810	8192	15189	78619
51000	55778	3807	8318	15358	79454
51500	56319	3803	8443	15527	80289
52000	56860	3800	8569	15696	81125
52500	57401	3797	8694	15865	81960
53000	57942	3793	8820	16033	82796
53500	58483	3790	8946	16202	83631
54000	59024	3787	9071	16371	84467
54500	59565	3783	9197	16540	85302
55000	60106	3780	9322	16709	86137
55500	60647	3777	9448	16878	86973
56000	61188	3773	9573	17046	87808
56500	61729	3770	9699	17215	88644
57000	62270	3767	9825	17384	89479
57500	62811	3764	9950	17553	90315
58000	63352	3760	10076	17722	91150
58500	63893	3757	10201	17891	91985
59000	64434	3754	10327	18060	92821
59500	64975	3750	10453	18228	93656
60000	65516	3747	10578	18397	94492

SCHEDULE A-11

1987 Detailed Income Calculation for Canada

Your Cash Income

	= _____
1. Full Cash Income	= Cash Income × 1.083 = _____
2. Of which Income from Government	= $ 3,750 = _____
3. Hidden Income	= Cash Income × 0.174 = _____
4. Hidden Purchasing Power Loss	= Cash Income × 0.304 = _____
	= _____
Total Income before Tax	= 1 + 3 + 4 = _____

EXAMPLE:

Your Cash Income

	= $ 70,000
1. Full Cash Income	= $ 70,000 × 1.083 = $ 75,810
2. Of which Income from Government	= $ 3,750 = $ 3,750
3. Hidden Income	= $ 70,000 × 0.174 = $ 12,180
4. Hidden Purchasing Power Loss	= $ 70,000 × 0.304 = $ 21,280
Total Income before Tax	= $109,270

HOW TO USE THE TAX TABLES

Tables A-12 to A-22 are the 1987 Tax Tables for each of the ten provinces and Canada as a whole. You will be able to locate within $500 your cash income in the first column of each Tax Table. You will then be able to establish for the province in which you reside, how much income you spent on each tax. The final column shows your total tax bill.

Step 1. Calculate your family's cash income as you did in Step 1 and Step 2 of the income calculation.

Step 2. If your family's cash income exceeded $60,000, skip to Step 5. If not, proceed to Step 3.

Step 3. Locate the line in the Tax Table that has your cash income in the first column.
         If your cash income was $21,000 for 1987, locate $21,000 in the 1987 Tax Table for your province of residence.

Step 4. Read off the tax sub-totals and total tax paid.
         eg. Alberta

Your Cash Income $	Profits Tax $	Income Tax $	Sales Tax $	Liquor, Tobacco, Amusement and Other Excise Taxes $	Auto, Fuel & Motor Vehicle Licence Taxes $
21000	2537	2293	374	724	124

Social Security, Pension, Medical & Hospital Taxes $	Property Tax $	Natural Resources Taxes $	Import Duties $	Other Taxes $	Total Taxes $
1325	1014	1448	98	102	10039

Step 5. If your cash income exceeded $60,000, you will have to use the Detailed Tax Calculation Schedules which accompany each Tax Table.

TABLE A-12
1987 Tax Table for the Province of Alberta

Your Cash Income	Profits Tax	Income Tax	Sales Tax	Liquor, Tobacco, Amusement and Other Excise Taxes	Auto, Fuel & Motor Vehicle Licence Taxes	Social Security, Pension, Medical & Hospital Taxes	Property Tax	Natural Resources Taxes	Import Duties	Other Taxes	Total Taxes
						(Dollars per family)					
5000	405	75	57	111	19	411	162	231	15	16	1501
5500	394	82	66	128	22	440	158	225	17	16	1549
6000	384	90	75	144	25	470	154	219	20	15	1596
6500	374	98	83	161	28	499	150	213	22	15	1643
7000	364	106	92	178	30	529	145	208	24	14	1690
7500	354	114	100	194	33	558	141	202	26	13	1737
8000	344	122	109	211	36	588	137	196	29	13	1784
8500	382	146	105	203	35	571	153	218	27	15	1855
9000	421	170	101	195	33	555	168	240	26	16	1925
9500	460	194	96	187	32	538	184	262	25	18	1996
10000	498	218	92	179	31	521	199	284	24	20	2067
10500	537	242	88	171	29	505	215	306	23	21	2137
11000	734	302	103	200	34	543	293	419	27	30	2685
11500	931	361	119	230	39	580	372	531	31	38	3232
12000	1128	420	134	259	44	618	451	644	35	46	3779
12500	1325	479	149	289	49	655	530	756	39	54	4326
13000	1522	538	165	319	54	693	608	869	43	62	4873
13500	1719	597	180	348	59	731	687	981	47	70	5420
14000	1916	657	195	378	65	768	766	1094	51	78	5967
14500	2113	716	210	407	70	806	845	1206	55	86	6514
15000	2310	775	226	437	75	843	923	1318	59	95	7061
15500	2323	898	237	459	78	881	928	1325	62	95	7288
16000	2335	1021	249	482	82	919	933	1332	65	95	7515
16500	2347	1144	260	504	86	957	938	1339	68	96	7741
17000	2359	1267	272	527	90	995	943	1346	71	96	7968
17500	2372	1390	284	549	94	1034	948	1353	74	96	8194
18000	2384	1513	295	572	98	1072	953	1360	77	97	8421
18500	2396	1636	307	594	102	1110	958	1367	80	97	8647
19000	2409	1759	318	617	105	1148	963	1374	84	97	8874

TABLE A-12 continued
1987 Tax Table for the Province of Alberta

Your Cash Income	Profits Tax	Income Tax	Sales Tax	Liquor, Tobacco, Amusement and Other Excise Taxes	Auto, Fuel & Motor Vehicle Licence Taxes	Social Security, Pension, Medical & Hospital Taxes	Property Tax	Natural Resources Taxes	Import Duties	Other Taxes	Total Taxes
						(Dollars per family)					
19500	2421	1882	330	639	109	1186	968	1381	87	98	9100
20000	2433	2005	342	662	113	1224	972	1388	90	98	9327
20500	2445	2128	353	684	117	1262	977	1395	93	98	9553
21000	2537	2293	374	724	124	1325	1014	1448	98	102	10039
21500	2628	2458	395	764	131	1388	1050	1500	103	105	10522
22000	2719	2623	415	804	137	1451	1087	1552	109	109	11006
22500	2810	2788	436	844	144	1513	1123	1604	114	113	11490
23000	2902	2953	457	884	151	1576	1160	1656	120	116	11975
23500	2993	3118	477	924	158	1639	1196	1708	125	120	12459
24000	3084	3284	498	964	165	1702	1233	1760	131	123	12943
24500	3175	3449	519	1004	172	1765	1269	1812	136	127	13427
25000	3267	3614	539	1044	178	1828	1305	1864	141	130	13912
25500	3358	3779	560	1084	185	1891	1342	1916	147	134	14396
26000	3373	3932	574	1111	190	1937	1348	1925	151	134	14673
26500	3387	4085	588	1138	195	1982	1354	1933	154	135	14951
27000	3402	4238	602	1165	199	2028	1360	1942	158	135	15228
27500	3417	4390	616	1192	204	2074	1366	1950	161	135	15505
28000	3432	4543	630	1219	208	2119	1372	1958	165	136	15783
28500	3447	4696	644	1246	213	2165	1378	1967	169	136	16060
29000	3462	4849	657	1273	218	2211	1383	1975	172	137	16338
29500	3476	5002	671	1300	222	2256	1389	1984	176	137	16615
30000	3491	5155	685	1327	227	2302	1395	1992	180	138	16892
30500	3506	5308	699	1354	231	2347	1401	2001	183	138	17170
31000	3521	5461	713	1381	236	2393	1407	2009	187	138	17447
31500	3582	5645	732	1418	242	2452	1431	2044	192	141	17879
32000	3643	5829	751	1454	249	2511	1456	2079	197	143	18310
32500	3703	6012	770	1491	255	2570	1480	2113	202	145	18741
33000	3764	6196	789	1527	261	2629	1504	2148	207	148	19173
33500	3825	6380	808	1564	267	2688	1529	2183	212	150	19604

34000	3886	6564	826	1600	273	2747	1553	2217	217	152	20036
34500	3946	6748	845	1637	280	2806	1577	2252	222	154	20467
35000	4007	6932	864	1673	286	2865	1602	2287	227	157	20899
35500	4068	7116	883	1710	292	2924	1626	2321	232	159	21330
36000	4001	7266	897	1738	297	2976	1599	2283	235	156	21448
36500	3933	7416	912	1765	302	3029	1572	2244	239	153	21565
37000	3866	7567	926	1793	306	3081	1545	2206	243	150	21683
37500	3798	7717	940	1821	311	3134	1518	2167	247	147	21800
38000	3731	7868	954	1848	316	3187	1491	2129	250	143	21917
38500	3663	8018	969	1876	321	3239	1464	2090	254	140	22035
39000	3596	8168	983	1904	325	3292	1437	2052	258	137	22152
39500	3528	8319	997	1932	330	3344	1410	2013	262	134	22270
40000	3461	8469	1012	1959	335	3397	1383	1975	265	131	22387
40500	3393	8620	1026	1987	340	3449	1356	1936	269	128	22504
41000	3326	8770	1040	2015	344	3502	1329	1898	273	125	22622
41500	3358	8924	1059	2050	350	3561	1342	1916	278	126	22964
42000	3390	9078	1077	2086	356	3620	1355	1935	282	127	23307
42500	3422	9232	1095	2121	363	3680	1368	1953	287	128	23649
43000	3454	9386	1114	2157	369	3739	1380	1971	292	129	23992
43500	3486	9541	1132	2193	375	3798	1393	1989	297	130	24334
44000	3518	9695	1151	2228	381	3857	1406	2008	302	131	24677
44500	3550	9849	1169	2264	387	3917	1419	2026	307	132	25019
45000	3582	10003	1187	2299	393	3976	1432	2044	311	133	25362
45500	3614	10157	1206	2335	399	4035	1445	2063	316	135	25704
46000	3638	10342	1221	2364	404	4084	1454	2076	320	135	26037
46500	3662	10527	1235	2393	409	4132	1463	2090	324	136	26371
47000	3685	10712	1250	2422	414	4181	1473	2103	328	137	26704
47500	3709	10897	1265	2450	419	4229	1482	2117	332	138	27038
48000	3733	11082	1280	2479	424	4277	1492	2130	336	138	27371
48500	3756	11267	1295	2508	429	4326	1501	2144	340	139	27704
49000	3780	11452	1310	2537	434	4374	1511	2157	344	140	28038
49500	3804	11637	1325	2566	439	4422	1520	2171	347	141	28371
50000	3827	11821	1340	2595	443	4471	1530	2184	351	141	28705
50500	3851	12006	1355	2624	448	4519	1539	2198	355	142	29038
51000	3921	12164	1369	2650	453	4560	1567	2237	359	145	29425
51500	3991	12321	1382	2677	457	4601	1595	2277	363	148	29812
52000	4061	12478	1396	2703	462	4642	1623	2317	366	151	30198
52500	4130	12635	1410	2730	467	4683	1651	2357	370	153	30585
53000	4200	12792	1423	2756	471	4724	1679	2397	373	156	30972
53500	4270	12949	1437	2783	476	4765	1707	2437	377	159	31359

TABLE A-12 continued
1987 Tax Table for the Province of Alberta

Your Cash Income	Profits Tax	Income Tax	Sales Tax	Liquor, Tobacco, Amusement and Other Excise Taxes	Auto, Fuel & Motor Vehicle Licence Taxes	Social Security, Pension, Medical & Hospital Taxes	Property Tax	Natural Resources Taxes	Import Duties	Other Taxes	Total Taxes
					(Dollars per family)						
54000	4340	13106	1451	2810	480	4806	1734	2477	380	162	31746
54500	4410	13263	1464	2836	485	4847	1762	2516	384	164	32132
55000	4479	13420	1478	2863	489	4889	1790	2556	388	167	32519
55500	4549	13577	1492	2889	494	4930	1818	2596	391	170	32906
56000	4619	13735	1506	2916	498	4971	1846	2636	395	173	33293
56500	4689	13892	1519	2942	503	5012	1874	2676	398	175	33680
57000	4759	14049	1533	2969	507	5053	1902	2716	402	178	34066
57500	4829	14206	1547	2995	512	5094	1930	2755	406	181	34453
58000	4898	14363	1560	3022	516	5135	1958	2795	409	184	34840
58500	4968	14520	1574	3048	521	5176	1986	2835	413	186	35227
59000	5038	14677	1588	3075	525	5217	2013	2875	416	189	35614
59500	5108	14834	1601	3101	530	5258	2041	2915	420	192	36000
60000	5178	14991	1615	3128	534	5299	2069	2955	424	195	36387

SCHEDULE A-12

1987 Detailed Tax Calculation for the Province of Alberta

1. Profit tax = Your Cash Income × 0.086 _____

2. Income tax = Your Cash Income × 0.250 _____

3. Sales tax = Your Cash Income × 0.027 _____

4. Liquor, tobacco, amusement
   & other excise taxes = Your Cash Income × 0.052 _____

5. Auto, fuel & motor
   vehicle licence fees = Your Cash Income × 0.009 _____

6. Social security, pension,
   medical & hospital taxes = Your Cash Income × 0.088 _____

7. Property tax = Your Cash Income × 0.034 _____

8. Natural resources taxes = Your Cash Income × 0.049 _____

9. Import duties = Your Cash Income × 0.007 _____

10. Other taxes = Your Cash Income × 0.003 _____

Total taxes 1 + 2 + 3 + 4 + 5 + 6 + 7 + 8 + 9 + 10

TABLE A-13
1987 Tax Table for the Province of British Columbia

Your Cash Income	Profits Tax	Income Tax	Sales Tax	Liquor, Tobacco, Amusement and Other Excise Taxes	Auto, Fuel & Motor Vehicle Licence Taxes	Social Security, Pension, Medical & Hospital Taxes	Property Tax	Natural Resources Taxes	Import Duties	Other Taxes	Total Taxes
					(Dollars per family)						
5000	90	65	90	60	21	425	89	56	24	6	926
5500	99	72	109	72	26	447	98	62	29	7	1022
6000	109	79	128	85	30	470	108	68	34	8	1119
6500	119	86	147	97	35	493	117	74	40	8	1215
7000	128	93	166	109	39	515	127	80	45	9	1311
7500	138	100	185	122	44	538	136	86	50	10	1407
8000	147	107	204	134	48	560	145	92	55	11	1504
8500	172	128	203	133	48	552	170	107	54	12	1579
9000	196	149	202	133	48	544	194	122	54	12	1653
9500	221	170	200	132	47	535	218	137	54	13	1728
10000	245	191	199	132	47	527	242	152	54	14	1803
10500	269	213	198	131	47	518	266	168	53	14	1878
11000	309	265	225	148	53	543	305	192	60	16	2116
11500	348	317	251	166	59	567	344	217	68	18	2355
12000	388	368	278	183	66	591	383	241	75	20	2594
12500	427	420	305	201	72	616	422	266	82	22	2833
13000	467	472	331	219	78	640	461	290	89	24	3072
13500	506	524	358	236	84	665	500	315	96	26	3311
14000	546	576	384	254	91	689	539	340	103	28	3550
14500	585	628	411	271	97	713	578	364	110	30	3789
15000	625	680	438	289	103	738	617	389	118	32	4028
15500	664	788	465	307	110	763	655	413	125	34	4325
16000	703	896	493	325	116	789	694	437	132	36	4621
16500	741	1004	520	343	123	815	732	461	140	38	4918
17000	780	1112	548	361	129	841	771	486	147	40	5215
17500	819	1220	575	380	136	867	809	510	155	42	5512
18000	858	1328	603	398	142	892	848	534	162	44	5809
18500	897	1436	630	416	149	918	886	558	169	46	6106
19000	936	1544	658	434	155	944	925	583	177	48	6403

19500	6700	50	184	607	963	970	162	452	685	1652	975
20000	6997	52	192	631	1002	996	168	470	713	1759	1014
20500	7294	54	199	655	1040	1021	175	489	740	1867	1053
21000	7628	56	212	660	1047	1084	186	521	789	2012	1060
21500	7963	58	225	665	1055	1147	198	553	837	2157	1068
22000	8297	60	238	669	1062	1210	209	585	886	2302	1075
22500	8631	62	251	674	1069	1273	221	617	934	2447	1083
23000	8966	64	264	678	1077	1336	232	649	983	2592	1090
23500	9300	66	277	683	1084	1399	243	681	1031	2737	1098
24000	9634	68	290	688	1091	1462	255	713	1080	2882	1105
24500	9969	70	303	692	1099	1525	266	745	1128	3026	1112
25000	10303	72	316	697	1106	1588	278	777	1177	3171	1120
25500	10637	74	330	702	1113	1651	289	809	1226	3316	1127
26000	10847	75	339	688	1093	1705	298	832	1261	3450	1106
26500	11057	76	349	675	1072	1758	306	855	1296	3584	1085
27000	11266	76	358	662	1051	1812	314	879	1331	3719	1064
27500	11476	77	367	649	1030	1865	323	902	1367	3853	1043
28000	11686	78	377	636	1009	1918	331	925	1402	3987	1022
28500	11895	79	386	623	989	1972	339	949	1437	4121	1001
29000	12105	79	396	610	968	2025	348	972	1473	4255	980
29500	12315	80	405	597	947	2078	356	995	1508	4390	959
30000	12524	81	415	583	926	2132	364	1018	1543	4524	938
30500	12734	82	424	570	905	2185	373	1042	1578	4658	917
31000	12944	82	434	557	884	2239	381	1065	1614	4792	895
31500	13299	84	444	575	912	2279	389	1089	1650	4954	924
32000	13655	86	453	592	940	2320	398	1113	1686	5115	952
32500	14011	88	463	610	968	2360	407	1137	1722	5276	980
33000	14366	91	473	627	996	2400	415	1160	1758	5438	1008
33500	14722	93	482	645	1023	2441	424	1184	1794	5599	1036
34000	15077	95	492	662	1051	2481	432	1208	1831	5760	1064
34500	15433	97	502	680	1079	2522	441	1232	1867	5922	1093
35000	15789	99	512	697	1107	2562	449	1256	1903	6083	1121
35500	16144	101	521	715	1135	2603	458	1280	1939	6244	1149
36000	16415	102	531	719	1141	2647	466	1303	1974	6376	1156
36500	16686	104	540	723	1148	2692	474	1326	2009	6508	1162
37000	16957	105	549	727	1154	2737	482	1349	2043	6640	1169
37500	17228	107	559	732	1161	2782	491	1372	2078	6772	1176
38000	17499	108	568	736	1168	2827	499	1394	2113	6904	1182
38500	17770	109	577	740	1174	2871	507	1417	2148	7036	1189
39000	18041	111	587	744	1181	2916	515	1440	2183	7168	1196
39500	18312	112	596	748	1187	2961	523	1463	2217	7300	1202

TABLE A-13 continued
1987 Tax Table for the Province of British Columbia

Your Cash Income	Profits Tax	Income Tax	Sales Tax	Liquor, Tobacco, Amusement and Other Excise Taxes	Auto, Fuel & Motor Vehicle Licence Taxes	Social Security, Pension, Medical & Hospital Taxes	Property Tax	Natural Resources Taxes	Import Duties	Other Taxes	Total Taxes
						(Dollars per family)					
40000	1209	7432	2252	1486	532	3006	1194	752	606	114	18583
40500	1216	7564	2287	1509	540	3050	1201	756	615	115	18853
41000	1222	7696	2322	1532	548	3095	1207	761	624	115	19124
41500	1173	7832	2362	1559	558	3164	1159	730	635	117	19288
42000	1124	7967	2403	1586	567	3232	1110	699	646	117	19452
42500	1075	8102	2444	1613	577	3301	1061	669	657	117	19615
43000	1026	8237	2484	1639	586	3369	1013	638	668	118	19779
43500	976	8372	2525	1666	596	3438	964	608	679	118	19942
44000	927	8508	2565	1693	606	3507	916	577	690	118	20106
44500	878	8643	2606	1720	615	3575	867	546	701	118	20270
45000	829	8778	2647	1747	625	3644	819	516	712	118	20433
45500	780	8913	2687	1773	634	3712	770	485	723	119	20597
46000	873	9076	2717	1793	641	3726	863	544	731	122	21085
46500	967	9238	2747	1813	648	3739	955	602	739	126	21573
47000	1061	9400	2777	1833	655	3752	1047	660	747	129	22061
47500	1154	9563	2807	1852	663	3766	1140	718	755	133	22550
48000	1248	9725	2837	1872	670	3779	1232	776	763	136	23038
48500	1341	9887	2867	1892	677	3793	1325	835	771	140	23526
49000	1435	10049	2897	1912	684	3806	1417	893	779	143	24014
49500	1528	10212	2927	1931	691	3819	1509	951	787	147	24503
50000	1622	10374	2957	1951	698	3833	1602	1009	795	150	24991
50500	1715	10536	2987	1971	705	3846	1694	1068	803	154	25479
51000	1730	10674	3016	1991	712	3882	1709	1077	811	155	25757
51500	1744	10812	3046	2010	719	3918	1723	1086	819	157	26034
52000	1759	10950	3076	2030	726	3954	1737	1095	827	158	26312
52500	1773	11088	3106	2050	733	3990	1751	1103	835	160	26589
53000	1788	11226	3136	2069	740	4026	1766	1112	843	161	26867
53500	1802	11364	3166	2089	747	4062	1780	1121	851	163	27144

54000	1817	11501	3195	2109	754	4098	1794	1130	859	164	27422
54500	1831	11639	3225	2128	761	4134	1808	1139	867	166	27699
55000	1845	11777	3255	2148	768	4169	1823	1148	875	167	27977
55500	1860	11915	3285	2168	775	4205	1837	1157	883	169	28254
56000	1874	12053	3315	2188	782	4241	1851	1166	891	170	28532
56500	1889	12191	3345	2207	789	4277	1865	1175	899	171	28810
57000	1903	12329	3374	2227	797	4313	1880	1184	907	173	29087
57500	1918	12467	3404	2247	804	4349	1894	1193	915	174	29365
58000	1932	12604	3434	2266	811	4385	1908	1202	923	176	29642
58500	1947	12742	3464	2286	818	4421	1923	1211	931	177	29920
59000	1961	12880	3494	2306	825	4457	1937	1220	939	179	30197
59500	1975	13018	3524	2325	832	4493	1951	1229	947	180	30475
60000	1990	13156	3553	2345	839	4529	1965	1238	955	182	30752

SCHEDULE A-13

1987 Detailed Tax Calculation for the Province of British Columbia

1. Profit tax = Your Cash Income × 0.033 _____

2. Income tax = Your Cash Income × 0.219 _____

3. Sales tax = Your Cash Income × 0.059 _____

4. Liquor, tobacco, amusement
   & other excise taxes = Your Cash Income × 0.039 _____

5. Auto, fuel & motor
   vehicle licence fees = Your Cash Income × 0.014 _____

6. Social security, pension,
   medical & hospital taxes = Your Cash Income × 0.075 _____

7. Property tax = Your Cash Income × 0.033 _____

8. Natural resources taxes = Your Cash Income × 0.021 _____

9. Import duties = Your Cash Income × 0.016 _____

10. Other taxes = Your Cash Income × 0.003 _____

Total taxes 1 + 2 + 3 + 4 + 5 + 6 + 7 + 8 + 9 + 10

TABLE A-14
1987 Tax Table for the Province of Manitoba

Your Cash Income	Profits Tax	Income Tax	Sales Tax	Liquor, Tobacco, Amusement and Other Excise Taxes	Auto, Fuel & Motor Vehicle Licence Taxes	Social Security, Pension, Medical & Hospital Taxes	Property Tax	Natural Resources Taxes	Import Duties	Other Taxes	Total Taxes
					(Dollars per family)						
5000	62	59	98	30	19	109	72	10	12	53	524
5500	69	66	116	36	22	130	81	11	14	63	608
6000	77	72	134	41	26	151	90	13	16	72	691
6500	85	78	152	47	29	172	99	14	18	81	775
7000	92	84	170	53	32	193	109	15	20	91	858
7500	100	90	187	58	36	214	118	16	22	100	942
8000	108	97	205	64	39	235	127	18	24	110	1026
8500	138	116	204	63	39	224	162	23	24	112	1105
9000	169	135	203	63	39	214	198	28	24	113	1185
9500	199	154	202	63	38	203	234	33	24	115	1265
10000	230	174	201	62	38	193	270	38	24	117	1345
10500	260	193	199	62	38	183	305	43	24	119	1425
11000	291	240	234	73	45	219	342	48	28	139	1659
11500	323	287	270	84	51	255	379	53	32	158	1892
12000	354	334	305	95	58	292	416	58	36	178	2126
12500	386	381	340	105	65	328	453	63	40	198	2360
13000	417	428	375	116	72	365	490	68	45	218	2593
13500	448	476	410	127	78	401	527	73	49	238	2827
14000	480	523	445	138	85	438	563	78	53	257	3061
14500	511	570	481	149	92	474	600	84	57	277	3294
15000	542	617	516	160	98	510	637	89	61	297	3528
15500	579	715	553	171	105	548	680	95	66	318	3830
16000	615	813	590	183	113	586	722	101	70	339	4132
16500	651	911	627	195	120	623	765	107	75	361	4433
17000	687	1009	665	206	127	661	807	112	79	382	4735
17500	724	1106	702	218	134	699	850	118	83	403	5037
18000	760	1204	739	229	141	737	892	124	88	424	5339
18500	796	1302	776	241	148	774	935	130	92	445	5641
19000	832	1400	814	252	155	812	977	136	97	467	5942

TABLE A-14 continued
1987 Tax Table for the Province of Manitoba

Your Cash Income	Profits Tax	Income Tax	Sales Tax	Liquor, Tobacco, Amusement and Other Excise Taxes	Auto, Fuel & Motor Vehicle Licence Taxes	Social Security, Pension, Medical & Hospital Taxes	Property Tax	Natural Resources Taxes	Import Duties	Other Taxes	Total Taxes
						(Dollars per family)					
19500	869	1498	851	264	162	850	1020	142	101	488	6244
20000	905	1596	888	275	169	887	1063	148	106	509	6546
20500	941	1694	925	287	176	925	1105	154	110	530	6848
21000	943	1825	971	301	185	984	1107	154	115	553	7139
21500	944	1957	1017	315	194	1043	1109	154	121	576	7429
22000	946	2088	1062	329	203	1101	1111	155	126	598	7720
22500	948	2219	1108	344	211	1160	1113	155	132	621	8011
23000	949	2351	1154	358	220	1219	1115	155	137	644	8302
23500	951	2482	1200	372	229	1277	1117	156	143	666	8592
24000	953	2614	1245	386	237	1336	1119	156	148	689	8883
24500	954	2745	1291	400	246	1395	1121	156	154	712	9174
25000	956	2876	1337	414	255	1454	1123	156	159	734	9465
25500	958	3008	1383	429	264	1512	1125	157	164	757	9755
26000	982	3130	1423	441	271	1557	1153	161	169	779	10065
26500	1006	3251	1463	454	279	1603	1181	165	174	800	10375
27000	1030	3373	1503	466	287	1648	1209	168	179	822	10685
27500	1054	3495	1544	479	294	1693	1237	172	184	844	10995
28000	1078	3616	1584	491	302	1738	1266	176	188	866	11305
28500	1102	3738	1624	504	310	1783	1294	180	193	887	11615
29000	1126	3860	1664	516	317	1828	1322	184	198	909	11925
29500	1150	3982	1705	529	325	1874	1350	188	203	931	12234
30000	1174	4103	1745	541	333	1919	1378	192	208	952	12544
30500	1197	4225	1785	553	340	1964	1406	196	212	974	12854
31000	1221	4347	1825	566	348	2009	1435	200	217	996	13164
31500	1227	4493	1870	580	356	2065	1441	201	222	1018	13473
32000	1232	4639	1914	593	365	2121	1447	202	228	1040	13781
32500	1237	4786	1958	607	373	2177	1453	202	233	1063	14090
33000	1243	4932	2003	621	382	2232	1459	203	238	1085	14398
33500	1248	5078	2047	635	390	2288	1466	204	243	1107	14707

34000	15015	1129	249	205	1472	2344	399	648	2091	5225	1253
34500	15324	1152	254	206	1478	2400	407	662	2135	5371	1258
35000	15632	1174	259	207	1484	2456	416	676	2180	5518	1264
35500	15941	1196	264	208	1490	2512	424	690	2224	5664	1269
36000	16204	1215	269	209	1499	2558	431	701	2262	5784	1276
36500	16467	1234	273	210	1507	2605	438	713	2299	5903	1283
37000	16730	1253	278	211	1516	2651	446	725	2337	6023	1291
37500	16993	1272	282	212	1524	2698	453	736	2374	6143	1298
38000	17256	1292	287	214	1533	2744	460	748	2412	6263	1305
38500	17519	1311	291	215	1541	2791	467	759	2449	6382	1312
39000	17783	1330	296	216	1550	2837	474	771	2487	6502	1320
39500	18046	1349	300	217	1558	2884	481	783	2525	6622	1327
40000	18309	1368	305	218	1567	2931	489	794	2562	6741	1334
40500	18572	1387	309	219	1575	2977	496	806	2600	6861	1341
41000	18835	1406	314	221	1584	3024	503	818	2637	6981	1348
41500	19037	1424	318	216	1552	3084	511	830	2678	7104	1321
42000	19239	1442	323	212	1519	3144	518	843	2718	7226	1294
42500	19440	1459	328	207	1487	3204	526	855	2758	7349	1266
43000	19642	1477	333	203	1455	3265	534	868	2799	7471	1239
43500	19844	1495	338	198	1423	3325	541	880	2839	7594	1211
44000	20046	1512	342	194	1390	3385	549	893	2880	7717	1184
44500	20247	1530	347	189	1358	3445	557	905	2920	7839	1156
45000	20449	1548	352	185	1326	3505	564	918	2960	7962	1129
45500	20651	1566	357	180	1294	3566	572	930	3001	8085	1101
46000	21010	1589	362	186	1333	3609	580	943	3042	8232	1135
46500	21369	1612	367	191	1372	3653	588	956	3083	8379	1168
47000	21728	1635	372	197	1411	3697	596	969	3125	8526	1202
47500	22087	1658	376	202	1451	3741	604	982	3166	8674	1235
48000	22446	1681	381	208	1490	3785	612	994	3207	8821	1269
48500	22805	1704	386	213	1529	3828	619	1007	3248	8968	1302
49000	23164	1727	391	218	1568	3872	627	1020	3290	9115	1335
49500	23523	1750	396	224	1608	3916	635	1033	3331	9263	1369
50000	23882	1773	401	229	1647	3960	643	1046	3372	9410	1402
50500	24241	1796	406	235	1686	4003	651	1058	3414	9557	1436
51000	24511	1812	410	238	1708	4038	657	1068	3445	9682	1454
51500	24781	1829	413	241	1730	4073	663	1078	3475	9807	1473
52000	25050	1846	417	244	1751	4107	669	1087	3506	9932	1491
52500	25320	1862	421	247	1773	4142	674	1097	3537	10057	1510
53000	25590	1879	424	250	1795	4176	680	1106	3568	10182	1528
53500	25859	1896	428	253	1817	4211	686	1116	3599	10307	1547

TABLE A-14 continued
1987 Tax Table for the Province of Manitoba

Your Cash Income	Profits Tax	Income Tax	Sales Tax	Liquor, Tobacco, Amusement and Other Excise Taxes	Auto, Fuel & Motor Vehicle Licence Taxes	Social Security, Pension, Medical & Hospital Taxes	Property Tax	Natural Resources Taxes	Import Duties	Other Taxes	Total Taxes
						(Dollars per family)					
54000	1565	10432	3630	1125	692	4246	1838	256	432	1912	26129
54500	1584	10557	3661	1135	698	4280	1860	259	435	1929	26399
55000	1602	10682	3691	1145	704	4315	1882	262	439	1946	26668
55500	1621	10807	3722	1154	710	4349	1904	265	443	1962	26938
56000	1640	10933	3753	1164	716	4384	1926	268	446	1979	27207
56500	1658	11058	3784	1173	722	4419	1947	271	450	1996	27477
57000	1677	11183	3815	1183	727	4453	1969	274	454	2012	27747
57500	1695	11308	3846	1192	733	4488	1991	277	457	2029	28016
58000	1714	11433	3877	1202	739	4522	2013	280	461	2046	28286
58500	1732	11558	3907	1212	745	4557	2034	283	465	2062	28556
59000	1751	11683	3938	1221	751	4591	2056	286	468	2079	28825
59500	1769	11808	3969	1231	757	4626	2078	289	472	2096	29095
60000	1788	11933	4000	1240	763	4661	2100	292	476	2112	29365

SCHEDULE A-14

1987 Detailed Tax Calculation for the Province of Manitoba

1. Profit tax   = Your Cash Income × 0.030 = _____

2. Income tax   = Your Cash Income × 0.199 = _____

3. Sales tax   = Your Cash Income × 0.067 = _____

4. Liquor, tobacco, amusement
   & other excise taxes   = Your Cash Income × 0.021 = _____

5. Auto, fuel & motor
   vehicle licence fees   = Your Cash Income × 0.013 = _____

6. Social security, pension,
   medical & hospital taxes   = Your Cash Income × 0.078 = _____

7. Property tax   = Your Cash Income × 0.035 = _____

8. Natural resources taxes   = Your Cash Income × 0.005 = _____

9. Import duties   = Your Cash Income × 0.008 = _____

10. Other taxes   = Your Cash Income × 0.035 = _____

Total taxes 1 + 2 + 3 + 4 + 5 + 6 + 7 + 8 + 9 + 10

TABLE A-15
1987 Tax Table for the Province of New Brunswick

(Dollars per family)

Your Cash Income	Profits Tax	Income Tax	Sales Tax	Liquor, Tobacco, Amusement and Other Excise Taxes	Auto, Fuel & Motor Vehicle Licence Taxes	Social Security, Pension, Medical & Hospital Taxes	Property Tax	Natural Resources Taxes	Import Duties	Other Taxes	Total Taxes
5000	60	55	130	59	27	96	70	8	6	37	548
5500	67	61	133	60	27	97	77	9	7	38	575
6000	73	66	136	61	28	97	85	10	7	39	601
6500	80	72	138	62	28	98	93	11	7	39	628
7000	86	78	141	64	29	98	100	11	7	40	655
7500	93	84	144	65	29	99	108	12	7	41	682
8000	100	89	147	66	30	99	116	13	9	42	709
8500	124	107	185	83	38	126	144	16	11	53	884
9000	149	125	223	100	45	152	173	20	13	63	1060
9500	173	143	261	117	53	178	202	23	13	74	1236
10000	198	160	299	134	61	204	230	26	15	85	1412
10500	223	178	337	151	69	230	259	29	17	96	1588
11000	254	222	372	167	76	252	296	33	18	106	1796
11500	286	265	407	183	83	273	332	38	20	116	2003
12000	318	309	442	199	90	295	369	42	22	126	2211
12500	349	352	477	215	97	317	406	46	23	136	2418
13000	381	396	512	230	104	338	443	50	25	146	2626
13500	413	439	547	246	112	360	479	54	27	156	2833
14000	444	483	582	262	119	382	516	58	29	166	3041
14500	476	526	617	278	126	404	553	63	30	176	3248
15000	508	570	653	294	133	425	590	67	32	186	3456
15500	540	660	706	318	144	463	627	71	35	201	3764
16000	572	750	760	342	155	500	664	75	37	216	4072
16500	604	841	813	366	166	538	701	79	40	232	4380
17000	636	931	867	390	177	575	738	84	43	247	4688
17500	668	1022	921	414	188	613	776	88	45	262	4996
18000	700	1112	974	438	199	651	813	92	48	277	5304
18500	732	1202	1028	463	210	688	850	96	51	293	5612
19000	764	1293	1081	487	221	726	887	101	53	308	5920

19500	6228	323	56	105	924	763	232	511	1135	1383	796
20000	6536	338	58	109	962	801	242	535	1189	1474	828
20500	6843	354	61	113	999	838	253	559	1242	1564	860
21000	7181	375	65	113	1001	902	269	593	1317	1685	862
21500	7519	396	68	114	1003	966	284	626	1392	1807	864
22000	7857	417	72	114	1005	1030	299	660	1466	1928	865
22500	8195	439	76	114	1007	1094	314	694	1541	2049	867
23000	8533	460	79	115	1010	1158	330	727	1616	2171	869
23500	8871	481	83	115	1012	1221	345	761	1691	2292	871
24000	9209	503	87	115	1014	1285	360	794	1766	2413	873
24500	9547	524	91	115	1016	1349	375	828	1840	2534	875
25000	9885	545	94	116	1018	1413	391	862	1915	2656	877
25500	10223	566	98	114	1020	1477	406	895	1990	2777	878
26000	10479	583	101	113	1007	1530	418	922	2048	2890	867
26500	10735	600	104	111	993	1584	430	948	2107	3002	855
27000	10991	616	107	109	980	1637	442	974	2166	3114	844
27500	11247	633	109	108	967	1691	454	1001	2224	3227	832
28000	11503	650	112	106	953	1744	466	1027	2283	3339	821
28500	11759	666	115	105	940	1798	478	1054	2341	3451	809
29000	12015	683	118	103	926	1851	490	1080	2400	3564	798
29500	12270	700	121	102	913	1905	502	1106	2458	3676	786
30000	12526	716	124	100	900	1958	513	1133	2517	3789	774
30500	12782	733	127	100	886	2012	525	1159	2576	3901	763
31000	13038	750	130	99	873	2065	537	1185	2634	4013	751
31500	13488	775	134	103	911	2132	555	1225	2721	4148	784
32000	13937	799	138	107	949	2198	573	1264	2809	4284	817
32500	14387	824	142	112	987	2264	591	1303	2896	4419	849
33000	14837	849	147	116	1025	2331	609	1342	2983	4554	882
33500	15286	874	151	120	1063	2397	626	1382	3070	4689	915
34000	15736	899	155	125	1101	2463	644	1421	3157	4824	948
34500	16186	923	160	129	1139	2529	662	1460	3245	4959	980
35000	16636	948	164	133	1177	2596	680	1499	3332	5094	1013
35500	17085	973	168	138	1215	2662	697	1539	3419	5229	1046
36000	17342	992	171	135	1191	2724	711	1568	3485	5340	1025
36500	17600	1011	175	132	1167	2786	724	1598	3551	5451	1005
37000	17857	1029	178	130	1144	2849	738	1628	3617	5561	985
37500	18114	1048	181	127	1120	2911	751	1657	3683	5672	964
38000	18371	1067	184	124	1096	2973	765	1687	3749	5782	944
38500	18629	1086	188	122	1073	3035	778	1717	3815	5893	923
39000	18886	1105	191	119	1049	3098	792	1746	3881	6003	903
39500	19143	1123	194	116	1025	3160	805	1776	3947	6114	883

TABLE A-15 continued
1987 Tax Table for the Province of New Brunswick

Your Cash Income	Profits Tax	Income Tax	Sales Tax	Liquor, Tobacco, Amusement and Other Excise Taxes	Auto, Fuel & Motor Vehicle Licence Taxes	Social Security, Pension, Medical & Hospital Taxes	Property Tax	Natural Resources Taxes	Import Duties	Other Taxes	Total Taxes
						(Dollars per family)					
40000	862	6224	4013	1806	819	3222	1002	113	197	1142	19400
40500	842	6335	4079	1835	832	3284	978	111	201	1161	19658
41000	822	6445	4145	1865	846	3347	955	108	204	1180	19915
41500	840	6559	4200	1890	857	3389	976	111	207	1195	20223
42000	859	6672	4255	1915	868	3432	997	113	209	1211	20531
42500	877	6785	4310	1940	879	3474	1019	115	212	1227	20839
43000	896	6898	4366	1965	891	3517	1040	118	215	1243	21147
43500	914	7012	4421	1989	902	3560	1062	120	217	1258	21455
44000	933	7125	4476	2014	913	3602	1083	123	220	1274	21763
44500	951	7238	4531	2039	924	3645	1105	125	223	1290	22071
45000	970	7351	4587	2064	936	3687	1126	128	226	1305	22380
45500	988	7465	4642	2089	947	3730	1148	130	228	1321	22688
46000	1008	7600	4708	2119	960	3781	1171	133	232	1340	23053
46500	1029	7736	4774	2148	974	3833	1195	135	235	1359	23418
47000	1049	7872	4840	2178	987	3884	1219	138	238	1378	23784
47500	1069	8008	4906	2208	1001	3936	1242	141	241	1396	24149
48000	1090	8144	4972	2238	1014	3987	1266	143	245	1415	24514
48500	1110	8280	5038	2267	1028	4038	1290	146	248	1434	24880
49000	1131	8416	5104	2297	1041	4090	1313	149	251	1453	25245
49500	1151	8552	5170	2327	1055	4141	1337	151	254	1472	25610
50000	1171	8688	5236	2356	1068	4193	1361	154	258	1490	25976
50500	1192	8824	5303	2386	1082	4244	1384	157	261	1509	26341
51000	1211	8939	5345	2405	1090	4275	1407	159	263	1521	26616
51500	1231	9055	5387	2424	1099	4306	1429	162	265	1533	26891
52000	1250	9170	5429	2443	1108	4337	1452	164	267	1545	27165
52500	1269	9286	5471	2462	1116	4368	1475	167	269	1557	27440
53000	1289	9401	5513	2481	1125	4399	1497	170	271	1569	27715
53500	1308	9517	5555	2500	1133	4430	1520	172	273	1581	27990

54000	1328	9632	5597	2519	1142	4461	1542	175	275	1593	28265
54500	1347	9748	5639	2538	1150	4492	1565	177	277	1605	28539
55000	1367	9863	5682	2557	1159	4523	1588	180	279	1617	28814
55500	1386	9978	5724	2576	1168	4554	1610	182	282	1629	29089
56000	1406	10094	5766	2595	1176	4585	1633	185	284	1641	29364
56500	1425	10209	5808	2614	1185	4616	1655	187	286	1653	29639
57000	1444	10325	5850	2633	1193	4647	1678	190	288	1665	29913
57500	1464	10440	5892	2651	1202	4678	1701	193	290	1677	30188
58000	1483	10556	5934	2670	1211	4709	1723	195	292	1689	30463
58500	1503	10671	5976	2689	1219	4740	1746	198	294	1701	30738
59000	1522	10787	6019	2708	1228	4771	1768	200	296	1713	31013
59500	1542	10902	6061	2727	1236	4802	1791	203	298	1725	31287
60000	1561	11018	6103	2746	1245	4833	1813	205	300	1737	31562

SCHEDULE A-15

1987 Detailed Tax Calculation for the Province of New Brunswick

1. Profit tax = Your Cash Income × 0.026 _____

2. Income tax = Your Cash Income × 0.184 _____

3. Sales tax = Your Cash Income × 0.102 _____

4. Liquor, tobacco, amusement
   & other excise taxes = Your Cash Income × 0.046 _____

5. Auto, fuel & motor
   vehicle licence fees = Your Cash Income × 0.021 _____

6. Social security, pension,
   medical & hospital taxes = Your Cash Income × 0.081 _____

7. Property tax = Your Cash Income × 0.030 _____

8. Natural resources taxes = Your Cash Income × 0.003 _____

9. Import duties = Your Cash Income × 0.005 _____

10. Other taxes = Your Cash Income × 0.029 _____

Total taxes 1 + 2 + 3 + 4 + 5 + 6 + 7 + 8 + 9 + 10

TABLE A-16

1987 Tax Table for the Province of Newfoundland

Your Cash Income	Profits Tax	Income Tax	Sales Tax	Liquor, Tobacco, Amusement and Other Excise Taxes	Auto, Fuel & Motor Vehicle Licence Taxes	Social Security, Pension, Medical & Hospital Taxes	Property Tax	Natural Resources Taxes	Import Duties	Other Taxes	Total Taxes
					(Dollars per family)						
5000	58	58	144	42	29	123	22	11	3	40	530
5500	50	64	140	41	28	121	19	10	3	38	513
6000	41	70	137	39	27	119	16	8	3	35	496
6500	33	76	133	38	26	117	13	6	3	33	478
7000	25	82	129	37	26	115	9	5	3	31	461
7500	16	88	125	36	25	113	6	3	3	29	444
8000	8	94	121	35	24	110	3	2	3	27	427
8500	20	113	147	42	29	132	8	4	4	35	532
9000	32	131	172	50	34	154	12	6	5	42	638
9500	44	150	198	57	39	175	17	9	5	49	743
10000	56	169	224	65	45	197	21	11	6	56	848
10500	68	187	249	72	50	218	26	13	7	64	954
11000	109	233	284	82	56	243	42	21	7	77	1154
11500	150	279	318	92	63	267	57	29	8	90	1354
12000	191	325	352	102	70	291	73	37	9	103	1554
12500	232	371	387	112	77	315	89	45	10	117	1753
13000	273	416	421	122	84	340	104	53	11	130	1953
13500	314	462	455	132	91	364	120	61	12	143	2153
14000	355	508	490	142	97	388	136	69	12	156	2353
14500	396	554	524	152	104	412	152	77	13	170	2553
15000	437	600	558	161	111	437	167	85	15	183	2753
15500	475	695	620	179	123	486	182	93	16	202	3068
16000	512	790	681	197	135	536	196	100	17	220	3384
16500	550	885	742	215	148	586	210	107	19	239	3699
17000	587	980	803	232	160	636	225	115	20	257	4014
17500	625	1075	865	250	172	686	239	122	22	276	4330
18000	662	1170	926	268	184	736	253	129	23	295	4645
18500	700	1266	987	285	196	785	268	137	25	313	4961
19000	738	1361	1048	303	209	835	282	144	25	332	5276

TABLE A-16 continued
1987 Tax Table for the Province of Newfoundland

(Dollars per family)

Your Cash Income	Profits Tax	Income Tax	Sales Tax	Liquor, Tobacco, Amusement and Other Excise Taxes	Auto, Fuel & Motor Vehicle Licence Taxes	Social Security, Pension, Medical & Hospital Taxes	Property Tax	Natural Resources Taxes	Import Duties	Other Taxes	Total Taxes
19500	775	1456	1110	321	221	885	297	151	26	350	5591
20000	813	1551	1171	339	233	935	311	158	28	369	5907
20500	850	1646	1232	356	245	985	325	166	29	388	6222
21000	817	1774	1296	375	258	1050	312	159	30	397	6468
21500	783	1902	1360	393	270	1115	300	153	32	406	6714
22000	750	2029	1424	412	283	1180	287	146	33	415	6959
22500	716	2157	1488	430	296	1246	274	140	35	424	7205
23000	683	2285	1552	449	309	1311	261	133	36	433	7451
23500	649	2412	1615	467	321	1376	248	127	38	442	7696
24000	616	2540	1679	486	334	1441	236	120	39	451	7942
24500	582	2668	1743	504	347	1506	223	114	41	460	8188
25000	549	2796	1807	522	359	1572	210	107	42	470	8433
25500	515	2923	1871	541	372	1637	197	100	44	479	8679
26000	565	3042	1926	557	383	1679	216	110	45	498	9019
26500	614	3160	1980	573	394	1720	235	120	47	517	9359
27000	664	3278	2035	588	405	1762	254	130	48	535	9699
27500	714	3396	2090	604	416	1803	273	139	49	554	10039
28000	764	3515	2144	620	426	1845	292	149	50	573	10379
28500	813	3633	2199	636	437	1886	311	159	52	592	10718
29000	863	3751	2254	652	448	1928	330	168	53	611	11058
29500	913	3870	2309	668	459	1969	349	178	54	630	11398
30000	962	3988	2363	683	470	2011	368	188	56	649	11738
30500	1012	4106	2418	699	481	2052	387	197	57	668	12078
31000	1062	4224	2473	715	492	2094	406	207	58	687	12418
31500	1027	4367	2565	742	510	2186	393	200	60	702	12753
32000	993	4509	2658	769	529	2278	380	194	62	717	13088
32500	958	4651	2751	795	547	2370	367	187	65	732	13423
33000	924	4793	2843	822	565	2462	353	180	67	748	13758
33500	889	4936	2936	849	584	2554	340	173	69	763	14093

14428	778	71	167	327	2646	602	876	3028	5078	855	34000
14763	793	73	160	314	2738	621	902	3121	5220	820	34500
15098	808	76	153	301	2830	639	929	3213	5362	786	35000
15433	824	78	147	287	2922	657	956	3306	5505	752	35500
15773	842	80	147	288	2999	674	980	3389	5621	754	36000
16114	860	82	147	289	3075	691	1004	3473	5737	756	36500
16455	879	84	148	290	3152	707	1028	3556	5854	758	37000
16796	897	86	148	291	3229	724	1052	3639	5970	760	37500
17137	915	88	149	292	3305	740	1076	3722	6086	763	38000
17477	934	89	149	293	3382	757	1100	3806	6203	765	38500
17818	952	91	150	293	3459	773	1124	3889	6319	767	39000
18159	971	93	150	294	3535	790	1149	3972	6435	769	39500
18500	989	95	150	295	3612	806	1173	4055	6552	772	40000
18884	1007	97	151	296	3689	823	1197	4139	6668	774	40500
19181	1026	99	151	297	3765	840	1221	4222	6784	776	41000
19495	1042	101	150	295	3837	855	1243	4298	6904	770	41500
19808	1057	103	149	293	3909	870	1265	4375	7023	765	42000
20122	1073	105	148	290	3981	885	1287	4451	7142	759	42500
20435	1089	106	147	288	4052	900	1309	4528	7261	754	43000
20749	1105	108	146	286	4124	916	1331	4604	7380	748	43500
21062	1121	110	145	284	4196	931	1353	4681	7500	742	44000
21376	1136	112	144	282	4268	946	1376	4757	7619	737	44500
21689	1152	114	143	280	4340	961	1398	4834	7738	731	45000
22003	1168	115	141	278	4411	976	1420	4910	7857	726	45500
22294	1180	117	135	265	4486	991	1441	4985	8000	694	46000
22586	1191	119	129	253	4561	1006	1463	5059	8143	662	46500
22877	1203	121	123	241	4635	1021	1484	5133	8286	630	47000
23169	1215	122	117	229	4710	1036	1506	5208	8430	598	47500
23460	1226	124	110	216	4785	1050	1527	5282	8573	566	48000
23752	1238	126	104	204	4860	1065	1549	5357	8716	534	48500
24043	1249	128	98	192	4934	1080	1570	5431	8859	502	49000
24335	1261	129	92	180	5009	1095	1592	5505	9002	470	49500
24626	1273	131	85	168	5084	1110	1613	5580	9145	438	50000
24918	1284	133	79	155	5159	1124	1635	5654	9288	406	50500
25226	1300	134	89	174	5188	1133	1647	5696	9410	456	51000
25535	1316	135	99	193	5217	1141	1659	5738	9531	506	51500
25844	1333	136	108	212	5247	1149	1671	5779	9653	555	52000
26152	1349	137	118	232	5276	1158	1683	5821	9774	605	52500
26461	1365	138	128	251	5306	1166	1695	5863	9896	655	53000
26770	1381	139	137	270	5335	1174	1707	5904	10017	705	53500

TABLE A-16 continued
1987 Tax Table for the Province of Newfoundland

Your Cash Income	Profits Tax	Income Tax	Sales Tax	Liquor, Tobacco, Amusement and Other Excise Taxes	Auto, Fuel & Motor Vehicle Licence Taxes	Social Security, Pension, Medical & Hospital Taxes	Property Tax	Natural Resources Taxes	Import Duties	Other Taxes	Total Taxes
					(Dollars per family)						
54000	755	10139	5946	1719	1182	5365	289	147	140	1397	27078
54500	805	10260	5988	1731	1191	5394	308	157	141	1413	27387
55000	855	10382	6029	1743	1199	5423	327	167	142	1429	27696
55500	904	10503	6071	1755	1207	5453	346	176	143	1445	28004
56000	954	10625	6113	1767	1216	5482	365	186	144	1461	28313
56500	1004	10746	6154	1780	1224	5512	384	196	145	1477	28622
57000	1054	10868	6196	1792	1232	5541	403	206	146	1493	28931
57500	1104	10989	6238	1804	1240	5571	422	215	147	1510	29239
58000	1154	11111	6279	1816	1249	5600	441	225	148	1526	29548
58500	1204	11233	6321	1828	1257	5629	460	235	149	1542	29857
59000	1253	11354	6363	1840	1265	5659	480	244	150	1558	30165
59500	1303	11476	6404	1852	1274	5688	499	254	151	1574	30474
60000	1353	11597	6446	1864	1282	5718	518	264	152	1590	30783

SCHEDULE A-16

1987 Detailed Tax Calculation for the Province of Newfoundland

1. Profit tax = Your Cash Income × 0.022 ═══
2. Income tax = Your Cash Income × 0.193 ═══
3. Sales tax = Your Cash Income × 0.107 ═══
4. Liquor, tobacco, amusement
   & other excise taxes = Your Cash Income × 0.032 ═══
5. Auto, fuel & motor
   vehicle licence fees = Your Cash Income × 0.021 ═══
6. Social security, pension,
   medical & hospital taxes = Your Cash Income × 0.095 ═══
7. Property tax = Your Cash Income × 0.009 ═══
8. Natural resources taxes = Your Cash Income × 0.004 ═══
9. Import duties = Your Cash Income × 0.003 ═══
10. Other taxes = Your Cash Income × 0.026 ═══

Total taxes 1 + 2 + 3 + 4 + 5 + 6 + 7 + 8 + 9 + 10

TABLE A-17
1987 Tax Table for the Province of Nova Scotia

Your Cash Income	Profits Tax	Income Tax	Sales Tax	Liquor, Tobacco, Amusement and Other Excise Taxes	Auto, Fuel & Motor Vehicle Licence Taxes	Social Security, Pension, Medical & Hospital Taxes	Property Tax	Natural Resources Taxes	Import Duties	Other Taxes	Total Taxes
					(Dollars per family)						
5000	59	59	126	78	25	136	63	5	11	22	586
5500	60	66	130	80	26	140	64	5	12	22	603
6000	60	72	133	82	26	144	64	5	12	23	621
6500	60	78	136	84	27	148	65	5	12	23	638
7000	61	84	139	86	28	152	65	5	13	24	655
7500	61	90	142	88	28	156	66	5	13	24	673
8000	62	97	146	90	29	160	66	5	13	24	690
8500	78	116	173	107	35	188	84	6	16	30	832
9000	95	135	201	124	40	217	102	7	18	35	974
9500	111	154	229	141	46	245	119	9	21	41	1116
10000	128	174	257	158	51	274	137	10	23	46	1258
10500	145	193	285	176	57	302	155	11	26	51	1400
11000	174	240	312	193	62	325	187	13	28	59	1594
11500	204	287	340	210	68	348	219	16	31	66	1788
12000	234	334	367	227	73	371	251	18	33	74	1982
12500	264	381	395	244	79	395	283	20	36	81	2176
13000	293	428	423	261	84	418	314	23	38	88	2370
13500	323	475	450	278	90	441	346	25	41	96	2564
14000	353	522	478	295	95	464	378	27	43	103	2758
14500	383	569	505	312	101	487	410	30	45	111	2953
15000	412	616	533	329	106	510	442	32	48	118	3147
15500	433	714	588	363	117	571	464	33	53	127	3462
16000	453	812	642	397	128	632	486	35	58	136	3778
16500	474	910	697	430	139	693	508	37	63	144	4094
17000	494	1008	752	464	150	754	530	38	68	153	4410
17500	515	1106	807	498	161	815	551	40	73	162	4726
18000	535	1203	861	532	172	876	573	41	78	171	5042
18500	555	1301	916	565	183	937	595	43	82	179	5357
19000	576	1399	971	599	193	998	617	44	87	188	5673

19500	5989	197	92	46	639	1059	204	633	1025	1497	596
20000	6305	206	97	48	661	1120	215	667	1080	1595	617
20500	6621	214	102	49	683	1181	226	700	1135	1692	637
21000	6987	223	108	50	696	1258	239	740	1199	1824	650
21500	7354	231	114	51	710	1335	252	780	1264	1955	662
22000	7720	240	120	52	723	1411	265	820	1328	2086	675
22500	8086	248	125	53	736	1488	278	860	1393	2218	687
23000	8453	257	131	54	750	1565	291	900	1458	2349	699
23500	8819	265	137	55	763	1642	303	940	1522	2480	712
24000	9185	274	143	56	776	1718	316	979	1587	2612	724
24500	9552	282	149	57	790	1795	329	1019	1651	2743	737
25000	9918	291	154	58	803	1872	342	1059	1716	2874	749
25500	10284	299	160	59	816	1949	355	1099	1781	3005	762
26000	10568	304	165	58	806	2022	366	1133	1835	3127	752
26500	10851	308	170	57	796	2095	377	1167	1890	3249	743
27000	11135	312	175	57	787	2168	388	1200	1945	3370	734
27500	11418	316	180	56	777	2241	399	1234	2000	3492	725
28000	11702	320	185	55	767	2314	409	1268	2054	3613	716
28500	11985	324	190	55	757	2387	420	1302	2109	3735	706
29000	12269	329	195	54	747	2460	431	1336	2164	3857	697
29500	12552	333	200	53	737	2533	442	1369	2219	3978	688
30000	12836	337	205	52	727	2606	453	1403	2274	4100	679
30500	13119	341	210	52	718	2679	464	1437	2328	4222	670
31000	13402	345	214	51	708	2752	475	1471	2383	4343	660
31500	13778	353	221	51	712	2835	488	1513	2451	4489	665
32000	14153	360	227	52	717	2919	502	1554	2518	4636	669
32500	14528	368	233	52	722	3003	515	1596	2586	4782	673
33000	14904	375	239	52	726	3086	529	1637	2653	4928	678
33500	15279	383	245	53	731	3170	542	1679	2721	5074	682
34000	15654	390	251	53	735	3254	556	1721	2788	5221	686
34500	16030	398	257	53	740	3337	569	1762	2855	5367	690
35000	16405	406	263	54	745	3421	583	1804	2923	5513	695
35500	16780	413	269	54	749	3505	596	1846	2990	5659	699
36000	17111	424	273	58	799	3533	603	1869	3028	5779	746
36500	17441	435	276	61	849	3562	611	1892	3065	5899	792
37000	17771	446	279	65	899	3590	618	1915	3102	6018	839
37500	18101	457	283	68	949	3619	626	1938	3139	6138	885
38000	18431	468	286	72	999	3647	633	1961	3177	6257	932
38500	18762	479	289	76	1049	3676	641	1984	3214	6377	979
39000	19092	490	293	79	1099	3704	648	2007	3251	6497	1025
39500	19422	501	296	83	1149	3732	655	2029	3288	6616	1072

TABLE A-17 continued
1987 Tax Table for the Province of Nova Scotia

(Dollars per family)

Your Cash Income	Profits Tax	Income Tax	Sales Tax	Liquor, Tobacco, Amusement and Other Excise Taxes	Auto, Fuel & Motor Vehicle Licence Taxes	Social Security, Pension, Medical & Hospital Taxes	Property Tax	Natural Resources Taxes	Import Duties	Other Taxes	Total Taxes
40000	1118	6736	3325	2052	663	3761	1199	86	299	512	19752
40500	1165	6856	3363	2075	670	3789	1249	90	303	523	20082
41000	1212	6975	3400	2098	678	3818	1298	94	306	534	20413
41500	1186	7098	3463	2137	690	3908	1271	92	312	537	20693
42000	1160	7220	3526	2176	703	3998	1244	90	317	539	20973
42500	1135	7343	3589	2215	715	4088	1216	88	323	542	21254
43000	1109	7465	3652	2254	728	4178	1189	86	329	544	21534
43500	1084	7588	3715	2293	740	4268	1161	84	334	547	21815
44000	1058	7710	3778	2332	753	4358	1134	82	340	549	22095
44500	1033	7833	3842	2371	766	4448	1107	80	346	551	22375
45000	1007	7956	3905	2410	778	4538	1079	78	351	554	22656
45500	981	8078	3968	2449	791	4628	1052	76	357	556	22936
46000	978	8225	4025	2484	802	4702	1048	76	362	562	23263
46500	974	8372	4082	2519	814	4776	1044	75	367	567	23589
47000	970	8519	4139	2554	825	4849	1040	75	373	572	23916
47500	966	8667	4196	2590	836	4923	1035	75	378	577	24242
48000	962	8814	4253	2625	848	4997	1031	74	383	583	24569
48500	958	8961	4310	2660	859	5070	1027	74	388	588	24896
49000	955	9108	4367	2695	870	5144	1023	74	393	593	25222
49500	951	9255	4424	2730	882	5218	1019	73	398	598	25549
50000	947	9402	4481	2766	893	5292	1015	73	403	603	25875
50500	943	9549	4538	2801	904	5365	1011	73	408	609	26202
51000	962	9674	4582	2828	913	5413	1031	74	412	616	26506
51500	980	9799	4626	2855	922	5462	1051	76	416	623	26810
52000	999	9924	4670	2882	931	5510	1070	77	420	631	27115
52500	1017	10049	4714	2909	940	5558	1090	79	424	638	27419
53000	1036	10174	4758	2937	948	5607	1110	80	428	645	27723
53500	1054	10299	4802	2964	957	5655	1130	81	432	653	28027

54000	1073	10424	4846	2991	966	5703	1150	83	436	660	28332
54500	1091	10549	4890	3018	975	5751	1170	84	440	668	28636
55000	1110	10674	4934	3045	983	5800	1190	86	444	675	28940
55500	1129	10799	4978	3072	992	5848	1209	87	448	682	29245
56000	1147	10924	5022	3100	1001	5896	1229	89	452	690	29549
56500	1166	11049	5066	3127	1010	5945	1249	90	456	697	29853
57000	1184	11173	5110	3154	1018	5993	1269	91	460	704	30158
57500	1203	11298	5154	3181	1027	6041	1289	93	464	712	30462
58000	1221	11423	5198	3208	1036	6089	1309	94	468	719	30766
58500	1240	11548	5242	3235	1045	6138	1329	96	472	726	31070
59000	1258	11673	5286	3263	1054	6186	1348	97	476	734	31375
59500	1277	11798	5330	3290	1062	6234	1368	99	480	741	31679
60000	1295	11923	5374	3317	1071	6283	1388	100	484	748	31983

SCHEDULE A-17

1987 Detailed Tax Calculation for the Province of Nova Scotia

1. Profit tax = Your Cash Income × 0.022 = _____

2. Income tax = Your Cash Income × 0.199 = _____

3. Sales tax = Your Cash Income × 0.089 = _____

4. Liquor, tobacco, amusement
   & other excise taxes = Your Cash Income × 0.055 = _____

5. Auto, fuel & motor
   vehicle licence fees = Your Cash Income × 0.018 = _____

6. Social security, pension,
   medical & hospital taxes = Your Cash Income × 0.105 = _____

7. Property tax = Your Cash Income × 0.023 = _____

8. Natural resources taxes = Your Cash Income × 0.002 = _____

9. Import duties = Your Cash Income × 0.008 = _____

10. Other taxes = Your Cash Income × 0.012 = _____

Total taxes 1 + 2 + 3 + 4 + 5 + 6 + 7 + 8 + 9 + 10

TABLE A-18
1987 Tax Table for the Province of Ontario

Your Cash Income	Profits Tax	Income Tax	Sales Tax	Liquor, Tobacco, Amusement and Other Excise Taxes	Auto, Fuel & Motor Vehicle Licence Taxes	Social Security, Pension, Medical & Hospital Taxes	Property Tax	Natural Resources Taxes	Import Duties	Other Taxes	Total Taxes
						(Dollars per family)					
5000	136	62	198	71	29	624	149	6	35	36	1346
5500	160	68	221	79	33	640	175	7	39	41	1464
6000	183	75	244	87	36	656	201	9	44	47	1581
6500	207	81	267	95	39	671	227	10	48	52	1698
7000	231	87	290	104	43	687	253	11	52	57	1815
7500	255	94	313	112	46	703	279	12	56	63	1932
8000	278	100	336	120	50	718	304	13	60	68	2049
8500	277	120	324	116	48	708	304	13	58	67	2036
9000	277	140	312	111	46	698	303	13	56	66	2022
9500	276	160	300	107	44	688	302	13	53	65	2009
10000	275	180	288	103	42	678	301	13	51	65	1996
10500	274	200	275	98	41	668	300	13	49	64	1983
11000	357	249	323	115	48	695	391	17	58	81	2334
11500	440	298	371	133	55	723	482	21	66	97	2686
12000	523	347	419	150	62	750	573	24	75	114	3030
12500	606	396	467	167	69	778	663	28	83	131	3389
13000	689	445	515	184	76	805	754	32	92	148	3740
13500	772	494	563	201	83	833	845	36	100	165	4092
14000	855	543	611	218	90	860	936	40	109	182	4444
14500	938	592	659	235	97	887	1026	44	117	199	4795
15000	1021	641	707	252	104	915	1117	48	126	216	5147
15500	1044	742	752	268	111	949	1142	49	134	222	5414
16000	1067	844	797	285	118	983	1168	50	142	229	5681
16500	1090	946	841	301	124	1017	1193	51	150	236	5948
17000	1113	1047	886	317	131	1051	1218	52	158	243	6215
17500	1136	1149	931	333	137	1085	1243	53	166	250	6482
18000	1159	1251	976	349	144	1119	1268	54	174	256	6750
18500	1182	1352	1021	365	151	1153	1293	55	182	263	7017
19000	1205	1454	1066	381	157	1187	1319	56	190	270	7284

TABLE A-18 continued
1987 Tax Table for the Province of Ontario

Your Cash Income	Profits Tax	Income Tax	Sales Tax	Liquor, Tobacco, Amusement and Other Excise Taxes	Auto, Fuel & Motor Vehicle Licence Taxes	Social Security, Pension, Medical & Hospital Taxes	Property Tax	Natural Resources Taxes	Import Duties	Other Taxes	Total Taxes
					(Dollars per family)						
19500	1228	1556	1111	397	164	1221	1344	57	198	277	7551
20000	1251	1657	1155	413	170	1255	1369	58	206	283	7818
20500	1274	1759	1200	429	177	1289	1394	59	214	290	8085
21000	1310	1895	1272	454	188	1343	1433	61	227	301	8483
21500	1345	2032	1343	480	198	1397	1472	63	239	311	8882
22000	1381	2168	1415	505	209	1452	1511	64	252	322	9280
22500	1417	2305	1486	531	219	1506	1550	66	265	333	9678
23000	1452	2441	1558	556	230	1560	1589	68	278	343	10076
23500	1488	2578	1629	582	240	1615	1628	69	290	354	10474
24000	1524	2714	1701	607	251	1669	1668	71	303	365	10872
24500	1560	2851	1772	633	261	1723	1707	73	316	375	11270
25000	1595	2987	1844	659	272	1777	1746	74	329	386	11669
25500	1631	3124	1915	684	283	1832	1785	76	341	396	12067
26000	1674	3250	1963	701	289	1865	1832	78	350	407	12409
26500	1718	3376	2010	718	296	1898	1880	80	358	417	12751
27000	1761	3503	2057	735	303	1931	1927	82	367	427	13093
27500	1805	3629	2105	752	310	1963	1975	84	375	438	13436
28000	1848	3755	2152	769	317	1996	2022	86	383	448	13778
28500	1891	3882	2199	785	324	2029	2070	88	392	458	14120
29000	1935	4008	2247	802	331	2062	2117	90	400	469	14462
29500	1978	4135	2294	819	338	2095	2165	92	409	479	14805
30000	2022	4261	2341	836	345	2128	2212	94	417	489	15147
30500	2065	4387	2389	853	352	2161	2260	96	426	500	15489
31000	2109	4514	2436	870	359	2194	2307	98	434	510	15831
31500	2047	4666	2505	895	369	2261	2240	96	446	504	16028
32000	1985	4818	2574	919	380	2328	2172	93	459	499	16225
32500	1923	4970	2643	944	390	2395	2105	90	471	493	16423
33000	1861	5122	2712	968	400	2462	2037	87	483	487	16620
33500	1800	5274	2781	993	410	2529	1969	84	496	482	16817

17014	476	508	81	1902	2596	420	1018	2850	5426	1738	34000
17211	470	520	78	1834	2663	430	1042	2919	5578	1676	34500
17408	465	532	75	1767	2730	441	1067	2988	5730	1614	35000
17605	459	545	72	1699	2797	451	1092	3056	5882	1552	35500
17828	460	553	72	1684	2840	458	1109	3106	6006	1539	36000
18051	461	562	71	1669	2884	465	1127	3156	6130	1526	36500
18275	462	571	71	1655	2927	473	1145	3205	6255	1512	37000
18498	463	580	70	1640	2971	480	1162	3255	6379	1499	37500
18722	464	589	69	1625	3014	487	1180	3304	6503	1485	38000
18945	465	598	69	1611	3057	495	1198	3354	6628	1472	38500
19168	466	606	68	1596	3101	502	1215	3403	6752	1458	39000
19392	467	615	67	1581	3144	509	1233	3453	6876	1445	39500
19615	468	624	67	1566	3188	517	1251	3502	7001	1431	40000
19838	469	633	66	1552	3231	524	1268	3552	7125	1418	40500
20062	470	642	66	1537	3274	531	1286	3601	7249	1405	41000
20439	482	651	68	1592	3312	539	1306	3656	7377	1455	41500
20816	494	661	70	1648	3350	547	1325	3710	7504	1506	42000
21193	506	671	73	1703	3388	555	1345	3765	7631	1556	42500
21571	518	681	75	1758	3426	563	1364	3820	7759	1607	43000
21948	530	690	77	1813	3464	571	1384	3874	7886	1657	43500
22325	542	700	80	1869	3502	579	1403	3929	8013	1708	44000
22702	554	710	82	1924	3540	588	1423	3983	8141	1758	44500
23079	566	720	84	1979	3578	596	1442	4038	8268	1809	45000
23457	578	729	87	2035	3616	604	1462	4092	8396	1859	45500
23811	586	740	88	2061	3660	612	1482	4150	8548	1883	46000
24164	594	750	89	2087	3705	621	1503	4208	8701	1907	46500
24518	601	760	90	2113	3750	629	1524	4266	8854	1931	47000
24872	609	771	91	2139	3795	638	1544	4324	9007	1955	47500
25226	617	781	92	2165	3839	646	1565	4382	9160	1978	48000
25580	625	791	93	2191	3884	655	1586	4440	9313	2002	48500
25934	632	801	95	2217	3929	663	1606	4498	9466	2026	49000
26287	640	812	96	2243	3974	672	1627	4556	9619	2050	49500
26641	648	822	97	2269	4018	680	1648	4613	9772	2074	50000
26995	656	832	98	2295	4063	689	1668	4671	9924	2097	50500
27299	663	841	99	2320	4100	696	1686	4720	10054	2120	51000
27604	670	850	100	2346	4137	703	1703	4768	10184	2143	51500
27908	677	858	101	2371	4174	710	1720	4817	10314	2166	52000
28213	684	867	102	2396	4211	718	1738	4865	10444	2189	52500
28517	691	876	103	2421	4248	725	1755	4914	10574	2212	53000
28822	698	884	104	2446	4285	732	1772	4962	10704	2235	53500

TABLE A-18 continued
1987 Tax Table for the Province of Ontario

Your Cash Income	Profits Tax	Income Tax	Sales Tax	Liquor, Tobacco, Amusement and Other Excise Taxes.	Auto, Fuel & Motor Vehicle Licence Taxes	Social Security, Pension, Medical & Hospital Taxes	Property Tax	Natural Resources Taxes	Import Duties	Other Taxes	Total Taxes
						(Dollars per family)					
54000	2258	10833	5010	1789	739	4322	2471	105	893	705	29126
54500	2281	10963	5059	1807	746	4359	2496	106	901	712	29431
55000	2304	11093	5107	1824	753	4396	2521	108	910	719	29735
55500	2327	11223	5156	1841	760	4433	2547	109	919	726	30040
56000	2350	11353	5204	1859	768	4470	2572	110	927	733	30344
56500	2373	11483	5252	1876	775	4507	2597	111	936	740	30649
57000	2396	11613	5301	1893	782	4544	2622	112	945	747	30953
57500	2419	11742	5349	1910	789	4581	2647	113	953	754	31258
58000	2442	11872	5398	1928	796	4617	2672	114	962	761	31562
58500	2465	12002	5446	1945	803	4654	2697	115	970	768	31866
59000	2488	12132	5495	1962	810	4691	2722	116	979	775	32171
59500	2511	12262	5543	1980	818	4728	2748	117	988	782	32475
60000	2534	12392	5591	1997	825	4765	2773	118	996	789	32780

SCHEDULE A-18

1987 Detailed Tax Calculation for the Province of Ontario

1. Profit tax = Your Cash Income × 0.042 _____

2. Income tax = Your Cash Income × 0.207 _____

3. Sales tax = Your Cash Income × 0.093 _____

4. Liquor, tobacco, amusement
   & other excise taxes = Your Cash Income × 0.033 _____

5. Auto, fuel & motor
   vehicle licence fees = Your Cash Income × 0.014 _____

6. Social security, pension,
   medical & hospital taxes = Your Cash Income × 0.079 _____

7. Property tax = Your Cash Income × 0.046 _____

8. Natural resources taxes = Your Cash Income × 0.002 _____

9. Import duties = Your Cash Income × 0.017 _____

10. Other taxes = Your Cash Income × 1.013 _____

Total taxes 1 + 2 + 3 + 4 + 5 + 6 + 7 + 8 + 9 + 10

TABLE A-19
1987 Tax Table for the Province of Prince Edward Island

Your Cash Income	Profits Tax	Income Tax	Sales Tax	Liquor, Tobacco, Amusement and Other Excise Taxes	Auto, Fuel & Motor Vehicle Licence Taxes	Social Security, Pension, Medical & Hospital Taxes	Property Tax	Natural Resources Taxes	Import Duties	Other Taxes	Total Taxes
					(Dollars per family)						
5000	71	48	119	45	34	140	87	1	2	10	558
5500	75	53	115	43	33	134	92	1	2	10	559
6000	79	59	111	42	32	128	96	1	2	10	561
6500	82	64	108	41	31	123	101	1	2	10	562
7000	86	69	104	39	30	117	105	2	2	9	563
7500	90	74	101	38	29	111	110	2	2	9	565
8000	94	79	97	37	28	105	115	2	2	9	566
8500	119	95	120	45	35	129	145	3	3	11	702
9000	143	110	143	54	41	154	176	3	3	13	839
9500	168	126	166	62	48	178	206	3	3	15	975
10000	193	142	189	71	55	202	237	3	4	17	1112
10500	218	157	212	80	61	226	267	4	4	19	1248
11000	225	196	234	88	68	254	275	4	4	21	1369
11500	231	234	257	97	74	283	283	4	5	23	1490
12000	237	273	279	105	81	311	291	4	5	25	1611
12500	244	311	302	114	87	339	298	4	5	27	1731
13000	250	349	324	122	94	368	306	4	6	29	1852
13500	256	388	347	130	100	396	314	4	6	31	1973
14000	263	426	369	139	107	425	322	5	7	33	2094
14500	269	465	392	147	113	453	330	5	7	35	2215
15000	275	503	414	156	120	481	337	5	7	36	2336
15500	299	583	450	169	130	523	366	5	8	40	2572
16000	322	663	485	183	140	564	394	6	9	43	2808
16500	345	743	521	196	151	605	423	6	9	46	3045
17000	369	823	556	209	161	647	451	6	10	49	3281
17500	392	902	592	223	171	688	480	7	11	52	3517
18000	415	982	627	236	181	730	508	8	11	55	3754
18500	438	1062	663	249	192	771	537	8	12	58	3990
19000	462	1142	698	263	202	812	565	8	13	62	4226

19500	485	1222	734	276	212	854	594	8	13	65	4463
20000	508	1302	769	289	223	895	622	9	14	68	4699
20500	532	1382	805	303	233	937	651	9	14	71	4935
21000	508	1489	842	317	244	993	622	9	15	74	5112
21500	484	1596	880	331	255	1050	592	8	16	78	5289
22000	460	1703	917	345	266	1106	563	8	16	81	5465
22500	436	1810	955	359	276	1163	534	8	17	84	5642
23000	412	1917	992	373	287	1220	504	7	18	87	5819
23500	388	2025	1030	388	298	1276	475	7	19	91	5995
24000	364	2132	1068	402	309	1333	446	6	19	94	6172
24500	340	2239	1105	416	320	1389	416	6	20	97	6349
25000	316	2346	1143	430	331	1446	387	6	21	101	6525
25500	292	2453	1180	444	342	1503	358	5	21	104	6702
26000	328	2553	1219	459	353	1545	402	5	22	107	6994
26500	364	2652	1258	474	364	1588	445	6	23	111	7285
27000	400	2751	1297	488	376	1631	489	6	23	114	7577
27500	435	2850	1336	503	387	1674	533	7	24	118	7868
28000	471	2950	1376	518	398	1717	577	8	25	121	8160
28500	507	3049	1415	532	409	1759	621	8	25	125	8451
29000	543	3148	1454	547	421	1802	665	9	26	128	8743
29500	579	3247	1493	562	432	1845	708	9	27	132	9034
30000	614	3347	1532	576	443	1888	752	10	28	135	9326
30500	650	3446	1571	591	455	1931	796	11	28	138	9617
31000	686	3545	1610	606	466	1973	840	11	29	142	9909
31500	685	3665	1654	622	479	2032	839	12	30	146	10163
32000	685	3784	1697	639	491	2091	839	12	31	150	10418
32500	685	3903	1741	655	504	2149	838	12	31	153	10672
33000	684	4023	1785	672	516	2208	838	12	32	157	10926
33500	684	4142	1828	688	529	2266	837	12	33	161	11181
34000	683	4262	1872	704	542	2325	837	12	34	165	11435
34500	683	4381	1916	721	554	2384	836	12	34	169	11689
35000	682	4500	1959	737	567	2442	836	12	35	173	11944
35500	682	4620	2003	754	580	2501	835	12	36	176	12198
36000	687	4717	2046	770	592	2557	841	12	37	180	12438
36500	691	4815	2089	786	605	2613	846	12	38	184	12678
37000	696	4913	2132	802	617	2669	852	12	38	188	12918
37500	700	5010	2174	818	629	2725	858	12	39	192	13158
38000	705	5108	2217	834	642	2782	863	12	40	195	13398
38500	709	5206	2260	850	654	2838	869	12	41	199	13638
39000	714	5303	2303	867	666	2894	874	12	41	203	13878
39500	719	5401	2346	883	679	2950	880	12	42	207	14118

TABLE A-19 continued
1987 Tax Table for the Province of Prince Edward Island

(Dollars per family)

Your Cash Income	Profits Tax	Income Tax	Sales Tax	Liquor, Tobacco, Amusement and Other Excise Taxes	Auto, Fuel & Motor Vehicle Licence Taxes	Social Security, Pension, Medical & Hospital Taxes	Property Tax	Natural Resources Taxes	Import Duties	Other Taxes	Total Taxes
40000	723	5499	2389	899	691	3006	886	13	43	210	14358
40500	728	5596	2431	915	704	3062	891	13	44	214	14598
41000	732	5694	2474	931	716	3118	897	13	44	218	14838
41500	672	5794	2522	949	730	3198	822	12	45	222	14965
42000	611	5894	2569	967	744	3277	748	11	46	226	15092
42500	550	5994	2616	984	757	3357	673	10	47	231	15219
43000	489	6094	2664	1002	771	3436	599	8	48	235	15346
43500	428	6194	2711	1020	785	3516	524	7	49	239	15473
44000	367	6294	2758	1038	798	3595	450	6	50	243	15600
44500	306	6394	2806	1056	812	3675	375	5	50	247	15727
45000	245	6494	2853	1074	826	3754	300	4	51	251	15853
45500	184	6594	2900	1091	839	3834	226	3	52	256	15980
46000	20	6714	2936	1105	850	3863	307	4	53	259	16340
46500	316	6834	2971	1118	860	3893	388	5	53	262	16700
47000	382	6954	3006	1131	870	3922	468	7	54	265	17060
47500	448	7074	3041	1144	880	3952	549	8	55	268	17419
48000	514	7195	3076	1157	890	3981	630	9	55	271	17779
48500	580	7315	3111	1171	900	4011	711	10	56	274	18139
49000	647	7435	3146	1184	911	4040	792	11	57	277	18499
49500	713	7555	3181	1197	921	4070	873	12	57	280	18858
50000	779	7675	3216	1210	931	4099	953	14	58	283	19218
50500	845	7795	3251	1223	941	4129	1034	15	58	286	19578
51000	869	7897	3280	1234	949	4161	1064	15	59	289	19818
51500	893	7999	3309	1245	958	4194	1094	15	59	292	20058
52000	918	8101	3338	1256	966	4226	1124	16	60	294	20298
52500	942	8203	3367	1267	975	4258	1153	16	61	297	20539
53000	966	8305	3396	1278	983	4291	1183	17	61	299	20779
53500	991	8407	3425	1289	991	4323	1213	17	62	302	21019

54000	1015	8509	3454	1300	1000	4355	1243	18	62	304	21259
54500	1039	8611	3483	1311	1008	4387	1273	18	63	307	21499
55000	1064	8713	3512	1322	1016	4420	1302	18	63	309	21740
55500	1088	8815	3541	1332	1025	4452	1332	19	64	312	21980
56000	1112	8917	3570	1343	1033	4484	1362	19	64	315	22220
56500	1137	9019	3599	1354	1042	4517	1392	20	65	317	22460
57000	1161	9121	3628	1365	1050	4549	1422	20	65	320	22700
57500	1185	9223	3657	1376	1058	4581	1451	21	66	322	22941
58000	1210	9325	3686	1387	1067	4614	1481	21	66	325	23181
58500	1234	9427	3715	1398	1075	4646	1511	22	67	327	23421
59000	1258	9529	3744	1409	1083	4678	1541	22	67	330	23661
59500	1283	9631	3773	1420	1092	4711	1571	23	68	332	23901
60000	1307	9733	3802	1430	1100	4743	1601		68	335	24142

SCHEDULE A-19

1987 Detailed Tax Calculation for the Province of Prince Edward Island

1. Profit tax   = Your Cash Income × 0.022   = _____

2. Income tax   = Your Cash Income × 0.162   = _____

3. Sales tax   = Your Cash Income × 0.063   = _____

4. Liquor, tobacco, amusement
   & other excise taxes   = Your Cash Income × 0.024   = _____

5. Auto, fuel & motor
   vehicle licence fees   = Your Cash Income × 0.018   = _____

6. Social security, pension,
   medical & hospital taxes   = Your Cash Income × 0.079   = _____

7. Property tax   = Your Cash Income × 0.027   = _____

8. Natural resources taxes   = Your Cash Income × 0.0004   = _____

9. Import duties   = Your Cash Income × 0.001   = _____

10. Other taxes   = Your Cash Income × 0.006   = _____

Total taxes 1 + 2 + 3 + 4 + 5 + 6 + 7 + 8 + 9 + 10

TABLE A-20
1987 Tax Table for the Province of Quebec

Your Cash Income	Profits Tax	Income Tax	Sales Tax	Liquor, Tobacco, Amusement and Other Excise Taxes	Auto, Fuel & Motor Vehicle Licence Taxes	Social Security, Pension, Medical & Hospital Taxes	Property Tax	Natural Resources Taxes	Import Duties	Other Taxes	Total Taxes
						(Dollars per family)					
5000	34	72	131	48	28	844	33	2	19	43	1254
5500	49	79	147	54	31	855	48	2	21	50	1335
6000	63	87	162	60	34	865	62	3	23	57	1416
6500	78	94	178	65	38	875	77	4	25	64	1497
7000	93	102	193	71	41	885	91	4	27	70	1578
7500	108	109	208	77	44	895	105	5	29	77	1659
8000	123	117	224	82	48	906	120	6	32	84	1740
8500	149	140	230	85	49	906	146	7	33	90	1834
9000	176	163	237	87	50	906	172	8	33	96	1928
9500	203	186	243	89	52	906	198	9	34	102	2022
10000	229	209	250	92	53	906	224	10	35	108	2117
10500	256	233	256	94	54	906	250	12	36	114	2211
11000	292	289	291	107	62	928	286	13	41	130	2440
11500	329	346	326	120	69	950	322	15	46	146	2668
12000	365	403	361	133	77	973	357	16	51	162	2897
12500	402	460	395	145	84	995	393	18	56	177	3126
13000	438	517	430	158	91	1018	429	20	61	193	3354
13500	475	573	465	171	99	1040	464	21	66	209	3583
14000	511	630	500	184	106	1062	500	23	71	225	3811
14500	548	687	534	197	113	1085	536	25	76	241	4040
15000	584	744	569	209	121	1107	571	26	80	256	4269
15500	614	862	625	230	133	1149	600	28	88	277	4607
16000	644	980	681	251	145	1192	630	29	96	298	4945
16500	674	1098	737	271	157	1234	659	30	104	319	5284
17000	704	1216	794	292	168	1276	688	32	112	340	5622
17500	734	1334	850	312	180	1318	717	33	120	361	5960
18000	764	1452	906	333	192	1360	747	34	128	382	6299
18500	793	1570	962	354	204	1403	776	36	136	403	6637
19000	823	1688	1018	374	216	1445	805	37	144	424	6975

TABLE A-20 continued
1987 Tax Table for the Province of Quebec

Your Cash Income	Profits Tax	Income Tax	Sales Tax	Liquor, Tobacco, Amusement and Other Excise Taxes	Auto, Fuel & Motor Vehicle Licence Taxes	Social Security, Pension, Medical & Hospital Taxes	Property Tax	Natural Resources Taxes	Import Duties	Other Taxes	Total Taxes
						(Dollars per family)					
19500	853	1806	1074	395	228	1487	835	39	152	445	7314
20000	883	1925	1130	416	240	1529	864	40	160	466	7652
20500	913	2043	1186	436	252	1571	893	41	168	487	7990
21000	904	2201	1255	461	266	1633	884	41	177	505	8328
21500	895	2360	1323	487	281	1694	876	40	187	523	8665
22000	886	2518	1392	512	295	1755	867	40	197	542	9003
22500	877	2676	1460	537	310	1816	858	40	206	560	9340
23000	868	2835	1528	562	324	1877	849	39	216	579	9678
23500	859	2993	1597	587	339	1938	840	39	226	597	10015
24000	850	3152	1665	612	353	1999	832	38	235	615	10353
24500	841	3310	1734	637	368	2060	823	38	245	634	10690
25000	833	3469	1802	663	383	2121	814	38	255	652	11028
25500	824	3627	1870	688	397	2182	805	37	264	671	11366
26000	825	3774	1919	706	407	2224	807	37	271	685	11657
26500	827	3921	1968	724	418	2266	809	37	278	700	11948
27000	829	4068	2017	742	428	2308	811	37	285	714	12239
27500	831	4214	2066	760	439	2350	812	38	292	729	12530
28000	832	4361	2115	778	449	2392	814	38	299	743	12821
28500	834	4508	2164	796	459	2434	816	38	306	757	13112
29000	836	4655	2214	814	470	2476	817	38	313	772	13403
29500	837	4801	2263	832	480	2518	819	38	320	786	13695
30000	839	4948	2312	850	491	2560	821	38	327	801	13986
30500	841	5095	2361	868	501	2602	822	38	334	815	14277
31000	843	5242	2410	886	511	2644	824	38	341	830	14568
31500	859	5418	2466	907	523	2689	841	39	349	849	14940
32000	876	5595	2522	928	535	2734	857	40	357	868	15311
32500	893	5771	2579	948	547	2780	873	40	365	887	15683
33000	910	5948	2635	969	559	2825	890	41	372	906	16055
33500	927	6124	2691	990	571	2870	906	42	380	925	16426

34000-series											
34000	944	6301	2748	1010	583	2915	923	43	388	943	16798
34500	960	6477	2804	1031	595	2960	939	43	396	962	17170
35000	977	6654	2860	1052	607	3005	956	44	404	981	17541
35500	994	6830	2917	1073	619	3051	972	45	412	1000	17913
36000	1036	6975	2971	1092	631	3089	1013	47	420	1023	18295
36500	1078	7119	3025	1112	642	3127	1054	49	428	1045	18678
37000	1119	7263	3079	1132	654	3165	1095	51	435	1067	19060
37500	1161	7408	3133	1152	665	3203	1136	52	443	1089	19442
38000	1203	7552	3187	1172	677	3241	1177	54	451	1111	19825
38500	1245	7696	3241	1192	688	3279	1217	56	458	1134	20207
39000	1287	7841	3296	1212	700	3317	1258	58	466	1156	20589
39500	1328	7985	3350	1232	711	3355	1299	60	474	1178	20972
40000	1370	8130	3404	1252	723	3393	1340	62	481	1200	21354
40500	1412	8274	3458	1272	734	3431	1381	64	489	1223	21736
41000	1454	8418	3512	1291	746	3469	1422	66	496	1245	22119
41500	1389	8566	3563	1310	756	3527	1359	63	504	1250	22287
42000	1325	8714	3615	1329	767	3584	1296	60	511	1254	22455
42500	1260	8862	3666	1348	778	3642	1232	57	518	1259	22623
43000	1196	9010	3717	1367	789	3700	1169	54	525	1264	22791
43500	1131	9158	3768	1386	800	3758	1106	51	533	1268	22959
44000	1066	9306	3820	1405	811	3816	1043	48	540	1273	23127
44500	1002	9454	3871	1423	822	3874	980	45	547	1278	23295
45000	937	9601	3922	1442	833	3932	917	42	554	1283	23464
45500	873	9749	3973	1461	843	3990	853	39	562	1287	23632
46000	895	9927	4030	1482	855	4034	876	40	570	1307	24015
46500	918	10104	4086	1502	867	4077	898	41	578	1327	24399
47000	941	10282	4142	1523	879	4121	920	42	585	1347	24782
47500	963	10460	4198	1544	891	4165	942	43	593	1366	25166
48000	986	10637	4254	1564	903	4208	964	45	601	1386	25549
48500	1009	10815	4310	1585	915	4252	986	46	609	1406	25932
49000	1031	10992	4366	1606	927	4296	1009	47	617	1426	26313
49500	1054	11170	4422	1626	939	4340	1031	48	625	1446	26699
50000	1077	11347	4478	1647	951	4383	1053	49	633	1465	27083
50500	1099	11525	4534	1667	962	4427	1075	50	641	1485	27466
51000	1127	11676	4575	1682	971	4456	1102	51	647	1501	27787
51500	1154	11826	4615	1697	980	4485	1129	52	652	1517	28109
52000	1182	11977	4656	1712	988	4515	1156	53	658	1533	28430
52500	1209	12128	4696	1727	997	4544	1183	55	664	1549	28751
53000	1237	12279	4736	1742	1005	4573	1210	56	670	1565	29072
53500	1264	12430	4777	1757	1014	4602	1237	57	675	1581	29394

TABLE A-20 continued
1987 Tax Table for the Province of Quebec

Your Cash Income	Profits Tax	Income Tax	Sales Tax	Liquor, Tobacco, Amusement and Other Excise Taxes	Auto, Fuel & Motor Vehicle Licence Taxes	Social Security, Pension, Medical & Hospital Taxes	Property Tax	Natural Resources Taxes	Import Duties	Other Taxes	Total Taxes
					(Dollars per family)						
54000	1292	12580	4817	1771	1023	4631	1263	58	681	1597	29715
54500	1319	12731	4858	1786	1031	4661	1290	60	687	1613	30036
55000	1347	12882	4898	1801	1040	4690	1317	61	692	1629	30358
55500	1374	13033	4939	1816	1048	4719	1344	62	698	1645	30679
56000	1402	13184	4979	1831	1057	4748	1371	63	704	1661	31000
56500	1429	13334	5020	1846	1066	4777	1398	65	710	1677	31321
57000	1457	13485	5060	1861	1074	4806	1425	66	715	1693	31643
57500	1484	13636	5100	1876	1083	4836	1452	67	721	1709	31964
58000	1512	13787	5141	1890	1091	4865	1479	68	727	1726	32285
58500	1539	13938	5181	1905	1100	4894	1505	70	732	1742	32606
59000	1567	14088	5222	1920	1108	4923	1532	71	738	1758	32928
59500	1594	14239	5262	1935	1117	4952	1559	72	744	1774	33249
60000	1622	14390	5303	1950	1126	4982	1586	73	750	1790	33570

SCHEDULE A-20

1987 Detailed Tax Calculation for the Province of Quebec

1. Profit tax = Your Cash Income × 0.027 = _____

2. Income tax = Your Cash Income × 0.240 = _____

3. Sales tax = Your Cash Income × 0.088 = _____

4. Liquor, tobacco, amusement
   & other excise taxes = Your Cash Income × 0.032 = _____

5. Auto, fuel & motor
   vehicle licence fees = Your Cash Income × 0.019 = _____

6. Social security, pension,
   medical & hospital taxes = Your Cash Income × 0.083 = _____

7. Property tax = Your Cash Income × 0.026 = _____

8. Natural resources taxes = Your Cash Income × 0.001 = _____

9. Import duties = Your Cash Income × 0.012 = _____

10. Other taxes = Your Cash Income × 0.030 = _____

Total taxes 1 + 2 + 3 + 4 + 5 + 6 + 7 + 8 + 9 + 10

TABLE A-21
1987 Tax Table for the Province of Saskatchewan

Your Cash Income	Profits Tax	Income Tax	Sales Tax	Liquor, Tobacco, Amusement and Other Excise Taxes	Auto, Fuel & Motor Vehicle Licence Taxes	Social Security, Pension, Medical & Hospital Taxes	Property Tax	Natural Resources Taxes	Import Duties	Other Taxes	Total Taxes
					(Dollars per family)						
5000	190	64	60	57	11	56	206	326	4	1	975
5500	181	71	81	76	15	90	197	312	5	−4	1024
6000	173	78	102	96	19	123	187	297	7	−8	1073
6500	164	84	122	115	23	157	178	282	8	−13	1122
7000	156	91	143	135	27	191	169	268	9	−17	1170
7500	147	98	164	154	30	224	160	253	11	−22	1219
8000	139	105	184	173	34	258	151	239	12	−26	1268
8500	191	125	185	174	34	248	207	328	12	−23	1483
9000	243	146	186	175	34	239	264	418	12	−20	1698
9500	295	167	186	175	35	230	321	508	12	−16	1913
10000	348	188	187	176	35	220	377	598	12	−13	2128
10500	400	208	188	177	35	211	434	688	12	−10	2342
11000	442	259	208	196	39	235	480	760	14	−11	2622
11500	484	310	229	216	43	259	526	833	15	−12	2901
12000	527	361	250	235	46	282	572	905	16	−14	3181
12500	569	412	270	255	50	306	617	978	18	−15	3460
13000	611	463	291	274	54	330	663	1051	19	−16	3740
13500	653	514	312	294	58	353	709	1123	20	−17	4019
14000	695	565	333	313	62	377	755	1196	22	−19	4298
14500	738	616	353	333	66	401	801	1268	23	−20	4578
15000	780	667	374	352	70	425	846	1341	25	−21	4857
15500	825	772	406	382	75	465	896	1419	27	−24	5242
16000	870	878	437	412	81	505	945	1496	29	−27	5626
16500	915	984	469	442	87	545	994	1574	31	−30	6010
17000	961	1090	501	471	93	585	1043	1652	33	−34	6394
17500	1006	1195	532	501	99	625	1092	1730	35	−37	6779
18000	1051	1301	564	531	105	665	1141	1807	37	−40	7163
18500	1096	1407	596	561	111	705	1190	1885	39	−43	7547
19000	1141	1513	628	591	117	746	1239	1963	41	−46	7931

8316	−49	43	2040	1288	786	123	621	659	1619	1187	19500
8700	−52	45	2118	1337	826	128	650	691	1724	1232	20000
9084	−55	47	2196	1386	866	134	680	723	1830	1277	20500
9413	−60	49	2233	1409	909	140	709	753	1972	1299	21000
9742	−64	51	2270	1433	951	146	737	783	2114	1320	21500
10071	−68	53	2307	1456	994	151	766	814	2256	1342	22000
10399	−73	55	2344	1480	1037	157	795	844	2398	1363	22500
10728	−77	57	2381	1503	1079	162	823	874	2540	1385	23000
11057	−82	59	2418	1526	1122	168	852	905	2682	1406	23500
11386	−86	61	2455	1550	1165	174	880	935	2824	1428	24000
11715	−90	63	2492	1573	1208	179	909	965	2966	1449	24500
12044	−95	65	2529	1597	1250	185	937	996	3108	1471	25000
12372	−99	67	2566	1620	1293	191	966	1026	3250	1492	25500
12707	−103	69	2612	1649	1333	196	994	1056	3381	1519	26000
13042	−107	71	2658	1678	1374	202	1022	1085	3513	1546	26500
13377	−111	73	2704	1707	1415	207	1049	1115	3645	1573	27000
13711	−115	75	2750	1736	1455	213	1077	1144	3776	1599	27500
14046	−118	77	2796	1765	1496	218	1105	1174	3908	1626	28000
14381	−122	79	2842	1794	1536	224	1133	1203	4039	1653	28500
14716	−126	81	2888	1823	1577	229	1161	1233	4171	1680	29000
15051	−130	83	2934	1852	1617	235	1189	1263	4302	1706	29500
15385	−134	85	2980	1881	1658	240	1217	1292	4434	1733	30000
15720	−138	87	3026	1910	1698	246	1244	1322	4565	1760	30500
16055	−142	89	3072	1939	1739	251	1272	1351	4697	1787	31000
16253	−149	91	3037	1917	1793	257	1303	1384	4855	1766	31500
16451	−157	93	3002	1895	1847	263	1333	1416	5013	1746	32000
16649	−164	95	2967	1873	1901	269	1364	1448	5171	1725	32500
16846	−171	97	2931	1850	1955	275	1394	1481	5329	1705	33000
17044	−179	99	2896	1828	2009	281	1425	1513	5487	1684	33500
17242	−186	101	2861	1806	2064	287	1455	1545	5645	1664	34000
17440	−194	103	2826	1784	2118	293	1485	1578	5804	1643	34500
17638	−201	105	2791	1761	2172	299	1516	1610	5962	1623	35000
17836	−209	108	2755	1739	2226	305	1546	1642	6120	1602	35500
18008	−215	109	2729	1723	2272	310	1573	1670	6249	1587	36000
18179	−221	111	2702	1706	2318	316	1599	1698	6379	1572	36500
18351	−227	113	2676	1689	2365	321	1625	1726	6508	1556	37000
18523	−234	115	2649	1672	2411	326	1651	1754	6637	1541	37500
18695	−240	117	2623	1656	2457	331	1678	1782	6767	1525	38000
18866	−246	119	2596	1639	2503	336	1704	1810	6896	1510	38500
19038	−252	120	2570	1622	2550	341	1730	1837	7025	1494	39000
19210	−258	122	2543	1605	2596	347	1756	1865	7155	1479	39500

TABLE A-21 continued
1987 Tax Table for the Province of Saskatchewan

Your Cash Income	Profits Tax	Income Tax	Sales Tax	Liquor, Tobacco, Amusement and Other Excise Taxes	Auto, Fuel & Motor Vehicle Licence Taxes	Social Security, Pension, Medical & Hospital Taxes	Property Tax	Natural Resources Taxes	Import Duties	Other Taxes	Total Taxes
					(Dollars per family)						
40000	1464	7284	1893	1782	352	2642	1589	2517	124	-265	19382
40500	1448	7413	1921	1809	357	2688	1572	2490	126	-271	19553
41000	1433	7543	1949	1835	362	2735	1555	2464	128	-277	19725
41500	1424	7675	1981	1865	368	2786	1546	2449	130	-284	19941
42000	1415	7808	2014	1896	374	2838	1536	2434	132	-291	20156
42500	1407	7940	2046	1926	380	2890	1527	2419	134	-297	20372
43000	1398	8073	2078	1957	386	2942	1517	2404	136	-304	20587
43500	1389	8205	2111	1987	392	2994	1508	2389	138	-311	20803
44000	1381	8338	2143	2018	398	3045	1499	2374	140	-317	21019
44500	1372	8470	2175	2048	404	3097	1489	2359	143	-324	21234
45000	1363	8603	2208	2078	410	3149	1480	2344	145	-331	21450
45500	1355	8735	2240	2109	416	3201	1470	2329	147	-337	21665
46000	1380	8895	2268	2135	421	3239	1498	2373	149	-341	22015
46500	1405	9054	2295	2161	427	3277	1525	2416	150	-344	22365
47000	1430	9213	2323	2187	432	3315	1552	2459	152	-348	22715
47500	1455	9372	2351	2213	437	3353	1579	2502	154	-352	23065
48000	1480	9531	2379	2240	442	3391	1607	2545	156	-355	23415
48500	1505	9690	2406	2266	447	3429	1634	2589	158	-359	23765
49000	1531	9849	2434	2292	452	3467	1661	2632	159	-363	24114
49500	1556	10008	2462	2318	458	3505	1689	2675	161	-366	24464
50000	1581	10167	2490	2344	463	3543	1716	2718	163	-370	24814
50500	1606	10326	2517	2370	468	3581	1743	2761	165	-374	25164
51000	1640	10461	2543	2394	473	3614	1781	2821	167	-376	25517
51500	1675	10596	2569	2419	477	3647	1818	2880	168	-379	25870
52000	1710	10732	2594	2443	482	3679	1856	2940	170	-382	26223
52500	1744	10867	2620	2467	487	3712	1893	2999	172	-384	26576
53000	1779	11002	2646	2491	492	3745	1930	3058	173	-387	26930
53500	1813	11137	2671	2515	496	3778	1968	3118	175	-390	27283

54000	1848	11272	2697	2539	501	3811	2005	3177	177	−392	27636
54500	1882	11407	2723	2564	506	3844	2043	3236	178	−395	27989
55000	1917	11542	2748	2588	511	3877	2080	3296	180	−398	28342
55500	1951	11677	2774	2612	516	3910	2118	3355	182	−400	28695
56000	1986	11813	2800	2636	520	3943	2155	3415	183	−403	29048
56500	2020	11948	2826	2660	525	3976	2193	3474	185	−406	29401
57000	2055	12083	2851	2684	530	4009	2230	3533	187	−408	29754
57500	2089	12218	2877	2709	535	4042	2268	3593	189	−411	30107
58000	2124	12353	2903	2733	539	4075	2305	3652	190	−414	30460
58500	2158	12488	2928	2757	544	4107	2343	3712	192	−416	30813
59000	2193	12623	2954	2781	549	4140	2380	3771	194	−419	31167
59500	2228	12758	2980	2805	554	4173	2418	3830	195	−421	31520
60000	2262	12893	3005	2830	559	4206	2455	3890	197	−424	31873

SCHEDULE A-21

1987 Detailed Tax Calculation for the Province of Saskatchewan

1. Profit tax = Your Cash Income × 0.038 = _____

2. Income tax = Your Cash Income × 0.215 = _____

3. Sales tax = Your Cash Income × 0.050 = _____

4. Liquor, tobacco, amusement
   & other excise taxes = Your Cash Income × 0.047 = _____

5. Auto, fuel & motor
   vehicle licence fees = Your Cash Income × 0.009 = _____

6. Social security, pension,
   medical & hospital taxes = Your Cash Income × 0.070 = _____

7. Property tax = Your Cash Income × 0.041 = _____

8. Natural resources taxes = Your Cash Income × 0.065 = _____

9. Import duties = Your Cash Income × 0.003 = _____

10. Other taxes = Your Cash Income × −0.007 = _____

Total taxes 1 + 2 + 3 + 4 + 5 + 6 + 7 + 8 + 9 + 10

TABLE A-22
1987 Tax Table for Canada

Your Cash Income	Profits Tax	Income Tax	Sales Tax	Liquor, Tobacco, Amusement and Other Excise Taxes	Auto, Fuel & Motor Vehicle Licence Taxes	Social Security, Pension, Medical & Hospital Taxes	Property Tax	Natural Resources Taxes	Import Duties	Other Taxes	Total Taxes
						(Dollars per family)					
5000	105	66	133	61	25	551	95	29	22	31	1117
5500	119	73	150	69	28	566	108	33	25	35	1204
6000	132	80	167	77	31	581	120	36	28	39	1290
6500	146	86	184	85	34	595	132	40	30	43	1376
7000	160	93	201	92	37	610	145	44	33	46	1462
7500	173	100	218	100	41	625	157	48	36	50	1549
8000	187	107	234	108	44	640	170	52	39	54	1635
8500	214	129	236	109	44	637	194	59	39	58	1718
9000	241	150	237	109	44	634	219	66	40	61	1802
9500	268	171	239	110	45	631	243	74	40	64	1886
10000	295	193	241	111	45	628	268	81	40	68	1969
10500	322	214	242	111	45	625	293	89	46	71	2053
11000	384	266	278	128	52	652	349	106	46	83	2344
11500	446	318	314	145	59	678	405	123	52	95	2636
12000	508	371	350	161	65	705	461	140	58	108	2927
12500	570	423	386	178	72	731	517	157	64	120	3218
13000	632	475	422	194	79	757	574	174	70	132	3509
13500	694	527	458	211	85	784	630	191	76	144	3801
14000	756	579	494	227	92	810	686	208	82	156	4092
14500	818	632	530	244	99	836	742	225	88	168	4383
15000	880	684	566	261	106	863	798	243	94	181	4674
15500	915	792	608	280	113	900	830	252	101	191	4983
16000	950	901	651	300	121	937	862	262	108	201	5292
16500	985	1009	693	319	129	975	894	272	115	211	5601
17000	1020	1118	735	338	137	1012	926	281	122	221	5910
17500	1056	1227	777	358	145	1049	958	291	129	230	6219
18000	1091	1335	820	377	153	1086	990	301	136	240	6528
18500	1126	1444	862	397	161	1124	1022	310	143	250	6838
19000	1161	1552	904	416	169	1161	1054	320	150	260	7147

TABLE A-22 continued
1987 Tax Table for Canada

Your Cash Income	Profits Tax	Income Tax	Sales Tax	Liquor, Tobacco, Amusement and Other Excise Taxes	Auto, Fuel & Motor Vehicle Licence Taxes	Social Security, Pension, Medical & Hospital Taxes	Property Tax	Natural Resources Taxes	Import Duties	Other Taxes	Total Taxes
						(Dollars per family)					
19500	1196	1661	946	436	176	1198	1086	330	156	270	7456
20000	1231	1769	989	455	184	1235	1118	339	163	280	7765
20500	1267	1878	1031	474	192	1273	1149	349	170	290	8074
21000	1278	2023	1090	502	203	1332	1160	352	180	300	8422
21500	1290	2169	1150	529	214	1391	1171	356	190	310	8770
22000	1302	2315	1210	557	226	1450	1182	359	200	319	9119
22500	1314	2460	1270	584	237	1509	1192	362	210	329	9467
23000	1326	2606	1329	612	248	1568	1203	365	220	339	9816
23500	1338	2752	1389	639	259	1627	1214	369	230	349	10164
24000	1349	2897	1449	667	270	1686	1225	372	240	358	10513
24500	1361	3043	1508	694	281	1745	1235	375	249	368	10861
25000	1373	3189	1568	722	292	1804	1246	379	259	378	11209
25500	1385	3334	1628	749	303	1863	1257	382	269	387	11558
26000	1401	3469	1671	769	312	1904	1272	386	276	395	11856
26500	1418	3604	1714	789	320	1946	1286	391	283	403	12155
27000	1434	3739	1758	809	328	1987	1301	395	291	411	12454
27500	1450	3874	1801	829	336	2029	1316	400	298	419	12752
28000	1467	4009	1844	849	344	2070	1331	404	305	427	13051
28500	1483	4144	1888	869	352	2112	1346	409	312	435	13349
29000	1499	4279	1931	889	360	2154	1361	413	319	443	13648
29500	1516	4414	1974	909	368	2195	1375	418	326	451	13946
30000	1532	4549	2018	929	376	2237	1390	422	334	459	14245
30500	1548	4684	2061	949	384	2278	1405	427	341	467	14543
31000	1565	4819	2104	969	392	2320	1420	431	348	475	14842
31500	1558	4981	2159	994	403	2377	1414	430	357	482	15154
32000	1552	5143	2214	1019	414	2434	1408	428	366	489	15465
32500	1546	5305	2269	1044	423	2491	1403	426	375	496	15777
33000	1539	5468	2323	1069	433	2548	1397	424	384	503	16088
33500	1533	5630	2378	1095	443	2605	1391	423	393	510	16400

16712	517	402	421	1385	2662	454	1120	2433	5792	1526	34000
17023	523	411	419	1379	2719	464	1145	2488	5954	1520	34500
17335	530	420	417	1374	2776	474	1170	2543	6117	1514	35000
17646	537	429	416	1368	2833	484	1195	2597	6279	1507	35500
17934	545	437	418	1377	2878	493	1216	2642	6411	1517	36000
18221	552	444	421	1386	2922	501	1237	2687	6544	1527	36500
18509	560	452	424	1395	2966	509	1258	2732	6677	1537	37000
18796	567	459	426	1404	3011	518	1278	2777	6810	1547	37500
19084	574	467	429	1412	3055	526	1299	2822	6942	1556	38000
19371	582	474	432	1421	3099	535	1320	2867	7075	1566	38500
19659	589	482	434	1430	3144	543	1340	2912	7208	1576	39000
19946	597	489	437	1439	3188	551	1361	2957	7341	1586	39500
20233	604	496	440	1448	3232	560	1382	3002	7473	1596	40000
20521	612	504	443	1457	3277	568	1403	3047	7606	1605	40500
20808	619	511	445	1466	3321	576	1423	3092	7739	1615	41000
21057	624	519	441	1452	3373	586	1446	3141	7875	1600	41500
21307	629	527	437	1439	3426	595	1468	3190	8011	1585	42000
21556	634	536	433	1425	3478	604	1491	3239	8147	1570	42500
21805	639	544	429	1411	3531	613	1513	3287	8283	1555	43000
22054	645	552	425	1398	3583	622	1536	3336	8419	1540	43500
22303	650	560	420	1384	3635	631	1558	3385	8554	1525	44000
22552	655	568	416	1370	3688	640	1581	3434	8690	1510	44500
22801	660	576	412	1357	3740	649	1603	3483	8826	1495	45000
23050	665	584	408	1343	3793	658	1625	3531	8962	1480	45500
23443	676	592	419	1380	3835	667	1647	3579	9126	1521	46000
23836	688	600	431	1417	3877	676	1670	3627	9289	1562	46500
24228	699	608	442	1454	3919	685	1692	3675	9452	1603	47000
24621	711	616	453	1491	3961	694	1714	3723	9615	1643	47500
25014	722	624	464	1528	4003	703	1736	3771	9778	1684	48000
25407	733	632	476	1565	4045	712	1758	3819	9942	1725	48500
25799	745	639	487	1602	4087	721	1780	3867	10105	1766	49000
26192	756	647	498	1640	4130	730	1802	3915	10268	1807	49500
26585	768	655	509	1677	4172	739	1824	3963	10431	1847	50000
26977	779	663	521	1714	4214	748	1846	4011	10594	1888	50500
27292	788	670	528	1739	4250	755	1864	4050	10733	1916	51000
27607	797	676	536	1763	4286	763	1883	4090	10872	1943	51500
27922	805	683	543	1788	4321	770	1901	4130	11010	1971	52000
28237	814	689	551	1813	4357	777	1919	4169	11149	1998	52500
28552	823	696	558	1838	4393	785	1937	4209	11288	2025	53000
28867	831	703	566	1863	4429	792	1955	4249	11426	2053	53500

TABLE A-22 continued
1987 Tax Table for Canada

Your Cash Income	Profits Tax	Income Tax	Sales Tax	Liquor, Tobacco, Amusement and Other Excise Taxes	Auto, Fuel & Motor Vehicle Licence Taxes	Social Security, Pension, Medical & Hospital Taxes	Property Tax	Natural Resources Taxes	Import Duties	Other Taxes	Total Taxes
					(Dollars per family)						
54000	2080	11565	4288	1974	799	4465	1888	574	709	840	29182
54500	2108	11703	4328	1992	807	4501	1913	581	716	849	29497
55000	2135	11842	4367	2010	814	4537	1938	589	722	858	29812
55500	2163	11981	4407	2028	822	4573	1963	596	729	866	30127
56000	2190	12119	4447	2047	829	4609	1988	604	735	875	30442
56500	2218	12258	4486	2065	836	4644	2013	611	742	884	30757
57000	2245	12397	4526	2083	844	4680	2038	619	748	892	31072
57500	2273	12535	4566	2101	851	4716	2062	626	755	901	31387
58000	2300	12674	4605	2120	859	4752	2087	634	762	910	31702
58500	2327	12812	4645	2138	866	4788	2112	642	768	919	32017
59000	2355	12951	4684	2156	873	4824	2137	649	775	927	32332
59500	2382	13090	4724	2174	881	4860	2162	657	781	936	32647
60000	2410	13228	4764	2193	888	4896	2187	664	788	945	32962

SCHEDULE A-22

1987 Detailed Tax Calculation for Canada

1. Profit tax   = Your Cash Income × 0.0402 = _____

2. Income tax   = Your Cash Income × 0.221 = _____

3. Sales tax   = Your Cash Income × 0.079 = _____

4. Liquor, tobacco, amusement
   & other excise taxes   = Your Cash Income × 0.037 = _____

5. Auto, fuel & motor
   vehicle licence fees   = Your Cash Income × 0.015 = _____

6. Social security, pension,
   medical & hospital taxes   = Your Cash Income × 0.082 = _____

7. Property tax   = Your Cash Income × 0.036 = _____

8. Natural resources taxes   = Your Cash Income × 0.011 = _____

9. Import duties   = Your Cash Income × 0.013 = _____

10. Other taxes   = Your Cash Income × 0.016 = _____

Total taxes 1 + 2 + 3 + 4 + 5 + 6 + 7 + 8 + 9 + 10

Notes

Preface

1. From conversations between one of the authors and Michael Parkin of the University of Western Ontario in May 1979, in connection with a Canadian Broadcasting Corporation program on taxation.

Chapter 1

1. A survey of the evolution of the Canadian tax system with emphasis on the sharing of tax revenues between the provinces and the federal government can be found in Perrin Lewis' chapter, "The Tangled Tale of Taxes and Transfers," in M. Walker (editor), *Canadian Confederation at the Crossroads*, The Fraser Institute, 1979.

2. Douglas Hartle, "An Open Letter to Allen Lambert..." *The Financial Post*, Feb. 11, 1979. Mr. Hartle was a senior civil servant in the federal Treasury Board during the latter period of the income tax explosion.

3. For a complete discussion of oil pricing and taxation, see G.C. Watkins and M.A. Walker (editors), *Oil in the Seventies*, The Fraser Institute, 1977.

4. A documentation of these developments can be found in Perrin Lewis, op. cit.

5. H.F. Campbell, "An Input-Output Analysis of the Commodity Structure of Indirect Taxes in Canada," *The Canadian Journal of Economics*, August 1975, p. 433.

6. This particular distinction is due to the work of E.K. Browning and W.R. Johnson of the University of Virginia who have completed a study of the burden of taxation in the United States. This study, *The Distribution of the Tax Burden* by Edgar K. Browning and William R. Johnson, 1979, has been published by the American Enterprise Institute.

7. These studies, published in 1976 and 1977 respectively, were *How Much Tax Do You Really Pay?*, M. Walker (editor), and *Income and Taxation in Canada 1961-1975*, S.C. Pipes and S. Star, The Fraser Institute.

8. E.K. Browning and William R. Johnson, *The Distribution of the Tax Burden*, American Enterprise Institute, 1979.

9. R.J. Wonnacott and Paul Wonnacott, *Free Trade Between the United States and Canada*, (Cambridge, Mass.: Harvard University Press, 1967), p. 299.

Chapter 2

1. K. Marx and Friedrich Engels, *Manifesto of the Communist Party*, 1848.

2. W.I. Gillespie, *In Search of Robin Hood*, C.D. Howe Research Institute, Montreal, 1978.

Chapter 3

1. Statistics Canada, *System of National Accounts*, National Income and Expenditure Accounts, Catalogue No. 13-201, Supply and Services Canada.

Chapter 4

1. Don McGillivray, "An Over-Simplified Look at our Complicated Taxes," *Financial Times of Canada*, November 8, 1976.

Glossary

Some of the Book's Principal Terms, Measures, and Concepts

About Indices

Index: a method of measuring the percentage changes from a base year of a certain item, such as the price, volume or value of food or the dollar amount of taxes. In order to construct an Index, the price, volume or value of the particular item being indexed in each year is divided by the price, volume or value of the item in the base year; it is then multiplied by 100. An Index has a value of 100 in the base year; in this book the base year chosen is 1961.

Consumer Price Index: measures the percentage change from a base year in the cost of purchasing a constant "basket" of goods and services representing the purchases by a particular population group in a specified time period. The Consumer Price Index or CPI, as it is often called, reflects price movements of some 300 items. The CPI is calculated monthly by Statistics Canada (see below).

Consumer Tax Index: measures the percentage change from a base year in the average Canadian family's tax bill. The Consumer Tax Index or CTI is composed of federal, provincial, and municipal taxes. The CTI, calculated by the Fraser Institute, was introduced by the Fraser Institute for the first time in Edition One, *How Much Tax Do You Really Pay?*

Balanced Budget Tax Index: is the same as the Consumer Tax Index except that included in the calculation is the amount of tax that would have to be raised if governments did not issue debt and were, in fact, balancing their budgets. This index was introduced by the Fraser Institute for the first time in Edition Two, *Tax Facts.*

Some Statistical Terms

Statistics Canada: is Canada's official statistical agency which is often referred to as "StatCan." Statistics Canada provided much of the published and unpublished data for this book. For a detailed listing of these sources, see the Bibliography.

Average Canadian Family: represents a family that had average income in a particular year. The averages were constructed from Statistics

Canada's expenditure surveys, details of which appear in the Bibliography.

Family Expenditure Survey: refers to the Statistics Canada surveys which show patterns of family expenditure for Canada by selected characteristics such as urban and/or rural area, family type, life cycle, income, age of head, tenure, occupation of head, education of head, country of origin and, if applicable, immigrant arrival year. The tables in these surveys which were integral to this book were those entitled, "Detailed Average Expenditure by Family Income for All Families and Unattached Individuals." From these tables it was possible to look at the spending patterns of the average family in each income class.

Family: refers to a group of persons dependent upon a common or pooled income for their major expenditure items and living in the same dwelling. The term also applies to a financially independent unattached individual living alone.

Shelter Expenditure: is included as one of the selected expenditure items in this book. It refers to expenditures on rented or owned living quarters, on repairs to these quarters; on mortgage interest and on other housing, such as vacation homes, lodging at university or at remote work locations. It also includes expenditures on water and heating fuel.

Income Concepts Used in the Book

Cash Income: is the income that a family would report when completing a government survey, such as the Family Expenditure Survey or the Census form. It includes income that one receives regularly, such as salary or wage income (before tax) and payments from government such as family allowances.

Full Cash Income: is cash income plus the extra income that is often omitted when a family speaks of its income. Items that are often excluded from cash income include bond or bank interest and dividend income.

Income from Government: is income that a family receives as payment from the government, whereas taxes are payments to the government. Therefore, income from the government can be considered a "negative tax." It is often referred to as a transfer payment. It includes such items as family allowance payments, old age security payments, veterans' grants, etc.

Hidden Income: is income that a family receives but probably does not consider to be a part of its income. Hidden income is largely made up of employer contributions to pension plans, medical premiums, and insurance plans. Another example is imputed non-farm rent. (For a more complete discussion of imputed non-farm rent see the Fraser Institute publication *Rent Control—A Popular Paradox,* p. 33).

Hidden Purchasing Power Loss: the prices of articles that the family buys are higher by the amount of hidden taxes which are paid to government by an intermediary and not at the point of final sale. For example, sales taxes paid by the manufacturer are typically added to the price charged to the wholesaler or retailer and are accordingly built into the final sales price but not called a tax. Therefore, the consumer actually loses purchasing power by the amount of these taxes. In this book, the purchasing power loss has been given back to the family as one of the components of total income before tax.

Total Income Before Tax: is the term used in this book to designate the amount of income the family would have received before paying tax. It is composed of full cash income which includes income from government (transfer payments), hidden income, and hidden purchasing power loss.

Deciles: all families were lined up according to total income before tax from lowest to highest and then divided into ten groups, i.e. the first decile contains the first 10 percent of families etc.

Transfer Payments: see "Income from Government" in this section.

About Taxes

Tax Burden: is the means of determining who ultimately pays tax and is synonymous with the term "tax incidence." Tax burden is measured by the decline in real purchasing power that results from the imposition of a tax.

Balanced Budget Tax Rate: is the tax rate that Canadians would face if governments had to balance their budgets and finance all expenditures from current tax revenue instead of issuing debt.

Deferred Taxation: the debt incurred by the various levels of government to finance the expenditures that cannot be met by current tax revenue is, in effect, deferred taxation because the debts and interest on them must ultimately be paid out of future tax revenue.

Direct Taxes: are taxes which are paid directly by the family. Examples of direct taxes are the personal income tax and provincial retail sales taxes. They are often referred to as explicit taxes.

Hidden Taxes: are taxes that are concealed in the price of articles that one buys. Hidden taxes are also referred to as implicit taxes. The most well-known form of the hidden tax is the indirect tax. Examples of hidden taxes are the tobacco tax, manufacturers' sales taxes and import duties.

Social Security Taxes: are composed of both federal and provincial taxes. The federal category includes employer and employee contributions to Public Service Pensions and to Unemployment Insurance. Provincial Social Security taxes include employer and employee contributions to Public Service Pensions, employer and employee contributions to Workers' Compensation and Industrial Employees' Vacations. Also included in this category as taxes are payments to the Canada and Quebec Pension Plans and Medical and Hospital Insurance Premiums.

Corporate Profits Tax: is the tax paid on the profits of a corporation.

Progressive, Proportional and Regressive Taxation: these are terms which refer to the proportionality of taxes on income. A tax is called proportional if it takes the same fraction of income from low income people as it does from high income people. (Unemployment Insurance payments and Canada Pension payments up to the maximum earnings level are examples of proportional taxes). A progressive tax is one that takes a greater proportion of income from high income people than from those with low incomes (income tax, for example). A regressive tax is one that takes a greater proportion of income from low income people than it does from high income people (sales tax, for example).

Negative Tax: see "Income from Government" in the previous section.

Taxation Powers Under the Constitution of Canada: the general scheme of taxation in the British North America Act might be summarized in this way:

1. the federal government is given an unlimited power to tax.

2. the provinces are also given what amounts to an unlimited power to tax "within the province," that is to say an unlimited power to tax persons within their jurisdiction and to impose taxes in respect to property located and income earned within the province. (They may not, however, levy indirect taxes). But their taxing powers are framed in such a way as to preclude them from imposing taxes which would have the effect of creating barriers to interprovincial trade, and generally from taxing persons and property outside the province.

Bibliography

Selected Sources

Bird, Richard M., *Growth of Government Spending in Canada*, Canadian Tax Foundation, July 1970.

Browning, Edgar K., "The Burden of Taxation," *Journal of Political Economy*, Volume 86, Number 4, August 1978.

Browning, Edgar K. and William R. Johnson, *The Distribution of the Tax Burden*, American Enterprise Institute, 1979.

Burrows, Marie, *Fiscal Positions of the Provinces: The 1983 Budgets*, Conference Board of Canada, Aeric, 1983.

Campbell, Harry F., "An Input-Output Analysis of the Commodity Structure of Indirect Taxes in Canada," *The Canadian Journal of Economics*, August 1975, p. 433.

Canadian Tax Foundation, *The National Finances—An Analysis of the Revenues and Expenditures of the Government of Canada, 1986-87*, Canadian Tax Foundation, 1987.

_____, *The National Finances—An Analysis of the Revenues and Expenditures of the Government of Canada, 1984-85*, Canadian Tax Foundation, 1985.

_____, *The National Finances—An Analysis of the Revenues and Expenditures of the Government of Canada, 1982-83*, Canadian Tax Foundation, 1983.

_____, *The National Finances—An Analysis of the Revenues and Expenditures of the Government of Canada, 1980-81*, Canadian Tax Foundation, 1981.

_____, *The National Finances—An Analysis of the Revenues and Expenditures of the Government of Canada, 1978-79*, Canadian Tax Foundation, 1979.

_____, *The National Finances—An Analysis of the Revenues and Expenditures of the Government of Canada, 1975-76*, Canadian Tax Foundation, 1976.

_____, *The National Finances—An Analysis of the Revenues and Expenditures of the Government of Canada, 1974-75*, Canadian Tax Foundation, 1975.

_____, *Provincial and Municipal Finances, 1985,* Canadian Tax Foundation, 1985.

_____, *Provincial and Municipal Finances, 1983,* Canadian Tax Foundation, 1983.

_____, *Provincial and Municipal Finances, 1979,* Canadian Tax Foundation, 1979.

_____, *Provincial and Municipal Finances, 1977,* Canadian Tax Foundation, 1977.

_____, *Provincial and Municipal Finances, 1975,* Canadian Tax Foundation, 1975.

Conference Board of Canada, *Provincial Outlook,* March 1986, Volume 1 No.1, Aeric.

_____, *Quarterly Provincial Forecast,* February 1984, Volume 8 No.3, Aeric.

Dodge, David A., "Impact of Tax, Transfer and Expenditure Policies of Government on the Distribution of Personal Incomes in Canada." *The Review of Income and Wealth, Series 21,* Number 1, March 1975, pp.1-52.

Gillespie, W. Irwin, *Incidence of Taxes and Public Expenditures in the Canadian Economy,* (Studies of the Royal Commission on Taxation, Number 2), 1966.

_____, *In Search of Robin Hood,* C.D. Howe Research Institute, 1978.

Goffman, Irving J., *The Burden of Canadian Taxation,* (Tax Paper Number 29), Canadian Tax Foundation , July 1972.

Marx, Karl and Friedrich Engels, *Manifesto of the Communist Party,* 1848.

Maslove, Allan M., *The Pattern of Taxation in Canada,* Economic Council of Canada, December 1972.

Meerman, Jacob P., "The Definition of Income in Studies of Budget Incidence and Income Distribution," *Review of Income and Wealth,* Series 20, Number 4, December 1974, pp. 512-22.

Musgrave, Richard A., and Peggy B. Musgrave, *Public Finance in Theory and Practice,* McGraw-Hill, Inc., 1973.

Pechman, Joseph A., and Benjamin A. Okner, *Who Bears the Tax Burden?* (Studies of Government Finance), The Brookings Institute, 1974.

Pipes, Sally C., and Michael A. Walker, *Tax Facts 5,* The Fraser Institute, 1986.

_____, *Tax Facts 4*, The Fraser Institute, 1984.

_____, *Tax Facts 3*, The Fraser Institute, 1982.

_____, *Tax Facts*, The Fraser Institute, 1979.

Star, Spencer and Sally C. Pipes, *Income and Taxation in Canada 1961-1975*, The Fraser Institute, 1977.

Walker, Michael, ed., Thomas Courchene, Perrin Lewis, Pierre Lortie, et al., *Canadian Confederation at the Crossroads: The Search for a Federal-Provincial Balance*, The Fraser Institiute, 1979.

Walker, Michael, ed., *How Much Tax Do You Really Pay?*, The Fraser Institute, 1976.

Walker, Michael, ed., David Laidler, Michael Parkin, Jackson Grayson, et al., *The Illusion of Wage and Price Control*, The Fraser Institute, 1976.

Walker, Michael and G. Campbell Watkins, editors, *Oil in the Seventies*, The Fraser Institute, 1977.

Wonnacott, Ronald J. and P. Wonnacott, *Free Trade Between the United States and Canada*, Harvard University Press, 1967.

Government Sources

Bank of Canada Review, Monthly.

Revenue Canada, *Taxation Statistics, 1987 Edition, Analyzing the Returns of Individuals for the 1985 Taxation Year and Miscellaneous Statistics.*

_____, *Taxation Statistics, 1985 Edition, Analyzing the Returns of Individuals for the 1983 Taxation Year and Miscellaneous Statistics.*

_____, *Taxation Statistics, 1983 Edition, Analyzing the Returns of Individuals for the 1981 Taxation Year and Miscellaneous Statistics.*

_____, Taxation Statistics, 1980 Edition, Analyzing the Returns of Individuals for the 1978 Taxation Year and Miscellaneous Statistics.

_____, *Taxation Statistics, 1978 Edition, Analyzing the Returns of Individuals for the 1976 Taxation Year and Miscellaneous Statistics.*

_____, *Taxation Statistics, 1976 Edition, Analyzing the Returns of Individuals for the 1974 Taxation Year and Miscellaneous Statistics.*

_____, *Taxation Statistics, 1974 Edition, Analyzing the Returns of Individuals for the 1972 Taxation Year and Miscellaneous Statistics.*

_____, *Taxation Statistics, 1973 Edition, Analyzing the Returns of Individuals for the 1971 Taxation Year and Miscellaneous Statistics.*

_____, *Taxation Statistics, 1971 Edition, Analyzing the Returns of Individuals for the 1969 Taxation Year and Miscellaneous Statistics.*

_____, *Taxation Statistics, 1970 Edition, Analyzing the Returns of Individuals for the 1968 Taxation Year and Miscellaneous Statistics.*

_____, *Taxation Statistics, 1963 Edition, Analyzing the Returns of Individuals for the 1961 Taxation Year.**

_____, *Taxation Statistics, 1962 Edition, Analyzing the Returns of Individuals for the 1960 Taxation Year.**

Statistics Canada, *Canada Year Book*, 1978, Supply and Services Canada, Ottawa.

_____, *The Control and Sale of Alcoholic Beverages in Canada, Fiscal Year ended March 31, 1985*, Catalogue No. 63-202 Annual, Supply and Services Canada.

_____, *The Control and Sale of Alcoholic Beverages in Canada, Fiscal Year ended March 31, 1984*, Catalogue No. 63-202 Annual, Supply and Services Canada, Ottawa.

_____, *The Control and Sale of Alcoholic Beverages in Canada, Fiscal Year ended March 31, 1982*, Catalogue No. 63-202 Annual, 1981 Supply and Services Canada, Ottawa.

_____, *The Control and Sale of Alcoholic Beverages in Canada, Fiscal Year ended March 31, 1981*, Catalogue No. 63-202 Annual, 1980 Supply and Services Canada, Ottawa.

_____, *Perspective Canada—A Compendium of Social Statistics*, Supply and Services Canada, Ottawa.

_____, *Canadian Statistical Review*, Catalogue No. 11-003 E. Monthly, Supply and Services Canada, Ottawa.

_____, *System of National Accounts, National Income and Expenditure Accounts, 1972-1986*, Catalogue No. 13-201 Annual, Supply and Services Canada, Ottawa.

_____, *System of National Accounts, National Income and Expenditure Accounts, 1970-1984*, Catalogue No. 13-201 Annual, Supply and Services Canada, Ottawa.

_____, *System of National Accounts, National Income and Expenditure Accounts, 1967-1981*, Catalogue No. 13-201 Annual, Supply and Services Canada, Ottawa.

_____, *System of National Accounts, National Income and Expenditure Accounts, First Quarter 1987*, Catalogue No. 13-001 Quarterly, Supply and Services Canada, Ottawa.

_____, *System of National Accounts, National Income and Expenditure Accounts, Fourth Quarter 1986*, Catalogue No. 13-001 Quarterly, Supply and Services Canada, Ottawa.

_____, *System of National Accounts, National Income and Expenditure Accounts, Fourth Quarter 1985*, Catalogue No. 13-001 Quarterly, Supply and Services Canada, Ottawa.

_____, *System of National Accounts, National Income and Expenditure Accounts, Third Quarter 1983*, Catalogue No. 13-001 Quarterly, Supply and Services Canada, Ottawa.

_____, *System of National Accounts, National Income and Expenditure Accounts, Fourth Quarter and Preliminary Annual 1980*, Catalogue No. 13-001, Supply and Services Canada, Ottawa.

_____, *System of National Accounts, National Income and Expenditure Accounts, Fourth Quarter and Preliminary Annual 1978*, Catalogue No. 13-001, Supply and Services Canada, Ottawa.

_____, *System of National Accounts, National Income and Expenditure Accounts, Fourth Quarter and Preliminary Annual 1976*, Catalogue No. 13-001, Supply and Services Canada, Ottawa.

_____, *System of National Accounts, National Income and Expenditure Accounts, Fourth Quarter and Preliminary Annual 1974*, Catalogue No. 13-001, Information Canada, Ottawa.

_____, *System of National Accounts, National Income and Expenditure Accounts, Fourth Quarter and Preliminary Annual 1972*, Catalogue No. 13-001, Information Canada, Ottawa.

_____, *System of National Accounts, National Income and Expenditure Accounts, Fourth Quarter and Preliminary Annual 1971*, Catalogue No. 13-001, Information Canada, Ottawa.

_____, *System of National Accounts, Financial Flow Accounts, Quarterly 1978*, Catalogue No. 13-002, Supply and Services Canada, Ottawa.

_____, *System of National Accounts, Financial Flow Accounts, Quarterly 1977*, Catalogue No. 13-002, Supply and Services Canada, Ottawa.

_____, *National Accounts, Income and Expenditure, 1962*, Catalogue No. 13-201, Information Canada, Ottawa.**

_____, *System of National Accounts, Provincial Economic Accounts, Experimental Data, 1969 to 1984*, Catalogue No. 13-213, Supply and Services Canada, Ottawa.

_____, *System of National Accounts, Provincial Economic Accounts, Experimental Data, 1963 to 1981*, Catalogue No. 13-213, Supply and Services Canada, Ottawa.

_____, *System of National Accounts, Canada's International Investment Position, 1978*, Catalogue No. 62-202, Annual, Supply and Services Canada, Ottawa.

_____, *Income Distribution by Size in Canada 1985*, Catalogue No. 13-207 Annual, Supply and Services Canada, Ottawa.

_____, *Income Distribution by Size in Canada 1984*, Catalogue No. 13-207 Annual, Supply and Services Canada, Ottawa.

_____, *Income Distribution by Size in Canada 1981*, Catalogue No. 13-207 Annual, Supply and Services Canada, Ottawa.

_____, *Income Distribution by Size in Canada 1980*, Catalogue No. 13-207 Annual, Supply and Services Canada, Ottawa.

_____, *Income Distribution by Size in Canada 1978*, Catalogue No. 13-207 Annual, Supply and Services Canada, Ottawa.

_____, *Income Distribution by Size in Canada 1976*, Catalogue No. 13-207 Annual, Supply and Services Canada, Ottawa.

_____, *Income Distribution by Size in Canada 1974*, Catalogue No. 13-207 Annual, Information Canada, Ottawa.

_____, *Income Distribution by Size in Canada 1972*, Catalogue No. 13-207 Annual, Information Canada, Ottawa.

_____, *Distribution of Non-Farm Incomes in Canada by Size, 1961*, Catalogue No. 13-521, Information Canada, Ottawa.

_____, *Income Distributions by Size in Canada, 1969*, Catalogue No. 13-544, Information Canada.

_____, *Farm Net Income, 1986*, Catalogue No. 21-202, Supply and Services Canada, Ottawa.

_____, *Farm Net Income, 1984*, Catalogue No. 21-202, Supply and Services Canada, Ottawa.

_____, *Farm Net Income, Agricultural Statistics Division, 1981*, Catalogue No. 21-202, Supply and Services Canada, Ottawa.

_____, *Farm Net Income*, 1978, Catalogue No. 21-202, Supply and Services Canada, Ottawa.

_____, *Prices and Price Indices*, Catalogue No. 62-001, Monthly, Supply and Services Canada, Ottawa.

_____, *Urban Family Expenditures, 1962*, Catalogue No. 62-525, Information Canada, Ottawa.**

_____, *Family Expenditure in Canada, Volume 1*, All Canada, 1969, Catalogue No. 62-535, Information Canada, Ottawa.

_____, *Family Expenditure in Canada, Volume 3*, Major Urban Centres, 1969, Catalogue No. 62-537, Information Canada, Ottawa.

_____, *Urban Family Expenditure, 1972*, Catalogue No. 62-541, Information Canada.

_____, *Urban Family Expenditure, 1974*, Catalogue No. 62-544, Occasional, Supply and Services Canada, Ottawa.

_____, *Urban Family Expenditure, 1976*, Catalogue No. 62-547, Occasional, Supply and Services Canada, Ottawa.

_____, *Urban Family Expenditure, 1978*, Catalogue No. 62-549, Supply and Services Canada, Ottawa.

_____, *Family Expenditure in Canada, All Canada, 1982*, Catalogue No. 62-555 Occasional, Supply and Services Canada, Ottawa.

_____, *Family Expenditure in Canada, Volume 3*, All Canada: Urban and Rural, 1978, Catalogue No. 62-551 Occasional, Supply and Services Canada, Ottawa.

_____, *Family Expenditure in Canada, 1982-Advance Information*, Statistics Canada Daily, No. 11-001E, Federal and Media Relations Division, Statistics Canada.

_____, *Quarterly Estimates of Canadian Balance of International Payments, System of National Accounts, First Quarter 1987*, Catalogue No. 67-001, Supply and Services Canada, Ottawa.

_____, *Quarterly Estimates of Canadian Balance of International Payments, System of National Accounts, Fourth Quarter 1986*, Catalogue No. 67-001, Supply and Services Canada, Ottawa.

_____, *Quarterly Estimates of Canadian Balance of International Payments, System of National Accounts, Fourth Quarter 1985*, Catalogue No. 67-001, Supply and Services Canada, Ottawa.

_____, *Quarterly Estimates of Canadian Balance of International Payments, System of National Accounts, Fourth Quarter 1980*, Catalogue No. 67-001, Supply and Services Canada, Ottawa.

_____, *Quarterly Estimates of Canadian Balance of International Payments, System of National Accounts, Fourth Quarter 1978*, Catalogue No. 67-001, Supply and Services Canada, Ottawa.

_____, *Quarterly Estimates of Canadian Balance of International Payments, System of National Accounts, Fourth Quarter 1976*, Catalogue No. 67-001, Supply and Services Canada, Ottawa.

_____, *Quarterly Estimates of Canadian Balance of International Payments, System of National Accounts, Fourth Quarter 1974*, Catalogue No. 67-001, Information Canada, Ottawa.

_____, *Quarterly Estimates of Canadian Balance of International Payments, System of National Accounts, Fourth Quarter 1972*, Catalogue No. 67-001, Information Canada, Ottawa.

_____, *Quarterly Estimates of Canadian Balance of International Payments, System of National Accounts, 1971*, Catalogue No. 67-201, Information Canada, Ottawa.

_____, *Quarterly Estimates of Canadian Balance of International Payments, System of National Accounts, 1963*, Catalogue No. 67-201, Information Canada, Ottawa.**

_____, *Canada's International Investment Position, 1981 to 1984*, Catalogue No. 67-202, Supply and Services Canada, Ottawa.

_____, *Canada's International Investment Position, 1978*, Catalogue No. 67-202, Supply and Services Canada, Ottawa.

_____, *Local Government Finance, Public Finance Division 1984*, Catalogue No. 68-204, Cansim Retrieval.

_____, *Local Government Finance, Revenue and Expenditure, Assets and Liabilities 1983*, Catalogue No. 68-204, Supply and Services Canada, Ottawa.

_____, *Local Government Finance, Revenue and Expenditure, Assets and Liabilities Actual, 1980*, Catalogue No. 68-204, Supply and Services Canada, Ottawa.

_____, *Local Government Finance, Public Finance Division,* Catalogue No. 68-203, Preliminary 1981, Estimates 1982, Supply and Services Canada, Ottawa.

_____, *Local Government Finance, Public Finance Division,* Catalogue No. 68-203, Preliminary 1980, Estimates 1981, Supply and Services Canada, Ottawa.

_____, *Local Government Finance, Revenue and Expenditure, Preliminary Estimates 1979,* Catalogue No. 68-203, Supply and Services Canada, Ottawa.

_____, *Local Government Finance, Revenue and Expenditure, Preliminary Estimates, 1978,* Catalogue No. 68-203, Supply and Services Canada, Ottawa.

_____, *Local Government Finance, Revenue and Expenditure, Preliminary Estimates, 1977,* Catalogue No. 68-203, Supply and Services Canada, Ottawa.

_____, *Local Government Finance, Revenue and Expenditure, Preliminary Estimates, 1976,* Catalogue No. 68-203, Supply and Services Canada, Ottawa.

_____, *Local Government Finance, Revenue and Expenditure, Preliminary Estimates, 1975,* Catalogue No. 68-203, Supply and Services Canada, Ottawa.

_____, *Local Government Finance, Revenue and Expenditure, Preliminary Estimates, 1974,* Catalogue No. 68-203, Information Canada, Ottawa.

_____, *Local Government Finance, Revenue and Expenditure, Preliminary Estimates, 1973,* Catalogue No. 68-203, Information Canada, Ottawa.

_____, *Local Government Finance, Revenue and Expenditure, Preliminary Estimates, 1972,* Catalogue No. 68-203, Information Canada, Ottawa.

_____, *Local Government Finance, Revenue and Expenditure, Preliminary Estimates, 1971,* Catalogue No. 68-203, Information Canada, Ottawa.

_____, *Local Government Finance, Revenue and Expenditure, Preliminary Estimates, 1969,* Catalogue No. 68-203, Information Canada, Ottawa.

_____, *Local Government Finance, Revenue and Expenditure, Preliminary Estimates, 1968,* Catalogue No. 68-203, Information Canada, Ottawa.

_____, *Local Government Finance, Revenue and Expenditure, Preliminary Estimates, 1961,* Catalogue No. 68-203, Information Canada, Ottawa.**

_____, *Local Government Finance, Revenue and Expenditure, Preliminary Estimates, 1960*, Catalogue No. 68-203, Information Canada, Ottawa.**

_____, *Provincial Government Finance, Revenue and Expenditure (estimates), 1981*, Catalogue 68-205 Annual, Supply and Services Canada, Ottawa.

_____, *Provincial Government Finance, Revenue and Expenditure, 1986*, Catalogue No. 68-207, Cansim Retrieval.

_____, *Provincial Government Finance, Revenue and Expenditure, 1983*, Catalogue No. 68-207, Supply and Services Canada, Ottawa.

_____, *Provincial Government Finance, Revenue and Expenditure, 1982*, Catalogue No. 68-207, Supply and Services Canada, Ottawa.

_____, *Provincial Government Finance, Revenue and Expenditure, 1980*, Catalogue No. 68-207, Supply and Services Canada, Ottawa.

_____, *Provincial Government Finance, Revenue and Expenditure, 1979*, Catalogue No. 68-207, Supply and Services Canada, Ottawa.

_____, *Provincial Government Finance, Revenue and Expenditure, 1978*, Catalogue No. 68-207, Supply and Services Canada, Ottawa.

_____, *Provincial Government Finance, Revenue and Expenditure, 1977*, Catalogue No. 68-207, Supply and Services Canada, Ottawa.

_____, *Provincial Government Finance, Revenue and Expenditure, 1976*, Catalogue No. 68-207, Supply and Services Canada, Ottawa.

_____, *Provincial Government Finance, Revenue and Expenditure, 1975*, Catalogue No. 68-207, Information Canada, Ottawa.

_____, *Provincial Government Finance, Revenue and Expenditure, 1974*, Catalogue No. 68-207, Information Canada, Ottawa.

_____, *Provincial Government Finance, Revenue and Expenditure, 1973*, Catalogue No. 68-207, Information Canada, Ottawa.

_____, *Provincial Government Finance, Revenue and Expenditure, 1972*, Catalogue No. 68-207, Information Canada, Ottawa.

_____, *Provincial Government Finance, Revenue and Expenditure, 1971*, Catalogue No. 68-207, Information Canada, Ottawa.

_____, *Provincial Government Finance, Revenue and Expenditure, 1969*, Catalogue No. 68-207, Information Canada, Ottawa.

_____, *Provincial Government Finance, Revenue and Expenditure, 1968*, Catalogue No. 68-207, Information Canada, Ottawa.

_____, *Provincial Government Finance, Revenue and Expenditure, 1961,* Catalogue No. 68-207, Information Canada, Ottawa.

_____, *Provincial Government Finance, Revenue and Expenditure, 1960,* Catalogue No. 68-207, Information Canada, Ottawa.

_____, *Federal Government Finance, Revenue and Expenditure, Assets and Liabilities, 1985,* Catalogue No. 68-211, Supply and Services Canada, Ottawa.

_____, *Federal Government Finance, Revenue and Expenditure, Assets and Liabilities, 1984,* Catalogue No. 68-211, Supply and Services Canada, Ottawa.

_____, *Federal Government Finance, Revenue and Expenditure, Assets and Liabilities, 1983,* Catalogue No. 68-211, Supply and Services Canada, Ottawa.

_____, *Federal Government Finance, Revenue and Expenditure, Assets and Liabilities, 1981,* Catalogue No. 68-211, Supply and Services Canada, Ottawa.

_____, *Federal Government Finance, Revenue and Expenditure, Assets and Liabilities, 1980,* Catalogue No. 68-211, Supply and Services Canada, Ottawa.

_____, *Federal Government Finance, Revenue and Expenditure, Assets and Liabilities, 1978,* Catalogue No. 68-211, Supply and Services Canada, Ottawa.

_____, *Federal Government Finance, Revenue and Expenditure, Assets and Liabilities, 1977,* Catalogue No. 68-211, Supply and Services Canada, Ottawa.

_____, *Federal Government Finance, Revenue and Expenditure, Assets and Liabilities, 1976,* Catalogue No. 68-211, Supply and Services Canada, Ottawa.

_____, *Federal Government Finance, Revenue and Expenditure, Assets and Liabilities, 1975,* Catalogue No. 68-211, Information Canada, Ottawa.

_____, *Federal Government Finance, Revenue and Expenditure, Assets and Liabilities, 1974,* Catalogue No. 68-211, Information Canada, Ottawa.

_____, *Federal Government Finance, Revenue and Expenditure, Assets and Liabilities 1973,* Catalogue No. 68-211, Information Canada, Ottawa.

_____, *Federal Government Finance, Revenue and Expenditure, Assets and Liabilities, 1972,* Catalogue No. 68-211, Information Canada, Ottawa.

_____, *Federal Government Finance, Revenue and Expenditure, Assets and Liabilities, 1971,* Catalogue No. 68-211, Information Canada, Ottawa.

_____, *Federal Government Finance, Revenue and Expenditure, Assets and Liabilities, 1969,* Catalogue No. 68-211, Information Canada, Ottawa.

_____, *Federal Government Finance, Revenue and Expenditure, Assets and Liabilities, 1968,* Catalogue No. 68-211, Information Canada, Ottawa.

_____, *Financial Statistics of the Government of Canada, 1961,* Catalogue No. 68-211, Information Canada, Ottawa.**

_____, *Financial Statistics of the Government of Canada, 1960,* Catalogue No. 68-211, Information Canada, Ottawa.**

_____, *Estimates of Labour Income, Labour Division, October-December 1986,* Catalogue No. 72-005 Quarterly, Supply and Services Canada, Ottawa.

_____, *Estimates of Labour Income, Labour Division, October-December 1985,* Catalogue No. 72-005 Quarterly, Supply and Services Canada, Ottawa.

_____, *Estimates of Labour Income, Labour Division, July-September 1983,* Catalogue No. 72-005 Quarterly, Supply and Services Canada, Ottawa.

_____, *Estimates of Labour Income, Quarterly, 1978,* Catalogue No. 72-005, Supply and Services Canada, Ottawa.

_____, *Quarterly Estimates of Population for Canada and the Provinces, October 1985,* Catalogue No. 91-001 Quarterly, Vol. 13. No. 4, Supply and Services Canada, Ottawa.

_____, *Quarterly Estimates of Population for Canada and the Provinces, October 1983,* Catalogue No. 91-001 Quarterly, Vol. 13. No. 4, Supply and Services Canada, Ottawa.

Statistiques Fiscales Des Particuliers du Québec, Analyse des Déclarations des Revenues des Contribuables de la Province de Québec pour l'Année 1983, Gouvernement du Québec, Ministère du Revenue.

_____, *Analyse des Déclarations des Revenues des Contribuables de la Province de Québec pour l'Année 1980 et 1981*, Gouvernement du Québec, Ministère du Revenue.

_____, *Analyse des Déclarations des Revenues des Contribuables de la Province de Québec pour l'Année 1977 et 1978*, Gouvernement du Québec, Ministère du Revenue.

---

*"Taxation Statistics" was published by the Department of National Revenue, Taxation Division, now Revenue Canada.

**This publication was published by the Dominion Bureau of Statistics, the former name of Statistics Canada.